THIS IS YOUR **PASSBOOK**® FOR ...

DISABILITY CLAIMS ADJUDICATOR TRAINEE

N L C ®

NATIONAL LEARNING CORPORATION®

passbooks.com

PASSBOOK® SERIES

THE *PASSBOOK® SERIES* has been created to prepare applicants and candidates for the ultimate academic battlefield – the examination room.

At some time in our lives, each and every one of us may be required to take an examination – for validation, matriculation, admission, qualification, registration, certification, or licensure.

Based on the assumption that every applicant or candidate has met the basic formal educational standards, has taken the required number of courses, and read the necessary texts, the *PASSBOOK® SERIES* furnishes the one special preparation which may assure passing with confidence, instead of failing with insecurity. Examination questions – together with answers – are furnished as the basic vehicle for study so that the mysteries of the examination and its compounding difficulties may be eliminated or diminished by a sure method.

This book is meant to help you pass your examination provided that you qualify and are serious in your objective.

The entire field is reviewed through the huge store of content information which is succinctly presented through a provocative and challenging approach – the question-and-answer method.

A climate of success is established by furnishing the correct answers at the end of each test.

You soon learn to recognize types of questions, forms of questions, and patterns of questioning. You may even begin to anticipate expected outcomes.

You perceive that many questions are repeated or adapted so that you can gain acute insights, which may enable you to score many sure points.

You learn how to confront new questions, or types of questions, and to attack them confidently and work out the correct answers.

You note objectives and emphases, and recognize pitfalls and dangers, so that you may make positive educational adjustments.

Moreover, you are kept fully informed in relation to new concepts, methods, practices, and directions in the field.

You discover that you arre actually taking the examination all the time: you are preparing for the examination by "taking" an examination, not by reading extraneous and/or supererogatory textbooks.

In short, this PASSBOOK®, used directedly, should be an important factor in helping you to pass your test.

DISABILITY CLAIMS ADJUDICATOR TRAINEE

DUTIES

Apply rules, regulations, policies, terminology, and procedures of Social Security Act to disability claims; review disability claims to obtain medical, educational, and vocational evidence; analyze and evaluate medical reports, test results, vocational and educational histories; recommend final disposition of disability claims.

SUBJECTS OF EXAMINATION:

The written test designed to evaluate knowledge, skills and/or abilities in the following areas:
1. Reading and analyzing written material;
2. Personal computer usage;
3. Effective expression; and
4. Effective working relationships.

HOW TO TAKE A TEST

I. YOU MUST PASS AN EXAMINATION

A. *WHAT EVERY CANDIDATE SHOULD KNOW*

Examination applicants often ask us for help in preparing for the written test. What can I study in advance? What kinds of questions will be asked? How will the test be given? How will the papers be graded?

As an applicant for a civil service examination, you may be wondering about some of these things. Our purpose here is to suggest effective methods of advance study and to describe civil service examinations.

Your chances for success on this examination can be increased if you know how to prepare. Those "pre-examination jitters" can be reduced if you know what to expect. You can even experience an adventure in good citizenship if you know why civil service exams are given.

B. *WHY ARE CIVIL SERVICE EXAMINATIONS GIVEN?*

Civil service examinations are important to you in two ways. As a citizen, you want public jobs filled by employees who know how to do their work. As a job seeker, you want a fair chance to compete for that job on an equal footing with other candidates. The best-known means of accomplishing this two-fold goal is the competitive examination.

Exams are widely publicized throughout the nation. They may be administered for jobs in federal, state, city, municipal, town or village governments or agencies.

Any citizen may apply, with some limitations, such as the age or residence of applicants. Your experience and education may be reviewed to see whether you meet the requirements for the particular examination. When these requirements exist, they are reasonable and applied consistently to all applicants. Thus, a competitive examination may cause you some uneasiness now, but it is your privilege and safeguard.

C. *HOW ARE CIVIL SERVICE EXAMS DEVELOPED?*

Examinations are carefully written by trained technicians who are specialists in the field known as "psychological measurement," in consultation with recognized authorities in the field of work that the test will cover. These experts recommend the subject matter areas or skills to be tested; only those knowledges or skills important to your success on the job are included. The most reliable books and source materials available are used as references. Together, the experts and technicians judge the difficulty level of the questions.

Test technicians know how to phrase questions so that the problem is clearly stated. Their ethics do not permit "trick" or "catch" questions. Questions may have been tried out on sample groups, or subjected to statistical analysis, to determine their usefulness.

Written tests are often used in combination with performance tests, ratings of training and experience, and oral interviews. All of these measures combine to form the best-known means of finding the right person for the right job.

II. HOW TO PASS THE WRITTEN TEST

A. NATURE OF THE EXAMINATION

To prepare intelligently for civil service examinations, you should know how they differ from school examinations you have taken. In school you were assigned certain definite pages to read or subjects to cover. The examination questions were quite detailed and usually emphasized memory. Civil service exams, on the other hand, try to discover your present ability to perform the duties of a position, plus your potentiality to learn these duties. In other words, a civil service exam attempts to predict how successful you will be. Questions cover such a broad area that they cannot be as minute and detailed as school exam questions.

In the public service similar kinds of work, or positions, are grouped together in one "class." This process is known as *position-classification*. All the positions in a class are paid according to the salary range for that class. One class title covers all of these positions, and they are all tested by the same examination.

B. FOUR BASIC STEPS

1) Study the announcement

How, then, can you know what subjects to study? Our best answer is: "Learn as much as possible about the class of positions for which you've applied." The exam will test the knowledge, skills and abilities needed to do the work.

Your most valuable source of information about the position you want is the official exam announcement. This announcement lists the training and experience qualifications. Check these standards and apply only if you come reasonably close to meeting them.

The brief description of the position in the examination announcement offers some clues to the subjects which will be tested. Think about the job itself. Review the duties in your mind. Can you perform them, or are there some in which you are rusty? Fill in the blank spots in your preparation.

Many jurisdictions preview the written test in the exam announcement by including a section called "Knowledge and Abilities Required," "Scope of the Examination," or some similar heading. Here you will find out specifically what fields will be tested.

2) Review your own background

Once you learn in general what the position is all about, and what you need to know to do the work, ask yourself which subjects you already know fairly well and which need improvement. You may wonder whether to concentrate on improving your strong areas or on building some background in your fields of weakness. When the announcement has specified "some knowledge" or "considerable knowledge," or has used adjectives like "beginning principles of…" or "advanced … methods," you can get a clue as to the number and difficulty of questions to be asked in any given field. More questions, and hence broader coverage, would be included for those subjects which are more important in the work. Now weigh your strengths and weaknesses against the job requirements and prepare accordingly.

3) Determine the level of the position

Another way to tell how intensively you should prepare is to understand the level of the job for which you are applying. Is it the entering level? In other words, is this the position in which beginners in a field of work are hired? Or is it an intermediate or advanced level? Sometimes this is indicated by such words as "Junior" or "Senior" in the class title. Other jurisdictions use Roman numerals to designate the level – Clerk I, Clerk II, for example. The word "Supervisor" sometimes appears in the title. If the level is not indicated by the title, check the description of duties. Will you be working under very close supervision, or will you have responsibility for independent decisions in this work?

4) Choose appropriate study materials

Now that you know the subjects to be examined and the relative amount of each subject to be covered, you can choose suitable study materials. For beginning level jobs, or even advanced ones, if you have a pronounced weakness in some aspect of your training, read a modern, standard textbook in that field. Be sure it is up to date and has general coverage. Such books are normally available at your library, and the librarian will be glad to help you locate one. For entry-level positions, questions of appropriate difficulty are chosen – neither highly advanced questions, nor those too simple. Such questions require careful thought but not advanced training.

If the position for which you are applying is technical or advanced, you will read more advanced, specialized material. If you are already familiar with the basic principles of your field, elementary textbooks would waste your time. Concentrate on advanced textbooks and technical periodicals. Think through the concepts and review difficult problems in your field.

These are all general sources. You can get more ideas on your own initiative, following these leads. For example, training manuals and publications of the government agency which employs workers in your field can be useful, particularly for technical and professional positions. A letter or visit to the government department involved may result in more specific study suggestions, and certainly will provide you with a more definite idea of the exact nature of the position you are seeking.

III. KINDS OF TESTS

Tests are used for purposes other than measuring knowledge and ability to perform specified duties. For some positions, it is equally important to test ability to make adjustments to new situations or to profit from training. In others, basic mental abilities not dependent on information are essential. Questions which test these things may not appear as pertinent to the duties of the position as those which test for knowledge and information. Yet they are often highly important parts of a fair examination. For very general questions, it is almost impossible to help you direct your study efforts. What we can do is to point out some of the more common of these general abilities needed in public service positions and describe some typical questions.

1) General information

Broad, general information has been found useful for predicting job success in some kinds of work. This is tested in a variety of ways, from vocabulary lists to questions about current events. Basic background in some field of work, such as sociology or economics, may be sampled in a group of questions. Often these are principles which have become familiar to most persons through exposure rather than through formal training. It is difficult to advise you how to study for these questions; being alert to the world around you is our best suggestion.

2) Verbal ability

An example of an ability needed in many positions is verbal or language ability. Verbal ability is, in brief, the ability to use and understand words. Vocabulary and grammar tests are typical measures of this ability. Reading comprehension or paragraph interpretation questions are common in many kinds of civil service tests. You are given a paragraph of written material and asked to find its central meaning.

3) Numerical ability

Number skills can be tested by the familiar arithmetic problem, by checking paired lists of numbers to see which are alike and which are different, or by interpreting charts and graphs. In the latter test, a graph may be printed in the test booklet which you are asked to use as the basis for answering questions.

4) Observation

A popular test for law-enforcement positions is the observation test. A picture is shown to you for several minutes, then taken away. Questions about the picture test your ability to observe both details and larger elements.

5) Following directions

In many positions in the public service, the employee must be able to carry out written instructions dependably and accurately. You may be given a chart with several columns, each column listing a variety of information. The questions require you to carry out directions involving the information given in the chart.

6) Skills and aptitudes

Performance tests effectively measure some manual skills and aptitudes. When the skill is one in which you are trained, such as typing or shorthand, you can practice. These tests are often very much like those given in business school or high school courses. For many of the other skills and aptitudes, however, no short-time preparation can be made. Skills and abilities natural to you or that you have developed throughout your lifetime are being tested.

Many of the general questions just described provide all the data needed to answer the questions and ask you to use your reasoning ability to find the answers. Your best preparation for these tests, as well as for tests of facts and ideas, is to be at your physical and mental best. You, no doubt, have your own methods of getting into an exam-taking mood and keeping "in shape." The next section lists some ideas on this subject.

IV. KINDS OF QUESTIONS

Only rarely is the "essay" question, which you answer in narrative form, used in civil service tests. Civil service tests are usually of the short-answer type. Full instructions for answering these questions will be given to you at the examination. But in case this is your first experience with short-answer questions and separate answer sheets, here is what you need to know:

1) Multiple-choice Questions

Most popular of the short-answer questions is the "multiple choice" or "best answer" question. It can be used, for example, to test for factual knowledge, ability to solve problems or judgment in meeting situations found at work.

A multiple-choice question is normally one of three types—

- It can begin with an incomplete statement followed by several possible endings. You are to find the one ending which *best* completes the statement, although some of the others may not be entirely wrong.
- It can also be a complete statement in the form of a question which is answered by choosing one of the statements listed.
- It can be in the form of a problem – again you select the best answer.

Here is an example of a multiple-choice question with a discussion which should give you some clues as to the method for choosing the right answer:

When an employee has a complaint about his assignment, the action which will *best* help him overcome his difficulty is to
    A. discuss his difficulty with his coworkers
    B. take the problem to the head of the organization
    C. take the problem to the person who gave him the assignment
    D. say nothing to anyone about his complaint

In answering this question, you should study each of the choices to find which is best. Consider choice "A" – Certainly an employee may discuss his complaint with fellow employees, but no change or improvement can result, and the complaint remains unresolved. Choice "B" is a poor choice since the head of the organization probably does not know what assignment you have been given, and taking your problem to him is known as "going over the head" of the supervisor. The supervisor, or person who made the assignment, is the person who can clarify it or correct any injustice. Choice "C" is, therefore, correct. To say nothing, as in choice "D," is unwise. Supervisors have and interest in knowing the problems employees are facing, and the employee is seeking a solution to his problem.

2) True/False Questions

The "true/false" or "right/wrong" form of question is sometimes used. Here a complete statement is given. Your job is to decide whether the statement is right or wrong.

SAMPLE: A roaming cell-phone call to a nearby city costs less than a non-roaming call to a distant city.

This statement is wrong, or false, since roaming calls are more expensive.
This is not a complete list of all possible question forms, although most of the others are variations of these common types. You will always get complete directions for

answering questions. Be sure you understand *how* to mark your answers – ask questions until you do.

V. RECORDING YOUR ANSWERS

Computer terminals are used more and more today for many different kinds of exams.

For an examination with very few applicants, you may be told to record your answers in the test booklet itself. Separate answer sheets are much more common. If this separate answer sheet is to be scored by machine – and this is often the case – it is highly important that you mark your answers correctly in order to get credit.

An electronic scoring machine is often used in civil service offices because of the speed with which papers can be scored. Machine-scored answer sheets must be marked with a pencil, which will be given to you. This pencil has a high graphite content which responds to the electronic scoring machine. As a matter of fact, stray dots may register as answers, so do not let your pencil rest on the answer sheet while you are pondering the correct answer. Also, if your pencil lead breaks or is otherwise defective, ask for another.

Since the answer sheet will be dropped in a slot in the scoring machine, be careful not to bend the corners or get the paper crumpled.

The answer sheet normally has five vertical columns of numbers, with 30 numbers to a column. These numbers correspond to the question numbers in your test booklet. After each number, going across the page are four or five pairs of dotted lines. These short dotted lines have small letters or numbers above them. The first two pairs may also have a "T" or "F" above the letters. This indicates that the first two pairs only are to be used if the questions are of the true-false type. If the questions are multiple choice, disregard the "T" and "F" and pay attention only to the small letters or numbers.

Answer your questions in the manner of the sample that follows:

32. The largest city in the United States is
   A. Washington, D.C.
   B. New York City
   C. Chicago
   D. Detroit
   E. San Francisco

1) Choose the answer you think is best. (New York City is the largest, so "B" is correct.)
2) Find the row of dotted lines numbered the same as the question you are answering. (Find row number 32)
3) Find the pair of dotted lines corresponding to the answer. (Find the pair of lines under the mark "B.")
4) Make a solid black mark between the dotted lines.

VI. BEFORE THE TEST

Common sense will help you find procedures to follow to get ready for an examination. Too many of us, however, overlook these sensible measures. Indeed, nervousness and fatigue have been found to be the most serious reasons why applicants fail to do their best on civil service tests. Here is a list of reminders:

- Begin your preparation early – Don't wait until the last minute to go scurrying around for books and materials or to find out what the position is all about.
- Prepare continuously – An hour a night for a week is better than an all-night cram session. This has been definitely established. What is more, a night a week for a month will return better dividends than crowding your study into a shorter period of time.
- Locate the place of the exam – You have been sent a notice telling you when and where to report for the examination. If the location is in a different town or otherwise unfamiliar to you, it would be well to inquire the best route and learn something about the building.
- Relax the night before the test – Allow your mind to rest. Do not study at all that night. Plan some mild recreation or diversion; then go to bed early and get a good night's sleep.
- Get up early enough to make a leisurely trip to the place for the test – This way unforeseen events, traffic snarls, unfamiliar buildings, etc. will not upset you.
- Dress comfortably – A written test is not a fashion show. You will be known by number and not by name, so wear something comfortable.
- Leave excess paraphernalia at home – Shopping bags and odd bundles will get in your way. You need bring only the items mentioned in the official notice you received; usually everything you need is provided. Do not bring reference books to the exam. They will only confuse those last minutes and be taken away from you when in the test room.
- Arrive somewhat ahead of time – If because of transportation schedules you must get there very early, bring a newspaper or magazine to take your mind off yourself while waiting.
- Locate the examination room – When you have found the proper room, you will be directed to the seat or part of the room where you will sit. Sometimes you are given a sheet of instructions to read while you are waiting. Do not fill out any forms until you are told to do so; just read them and be prepared.
- Relax and prepare to listen to the instructions
- If you have any physical problem that may keep you from doing your best, be sure to tell the test administrator. If you are sick or in poor health, you really cannot do your best on the exam. You can come back and take the test some other time.

VII. AT THE TEST

The day of the test is here and you have the test booklet in your hand. The temptation to get going is very strong. Caution! There is more to success than knowing the right answers. You must know how to identify your papers and understand variations in the type of short-answer question used in this particular examination. Follow these suggestions for maximum results from your efforts:

1) Cooperate with the monitor

The test administrator has a duty to create a situation in which you can be as much at ease as possible. He will give instructions, tell you when to begin, check to see that you are marking your answer sheet correctly, and so on. He is not there to guard you, although he will see that your competitors do not take unfair advantage. He wants to help you do your best.

2) Listen to all instructions

Don't jump the gun! Wait until you understand all directions. In most civil service tests you get more time than you need to answer the questions. So don't be in a hurry. Read each word of instructions until you clearly understand the meaning. Study the examples, listen to all announcements and follow directions. Ask questions if you do not understand what to do.

3) Identify your papers

Civil service exams are usually identified by number only. You will be assigned a number; you must not put your name on your test papers. Be sure to copy your number correctly. Since more than one exam may be given, copy your exact examination title.

4) Plan your time

Unless you are told that a test is a "speed" or "rate of work" test, speed itself is usually not important. Time enough to answer all the questions will be provided, but this does not mean that you have all day. An overall time limit has been set. Divide the total time (in minutes) by the number of questions to determine the approximate time you have for each question.

5) Do not linger over difficult questions

If you come across a difficult question, mark it with a paper clip (useful to have along) and come back to it when you have been through the booklet. One caution if you do this – be sure to skip a number on your answer sheet as well. Check often to be sure that you have not lost your place and that you are marking in the row numbered the same as the question you are answering.

6) Read the questions

Be sure you know what the question asks! Many capable people are unsuccessful because they failed to *read* the questions correctly.

7) Answer all questions

Unless you have been instructed that a penalty will be deducted for incorrect answers, it is better to guess than to omit a question.

8) Speed tests

It is often better NOT to guess on speed tests. It has been found that on timed tests people are tempted to spend the last few seconds before time is called in marking answers at random – without even reading them – in the hope of picking up a few extra points. To discourage this practice, the instructions may warn you that your score will be "corrected" for guessing. That is, a penalty will be applied. The incorrect answers will be deducted from the correct ones, or some other penalty formula will be used.

9) Review your answers

If you finish before time is called, go back to the questions you guessed or omitted to give them further thought. Review other answers if you have time.

10) Return your test materials

If you are ready to leave before others have finished or time is called, take ALL your materials to the monitor and leave quietly. Never take any test material with you. The monitor can discover whose papers are not complete, and taking a test booklet may be grounds for disqualification.

VIII. EXAMINATION TECHNIQUES

1) Read the general instructions carefully. These are usually printed on the first page of the exam booklet. As a rule, these instructions refer to the timing of the examination; the fact that you should not start work until the signal and must stop work at a signal, etc. If there are any *special* instructions, such as a choice of questions to be answered, make sure that you note this instruction carefully.

2) When you are ready to start work on the examination, that is as soon as the signal has been given, read the instructions to each question booklet, underline any key words or phrases, such as *least*, *best*, *outline*, *describe* and the like. In this way you will tend to answer as requested rather than discover on reviewing your paper that you *listed without describing*, that you selected the *worst* choice rather than the *best* choice, etc.

3) If the examination is of the objective or multiple-choice type – that is, each question will also give a series of possible answers: A, B, C or D, and you are called upon to select the best answer and write the letter next to that answer on your answer paper – it is advisable to start answering each question in turn. There may be anywhere from 50 to 100 such questions in the three or four hours allotted and you can see how much time would be taken if you read through all the questions before beginning to answer any. Furthermore, if you come across a question or group of questions which you know would be difficult to answer, it would undoubtedly affect your handling of all the other questions.

4) If the examination is of the essay type and contains but a few questions, it is a moot point as to whether you should read all the questions before starting to answer any one. Of course, if you are given a choice – say five out of seven and the like – then it is essential to read all the questions so you can eliminate the two that are most difficult. If, however, you are asked to answer all the questions, there may be danger in trying to answer the easiest one first because you may find that you will spend too much time on it. The best technique is to answer the first question, then proceed to the second, etc.

5) Time your answers. Before the exam begins, write down the time it started, then add the time allowed for the examination and write down the time it must be completed, then divide the time available somewhat as follows:

- If 3-1/2 hours are allowed, that would be 210 minutes. If you have 80 objective-type questions, that would be an average of 2-1/2 minutes per question. Allow yourself no more than 2 minutes per question, or a total of 160 minutes, which will permit about 50 minutes to review.
- If for the time allotment of 210 minutes there are 7 essay questions to answer, that would average about 30 minutes a question. Give yourself only 25 minutes per question so that you have about 35 minutes to review.

6) The most important instruction is to *read each question* and make sure you know what is wanted. The second most important instruction is to *time yourself properly* so that you answer every question. The third most important instruction is to *answer every question*. Guess if you have to but include something for each question. Remember that you will receive no credit for a blank and will probably receive some credit if you write something in answer to an essay question. If you guess a letter – say "B" for a multiple-choice question – you may have guessed right. If you leave a blank as an answer to a multiple-choice question, the examiners may respect your feelings but it will not add a point to your score. Some exams may penalize you for wrong answers, so in such cases *only*, you may not want to guess unless you have some basis for your answer.

7) Suggestions
   a. Objective-type questions
      1. Examine the question booklet for proper sequence of pages and questions
      2. Read all instructions carefully
      3. Skip any question which seems too difficult; return to it after all other questions have been answered
      4. Apportion your time properly; do not spend too much time on any single question or group of questions
      5. Note and underline key words – *all, most, fewest, least, best, worst, same, opposite,* etc.
      6. Pay particular attention to negatives
      7. Note unusual option, e.g., unduly long, short, complex, different or similar in content to the body of the question
      8. Observe the use of "hedging" words – *probably, may, most likely,* etc.
      9. Make sure that your answer is put next to the same number as the question
      10. Do not second-guess unless you have good reason to believe the second answer is definitely more correct
      11. Cross out original answer if you decide another answer is more accurate; do not erase until you are ready to hand your paper in
      12. Answer all questions; guess unless instructed otherwise
      13. Leave time for review

   b. Essay questions
      1. Read each question carefully
      2. Determine exactly what is wanted. Underline key words or phrases.
      3. Decide on outline or paragraph answer

4. Include many different points and elements unless asked to develop any one or two points or elements
5. Show impartiality by giving pros and cons unless directed to select one side only
6. Make and write down any assumptions you find necessary to answer the questions
7. Watch your English, grammar, punctuation and choice of words
8. Time your answers; don't crowd material

8) Answering the essay question

Most essay questions can be answered by framing the specific response around several key words or ideas. Here are a few such key words or ideas:

M's: manpower, materials, methods, money, management
P's: purpose, program, policy, plan, procedure, practice, problems, pitfalls, personnel, public relations
   a. Six basic steps in handling problems:
      1. Preliminary plan and background development
      2. Collect information, data and facts
      3. Analyze and interpret information, data and facts
      4. Analyze and develop solutions as well as make recommendations
      5. Prepare report and sell recommendations
      6. Install recommendations and follow up effectiveness

   b. Pitfalls to avoid
      1. *Taking things for granted* – A statement of the situation does not necessarily imply that each of the elements is necessarily true; for example, a complaint may be invalid and biased so that all that can be taken for granted is that a complaint has been registered
      2. *Considering only one side of a situation* – Wherever possible, indicate several alternatives and then point out the reasons you selected the best one
      3. *Failing to indicate follow up* – Whenever your answer indicates action on your part, make certain that you will take proper follow-up action to see how successful your recommendations, procedures or actions turn out to be
      4. *Taking too long in answering any single question* – Remember to time your answers properly

IX. AFTER THE TEST

Scoring procedures differ in detail among civil service jurisdictions although the general principles are the same. Whether the papers are hand-scored or graded by machine we have described, they are nearly always graded by number. That is, the person who marks the paper knows only the number – never the name – of the applicant. Not until all the papers have been graded will they be matched with names. If other tests, such as training and experience or oral interview ratings have been given, scores will be combined. Different parts of the examination usually have different weights. For example, the written test might count 60 percent of the final grade, and a rating of training and experience 40 percent. In many jurisdictions, veterans will have a certain number of points added to their grades.

After the final grade has been determined, the names are placed in grade order and an eligible list is established. There are various methods for resolving ties between those who get the same final grade – probably the most common is to place first the name of the person whose application was received first. Job offers are made from the eligible list in the order the names appear on it. You will be notified of your grade and your rank as soon as all these computations have been made. This will be done as rapidly as possible.

People who are found to meet the requirements in the announcement are called "eligibles." Their names are put on a list of eligible candidates. An eligible's chances of getting a job depend on how high he stands on this list and how fast agencies are filling jobs from the list.

When a job is to be filled from a list of eligibles, the agency asks for the names of people on the list of eligibles for that job. When the civil service commission receives this request, it sends to the agency the names of the three people highest on this list. Or, if the job to be filled has specialized requirements, the office sends the agency the names of the top three persons who meet these requirements from the general list.

The appointing officer makes a choice from among the three people whose names were sent to him. If the selected person accepts the appointment, the names of the others are put back on the list to be considered for future openings.

That is the rule in hiring from all kinds of eligible lists, whether they are for typist, carpenter, chemist, or something else. For every vacancy, the appointing officer has his choice of any one of the top three eligibles on the list. This explains why the person whose name is on top of the list sometimes does not get an appointment when some of the persons lower on the list do. If the appointing officer chooses the second or third eligible, the No. 1 eligible does not get a job at once, but stays on the list until he is appointed or the list is terminated.

X. HOW TO PASS THE INTERVIEW TEST

The examination for which you applied requires an oral interview test. You have already taken the written test and you are now being called for the interview test – the final part of the formal examination.

You may think that it is not possible to prepare for an interview test and that there are no procedures to follow during an interview. Our purpose is to point out some things you can do in advance that will help you and some good rules to follow and pitfalls to avoid while you are being interviewed.

What is an interview supposed to test?
The written examination is designed to test the technical knowledge and competence of the candidate; the oral is designed to evaluate intangible qualities, not readily measured otherwise, and to establish a list showing the relative fitness of each candidate – as measured against his competitors – for the position sought. Scoring is not on the basis of "right" and "wrong," but on a sliding scale of values ranging from "not passable" to "outstanding." As a matter of fact, it is possible to achieve a relatively low score without a single "incorrect" answer because of evident weakness in the qualities being measured.

Occasionally, an examination may consist entirely of an oral test – either an individual or a group oral. In such cases, information is sought concerning the technical knowledges and abilities of the candidate, since there has been no written examination for this purpose. More commonly, however, an oral test is used to supplement a written examination.

Who conducts interviews?

The composition of oral boards varies among different jurisdictions. In nearly all, a representative of the personnel department serves as chairman. One of the members of the board may be a representative of the department in which the candidate would work. In some cases, "outside experts" are used, and, frequently, a businessman or some other representative of the general public is asked to serve. Labor and management or other special groups may be represented. The aim is to secure the services of experts in the appropriate field.

However the board is composed, it is a good idea (and not at all improper or unethical) to ascertain in advance of the interview who the members are and what groups they represent. When you are introduced to them, you will have some idea of their backgrounds and interests, and at least you will not stutter and stammer over their names.

What should be done before the interview?

While knowledge about the board members is useful and takes some of the surprise element out of the interview, there is other preparation which is more substantive. It *is* possible to prepare for an oral interview – in several ways:

1) Keep a copy of your application and review it carefully before the interview

This may be the only document before the oral board, and the starting point of the interview. Know what education and experience you have listed there, and the sequence and dates of all of it. Sometimes the board will ask you to review the highlights of your experience for them; you should not have to hem and haw doing it.

2) Study the class specification and the examination announcement

Usually, the oral board has one or both of these to guide them. The qualities, characteristics or knowledges required by the position sought are stated in these documents. They offer valuable clues as to the nature of the oral interview. For example, if the job involves supervisory responsibilities, the announcement will usually indicate that knowledge of modern supervisory methods and the qualifications of the candidate as a supervisor will be tested. If so, you can expect such questions, frequently in the form of a hypothetical situation which you are expected to solve. NEVER go into an oral without knowledge of the duties and responsibilities of the job you seek.

3) Think through each qualification required

Try to visualize the kind of questions you would ask if you were a board member. How well could you answer them? Try especially to appraise your own knowledge and background in each area, *measured against the job sought*, and identify any areas in which you are weak. Be critical and realistic – do not flatter yourself.

4) Do some general reading in areas in which you feel you may be weak

For example, if the job involves supervision and your past experience has NOT, some general reading in supervisory methods and practices, particularly in the field of human relations, might be useful. Do NOT study agency procedures or detailed manuals. The oral board will be testing your understanding and capacity, not your memory.

5) Get a good night's sleep and watch your general health and mental attitude

You will want a clear head at the interview. Take care of a cold or any other minor ailment, and of course, no hangovers.

What should be done on the day of the interview?

Now comes the day of the interview itself. Give yourself plenty of time to get there. Plan to arrive somewhat ahead of the scheduled time, particularly if your appointment is in the fore part of the day. If a previous candidate fails to appear, the board might be ready for you a bit early. By early afternoon an oral board is almost invariably behind schedule if there are many candidates, and you may have to wait. Take along a book or magazine to read, or your application to review, but leave any extraneous material in the waiting room when you go in for your interview. In any event, relax and compose yourself.

The matter of dress is important. The board is forming impressions about you – from your experience, your manners, your attitude, and your appearance. Give your personal appearance careful attention. Dress your best, but not your flashiest. Choose conservative, appropriate clothing, and be sure it is immaculate. This is a business interview, and your appearance should indicate that you regard it as such. Besides, being well groomed and properly dressed will help boost your confidence.

Sooner or later, someone will call your name and escort you into the interview room. *This is it.* From here on you are on your own. It is too late for any more preparation. But remember, you asked for this opportunity to prove your fitness, and you are here because your request was granted.

What happens when you go in?

The usual sequence of events will be as follows: The clerk (who is often the board stenographer) will introduce you to the chairman of the oral board, who will introduce you to the other members of the board. Acknowledge the introductions before you sit down. Do not be surprised if you find a microphone facing you or a stenotypist sitting by. Oral interviews are usually recorded in the event of an appeal or other review.

Usually the chairman of the board will open the interview by reviewing the highlights of your education and work experience from your application – primarily for the benefit of the other members of the board, as well as to get the material into the record. Do not interrupt or comment unless there is an error or significant misinterpretation; if that is the case, do not hesitate. But do not quibble about insignificant matters. Also, he will usually ask you some question about your education, experience or your present job – partly to get you to start talking and to establish the interviewing "rapport." He may start the actual questioning, or turn it over to one of the other members. Frequently, each member undertakes the questioning on a particular area, one in which he is perhaps most competent, so you can expect each member to participate in the examination. Because time is limited, you may also expect some rather abrupt switches in the direction the questioning takes, so do not be upset by it. Normally, a board member will not pursue a single line of questioning unless he discovers a particular strength or weakness.

After each member has participated, the chairman will usually ask whether any member has any further questions, then will ask you if you have anything you wish to add. Unless you are expecting this question, it may floor you. Worse, it may start you off on an extended, extemporaneous speech. The board is not usually seeking more information. The question is principally to offer you a last opportunity to present further qualifications or to indicate that you have nothing to add. So, if you feel that a significant qualification or characteristic has been overlooked, it is proper to point it out in a sentence or so. Do not compliment the board on the thoroughness of their examination – they have been sketchy, and you know it. If you wish, merely say, "No thank you, I have nothing further to add." This is a point where you can "talk yourself out" of a good impression or fail to present an important bit of information. Remember, *you close the interview yourself.*

The chairman will then say, "That is all, Mr. _____, thank you." Do not be startled; the interview is over, and quicker than you think. Thank him, gather your belongings and take your leave. Save your sigh of relief for the other side of the door.

How to put your best foot forward

Throughout this entire process, you may feel that the board individually and collectively is trying to pierce your defenses, seek out your hidden weaknesses and embarrass and confuse you. Actually, this is not true. They are obliged to make an appraisal of your qualifications for the job you are seeking, and they want to see you in your best light. Remember, they must interview all candidates and a non-cooperative candidate may become a failure in spite of their best efforts to bring out his qualifications. Here are 15 suggestions that will help you:

1) Be natural – Keep your attitude confident, not cocky

If you are not confident that you can do the job, do not expect the board to be. Do not apologize for your weaknesses, try to bring out your strong points. The board is interested in a positive, not negative, presentation. Cockiness will antagonize any board member and make him wonder if you are covering up a weakness by a false show of strength.

2) Get comfortable, but don't lounge or sprawl

Sit erectly but not stiffly. A careless posture may lead the board to conclude that you are careless in other things, or at least that you are not impressed by the importance of the occasion. Either conclusion is natural, even if incorrect. Do not fuss with your clothing, a pencil or an ashtray. Your hands may occasionally be useful to emphasize a point; do not let them become a point of distraction.

3) Do not wisecrack or make small talk

This is a serious situation, and your attitude should show that you consider it as such. Further, the time of the board is limited – they do not want to waste it, and neither should you.

4) Do not exaggerate your experience or abilities

In the first place, from information in the application or other interviews and sources, the board may know more about you than you think. Secondly, you probably will not get away with it. An experienced board is rather adept at spotting such a situation, so do not take the chance.

5) If you know a board member, do not make a point of it, yet do not hide it
        Certainly you are not fooling him, and probably not the other members of the board. Do not try to take advantage of your acquaintanceship – it will probably do you little good.

6) Do not dominate the interview
        Let the board do that. They will give you the clues – do not assume that you have to do all the talking. Realize that the board has a number of questions to ask you, and do not try to take up all the interview time by showing off your extensive knowledge of the answer to the first one.

7) Be attentive
        You only have 20 minutes or so, and you should keep your attention at its sharpest throughout. When a member is addressing a problem or question to you, give him your undivided attention. Address your reply principally to him, but do not exclude the other board members.

8) Do not interrupt
        A board member may be stating a problem for you to analyze. He will ask you a question when the time comes. Let him state the problem, and wait for the question.

9) Make sure you understand the question
        Do not try to answer until you are sure what the question is. If it is not clear, restate it in your own words or ask the board member to clarify it for you. However, do not haggle about minor elements.

10) Reply promptly but not hastily
        A common entry on oral board rating sheets is "candidate responded readily," or "candidate hesitated in replies." Respond as promptly and quickly as you can, but do not jump to a hasty, ill-considered answer.

11) Do not be peremptory in your answers
        A brief answer is proper – but do not fire your answer back. That is a losing game from your point of view. The board member can probably ask questions much faster than you can answer them.

12) Do not try to create the answer you think the board member wants
        He is interested in what kind of mind you have and how it works – not in playing games. Furthermore, he can usually spot this practice and will actually grade you down on it.

13) Do not switch sides in your reply merely to agree with a board member
        Frequently, a member will take a contrary position merely to draw you out and to see if you are willing and able to defend your point of view. Do not start a debate, yet do not surrender a good position. If a position is worth taking, it is worth defending.

14) Do not be afraid to admit an error in judgment if you are shown to be wrong

      The board knows that you are forced to reply without any opportunity for careful consideration. Your answer may be demonstrably wrong. If so, admit it and get on with the interview.

15) Do not dwell at length on your present job

      The opening question may relate to your present assignment. Answer the question but do not go into an extended discussion. You are being examined for a *new* job, not your present one. As a matter of fact, try to phrase ALL your answers in terms of the job for which you are being examined.

Basis of Rating

      Probably you will forget most of these "do's" and "don'ts" when you walk into the oral interview room. Even remembering them all will not ensure you a passing grade. Perhaps you did not have the qualifications in the first place. But remembering them will help you to put your best foot forward, without treading on the toes of the board members.

      Rumor and popular opinion to the contrary notwithstanding, an oral board wants you to make the best appearance possible. They know you are under pressure – but they also want to see how you respond to it as a guide to what your reaction would be under the pressures of the job you seek. They will be influenced by the degree of poise you display, the personal traits you show and the manner in which you respond.

ABOUT THIS BOOK

      This book contains tests divided into Examination Sections. Go through each test, answering every question in the margin. At the end of each test look at the answer key and check your answers. On the ones you got wrong, look at the right answer choice and learn. Do not fill in the answers first. Do not memorize the questions and answers, but understand the answer and principles involved. On your test, the questions will likely be different from the samples. Questions are changed and new ones added. If you understand these past questions you should have success with any changes that arise. Tests may consist of several types of questions. We have additional books on each subject should more study be advisable or necessary for you. Finally, the more you study, the better prepared you will be. This book is intended to be the last thing you study before you walk into the examination room. Prior study of relevant texts is also recommended. NLC publishes some of these in our Fundamental Series. Knowledge and good sense are important factors in passing your exam. Good luck also helps. So now study this Passbook, absorb the material contained within and take that knowledge into the examination. Then do your best to pass that exam.

———

EXAMINATION SECTION

EXAMINATION SECTION

TEST 1

DIRECTIONS: Each question or incomplete statement is followed by several suggested answers or completions. Select the one that BEST answers the question or completes the statement. *PRINT THE LETTER OF THE CORRECT ANSWER IN THE SPACE AT THE RIGHT.*

1. The original Social Security Act of the United States was signed in the year 1.____
   A. 1966   B. 1935   C. 1953   D. 1922

2. Old Age, Survivors, and Disability Insurance (OASDI) tax rate for the year 2.____
   2014 is
   A. 9.9%   B. 10.4%   C. 12.10%   D. 12.4%

3. Supplemental Security Income (SSI) program of the United States is for 3.____
   support of low-income people
   A. who are 65 years or older
   B. who are 45 years or older
   C. who are in between 45 years to 65 years of age
   D. there is no age limit

4. SSI is funded from the 4.____
   A. Social Security Trust Fund
   B. U.S. Treasury General Funds
   C. Federal Old-Age and Survivors Insurance Trust Fund
   D. Social Security Administration Trust Fund

5. A person, younger than 65 years, can qualify for the Medicare program of 5.____
   Social Security Benefits
   A. if she/he is a cancer patient
   B. if she/he has permanent kidney failure
   C. if she/he is a cardiac patient
   D. any one of the above

6. Medicare program of Social Security Benefits bears complete medical expenses 6.____
   after the age of 65 years.
   A. True   B. False

7. What is the minimum age for applying for Social Security Retirement 7.____
   Benefits? At least
   A. 64 years and 9 months old   B. 63 years and 6 months old
   C. 62 years and 6 months old   D. 61 years and 9 months old

8. Supplemental Security Income (SSI) program covers disability benefits 8.____
   as well.
   A. True   B. False

9. Social Security pays benefits to people who cannot work because they have a medical condition that is expected to last at least _____ months or result in death.
   A. 12   B. 9   C. 6   D. 4

   9.____

10. A dependent single parent of a deceased worker, who is 62 years in age or older, would be receiving survivors benefit amount equal to _____ percent of the basic Social Security benefit.
   A. 85½   B. 82½   C. 75   D. 80½

   10.____

11. If a person is already receiving Medicare, he/she is not eligible to apply for retirement benefits.
   A. True   B. False

   11.____

12. If you are the divorced spouse of a worker who dies, you could get benefits just the same as a widow or widower, provided that your marriage lasted at least _____ years or more.
   A. 2   B. 3   C. 5   D. 10

   12.____

13. A disabled child must not be working and earning more than _____ per month (as per the specified amount for the year 2014) to be eligible for Social Security benefits.
   A. $1,000   B. $1,050   C. $1,070   D. $1,075

   13.____

14. The terminology of "marked and severe functional limitations" for a disabled child means that a child is having a
   A. physical disability
   B. mental functional limitation
   C. serious limitation in physical activities
   D. physical disability or a mental functional limitation

   14.____

15. The disability decision for a child is made by the
   A. application reviewers in the Social Security Administration Office
   B. Disability Determination Services of the State
   C. doctors and other trained staff of federal agencies
   D. all are authorized

   15.____

16. Disclosure of the social security number of any person is subjected to be penalized as per the laws of the United States.
   A. True   B. False

   16.____

17. Social Security pays _____ types of benefits.
   A. two   B. three   C. four   D. five

   17.____

18. A worker's base years for computing Social Security benefits are the years after
   A. 1935   B. 1950   C. 1955   D. 1960

   18.____

19. In the Social Security Act, the term "child" is used for a   19.____
    A. biological child   B. adopted child
    C. grandchild   D. all of the above

20. COLA stands for   20.____
    A. Compensations or Later Adjustments
    B. Compensations on Living Allowance
    C. Cost of Living Adjustment
    D. Compensations on Living Adjustment

21. Early Retirement reduced benefit amount is increased as the person   21.____
reaches the age of his/her full retirement
    A. as per the latest policy   B. by 10%
    C. by 15%   D. remains the same

22. The payment dates for Social Security benefits were revised after   22.____
    A. January 1, 2008   B. July 1, 2000
    C. May 1, 1997   D. March 1, 1995

23. SSA may make immediate SSI payments to a disabled child if he/she is   23.____
having
    A. HIV infection   B. total blindness
    C. a birth weight below 2 pounds   D. all of the above

24. According to data compiled by the Social Security Administration, the   24.____
expected (average) age of a man reaching age 65 today is _____ years.
    A. 82.4   B. 84.3   C. 80.5   D. 82.6

25. According to data compiled by the Social Security Administration, the   25.____
expected (average) age of a woman reaching age 65 today is
    A. 86.6   B. 84.3   C. 81.5   D. 82.6

KEY (CORRECT ANSWERS)

1.	B		11.	B
2.	D		12.	D
3.	A		13.	C
4.	B		14.	D
5.	B		15.	B
6.	B		16.	A
7.	D		17.	D
8.	A		18.	B
9.	A		19.	D
10.	B		20.	C

21.	D
22.	C
23.	D
24.	B
25.	A

TEST 2

DIRECTIONS: Each question or incomplete statement is followed by several suggested answers or completions. Select the one that BEST answers the question or completes the statement. *PRINT THE LETTER OF THE CORRECT ANSWER IN THE SPACE AT THE RIGHT.*

1.   The Social Security Administration was established in 1935 under U.S. law, codified at
    A. 21 U.S.C.   B. 42 U.S.C.   C. 24 U.S.C.   D. 29 U.S.C.

1.____

2.   The Social Security Administration (SSA) has a central office in
    A. Florida   B. California   C. Maryland   D. Washington

2.____

3.   The Social Security Administration (SSA) has _____ regional offices in the United States
    A. 1,700   B. 10   C. 50   D. 54

3.____

4.   Medicaid is a _____ program of Social Security benefits.
    A. private   B. district   C. state   D. federal

4.____

5.   The Social Security Administration (SSA) has defined _____ steps in the decision process for Disability Determination Services.
    A. 10   B. 5   C. 12   D. 7

5.____

6.   State and local government workers are entitled to the Social Security system under Title II, Section _____ of the Social Security Act.
    A. 218. Agreements
    B. 202. Old-age and Survivors Insurance Benefit Payments
    C. 207. Assignment
    D. all of the above

6.____

7.   "Residual Functional Capacity" for disabled applicants is defined as what the applicant can_____ in spite of his or her disability.
    A. understand   B. do
    C. memorize   D. all of the above

7.____

8.   In some special cases, a person may qualify to avail the disability benefits, like
    A. just by the presence of disability symptoms in the applicant
    B. a divorced spouse becoming eligible to avail the disability benefits
    C. a grandchild becomes eligible to avail the disability benefits
    D. all of the above

8.____

9.   The Office of Family Assistance, Family Support Administration, administers benefit payments under Title _____ of the Social Security Act.
    A. II   B. VII   C. XVI   D. XIV

9.____

10. If a person is born between the 11th through the 20th of the month, he would receive his payment on the _____ Wednesday of the month.
    A. first   B. second   C. third   D. fourth

10.____

11. Medicare is a national social insurance program having its collaboration with about _____ private insurance companies in the United States.
    A. ten   B. twenty   C. thirty   D. forty

11.____

12. In the Social Security Administration (SSA) office, CDI stands for
    A. Center for Disabled Insurance
    B. Cooperative Disability Investigations
    C. California Department of Insurance
    D. Center of Disability Investigations

12.____

13. As per the Social Security Administration (SSA) definitions, the common factors to determine disability are the ability to
    A. watch and hear   B. sit, stand, lift, bend, and stoop
    C. understand (mentally)   D. all of the above

13.____

14. Medicare is divided into _____ categories of social benefits.
    A. three   B. four   C. five   D. six

14.____

15. The early retirement age, as defined by the SSA, is _____ years.
    A. 60   B. 62   C. 63   D. 64

15.____

16. For payroll taxes of Social Security in the current year, the MAXIMUM amount of taxable earnings is
    A. $110,000   B. $112,000   C. $115,000   D. $117,000

16.____

17. AME stands for _____ in the standard terminologies of the Social Security Administration (SSA).
    A. Average Monthly Entitlements   B. Americans' Monthly Entitlements
    C. Average Monthly Earnings   D. none of the above

17.____

18. The MAXIMUM length of stay that Medicare will cover in a hospital patient stay is typically _____ days.
    A. 30   B. 60   C. 90   D. 100

18.____

19. Which of the following is NOT covered in the prescription drug plans of Medicare?
    A. Cost of prescription drugs
    B. Cost of drugs used for epilepsy and cancer
    C. Cost of drugs used for cosmetic purposes
    D. Cost of drug insurance premiums for Medicare

19.____

20. Disability Determination Services are the _____ agencies to make disability findings for the Social Security Administration.
    A. private   B. district   C. state   D. federal

20.____

21. A child under the age of 18 would be receiving survivors benefits in an   21.____
     amount equal to _____ percent.
     A. 75   B. 50   C. 85   D. 60

22. For the decade 2010-2019, Medicare has a projected budget of _____   22.____
     of the federal budget.
     A. 13.20%   B. 14.8%   C. 1.25%   D. 10.5%

23. Mental disabilities are determined based on the ability of a person to   23.____
     A. communicate with others
     B. understand oral and/or written instructions from others
     C. get along with others
     D. all of the above

24. The Social Security Administration reviews SSI payments for disabled   24.____
     children after
     A. they reach 22 years of age
     B. they reach 18 years of age
     C. every two years
     D. SSA does not review their decision

25. Disability benefits are payable to the spouse if he/she is   25.____
     A. also disabled   B. caring for your child
     C. 60 years or older   D. all of the above

_____

KEY (CORRECT ANSWERS)

1.	B		11.	C
2.	C		12.	B
3.	B		13.	B
4.	C		14.	B
5.	B		15.	B
6.	A		16.	D
7.	B		17.	C
8.	D		18.	C
9.	C		19.	C
10.	C		20.	C

21.	A
22.	B
23.	D
24.	B
25.	C

_____

TEST 3

DIRECTIONS: Each question or incomplete statement is followed by several suggested answers or completions. Select the one that BEST answers the question or completes the statement. *PRINT THE LETTER OF THE CORRECT ANSWER IN THE SPACE AT THE RIGHT.*

1. The Social Security Administration works
   A. as an Executive branch of government
   B. as a state agency in the United States
   C. as a private agency in the United States
   D. under the United States Secretary of Health and Human Services

1.____

2. A widow or widower of full retirement age would be receiving survivors benefits in an amount equal to _____ percent.
   A. 100   B. 50   C. 85   D. 60

2.____

3. Disability in adults is MOSTLY determined by their
   A. mental ability to get along with people
   B. physical functioning capacity
   C. residual functional capacity
   D. all of the above

3.____

4. ADL stands for
   A. Activities of Daily Living   B. Average Domestic Life
   C. Activities of Domestic Life   D. Activities in Disabled's Life

4.____

5. The Average Monthly Earnings of an applicant is determined by
   A. dividing the total earnings in the computation years by the number of months in those same years
   B. the annual income statement
   C. annual taxable amount of the computational year
   D. the monthly income of computation years

5.____

6. In the United States, the Social Security program is basically for
   A. old age people   B. survivors
   C. the disabled and blind   D. all of the above

6.____

7. In the United States, Social Security Disability is basically a
   A. social insurance program   B. health coverage plan
   C. remuneration program   D. all of the above

7.____

8. In fact, Social Security disability beneficiaries are more than _____ time(s) as likely to die in a year as other people the same age.
   A. one   B. two   C. three   D. four

8.____

9. Social Security Trust Funds are further dispersed into Federal _____
Insurance Trust Fund.
    A. Old Age and Survivors   B. Disability
    C. Hospital   D. all of the above

9.____

10. The Social Security Administration is providing Accessibility Commitment
under Section _____ of the Rehabilitation Act.
    A. 508   B. 503   C. 501   D. 509

10.____

11. *BrowseAloud* is a browser plug-in for people who
    A. cannot understand English   B. cannot read properly online
    C. are completely blind   D. cannot hear

11.____

12. A person is considered legally blind if his vision cannot be corrected to
better than _____ in his better eye.
    A. 20/200   B. 6/6   C. 20/20   D. 10/200

12.____

13. Blind people can avail Social Security benefits from the
    A. Social Security Disability Insurance Program
    B. Supplemental Security Income (SSI) program
    C. Medicare program
    D. both A and B

13.____

14. What is "disability freeze"?
It is a special
    A. rule that allows special disability cases to be considered in the office of
       the SSA
    B. rule that may help you get higher retirement or disability benefits
       someday
    C. disability insurance plan
    D. rule for people who are not legally blind

14.____

15. SSI payments are based on need. The income limits are defined by the
    A. states   B. Federal government
    C. SSA   D. public surveys

15.____

16. What is meant by the term "work incentives" in the Social Security
Administration?
They are the
    A. rules for people receiving disability benefits to work
    B. additional retirement benefits by SSA
    C. additional payment benefits from SSI
    D. incentives for the workers of SSA

16.____

17. Which one of the following is NOT a communication method of the SSA?
    A. Voice mail   B. 18-point size notice
    C. First Class mail   D. Braille notice

17.____

18. More than one in _____ 20-year-old Americans insured for disability   18.____
    benefits become disabled before reaching retirement age.
       A. four   B. ten   C. five   D. eight

19. Social Security Trust Funds are collected from   19.____
       A. Payroll Taxes
       B. Self-employed Contributions Act Tax
       C. Federal Insurance Contributions Act Tax
       D. all of the above

20. If a grandchild lives in the custody of his grandparent, the Social Security   20.____
    Administration will pay benefits to grandchildren when the grandparent
       A. becomes disabled   B. retires
       C. dies   D. all of the above

21. _____ formats of communication are offered by the SSA for blind people.   21.____
       A. Five   B. Six   C. Seven   D. Eight

22. Parents under the age of 24 need about _____ of work under Social   22.____
    Security for their children to receive Social Security benefits.
       A. half year   B. one year
       C. one to one-half year   D. two to two-half year

23. What are the number of working years of parents, required by the SSA,   23.____
    for offering complete Social Security benefits for children?
       A. 10   B. 15   C. 20   D. 25

24. The SSA evaluates the work status of legally blind people after the age of   24.____
       A. 50   B. 55   C. 60   D. 65

25. A legally blind person is getting benefits after the age of 55. If his earnings   25.____
    exceed the specific amount, then SSI would
       A. terminate his benefits   B. suspend his benefits
       C. reduce his benefits   D. penalize him

———————

KEY (CORRECT ANSWERS)

1.	A		11.	B
2.	A		12.	A
3.	C		13.	D
4.	A		14.	B
5.	A		15.	A
6.	D		16.	A
7.	A		17.	A
8.	C		18.	A
9.	D		19.	D
10.	A		20.	D

21.	C
22.	C
23.	A
24.	B
25.	B

TEST 4

1. The Social Security Act was originally signed by President   1.____
   A. Franklin D. Roosevelt   B. John F. Kennedy
   C. Harry S. Truman   D. Herbert Hoover

2. A person is considered legally blind if his visual field is   2.____
   A. 25 degrees or less   B. 25 degrees or more
   C. 20 degrees or more   D. 20 degrees or less

3. President _____ returned the Social Security Administration (SSA) to the   3.____
   status of an independent agency in the Executive branch of government.
   A. Barack Obama   B. George W. Bush
   C. George H.W. Bush   D. Bill Clinton

4. Current monthly income limitation is equal to _____ to avail Social Security   4.____
   disability benefits as a legally blind.
   A. $1,800   B. $1,500   C. $1,200   D. $1,000

5. A widow or widower (of any age) who is caring for a child (under age 16)   5.____
   would be receiving survivors benefit in an amount equal to _____ percent.
   A. 100   B 50   C. 75   D. 60

6. To avail grandparents-grandchildren Social Securi6ty benefits, the   6.____
   A. biological parents of the child must be deceased
   B. biological parents of the child must be disabled
   C. grandchild must be legally adopted by the grandparent
   D. all of the above

7. The amount of work you need to qualify for Social Security benefits depends   7.____
   on your age. The younger you are,
   A. the less work you need
   B. the more work you need
   C. specific work years are defined for specific age limits
   D. specific work years are defined for specific income ranges

8. The overall budget for Social Security benefits is nearly _____ of the   8.____
   Federal expenditures.
   A. 13%   B. 27%   C. 31%   D. 37%

9. People pay taxes when they work. This tax amount is   9.____
    A. saved in their personal account with the Social Security Administration
    B. being used right now to pay people who are getting benefits now
    C. saved as their insurance premium amount with the Social Security
        Administration
    D. divided in all three of the above mentioned accounts

10. People need to have recent work for availing accidental disability benefits.   10.____
    If the person is over age 30, he needs
    A. the last five years of work
    B. three years of work out of the last 5 years
    C. five years of work out of the last 10 years
    D. eight years of work out of the last 12 years

11. The current Medicare tax rate for employed people is   11.____
    A. 1.0%   B. 1.45%   C. 1.25%   D. 1.75%

12. _____ of Social Security tax goes to a trust fund that pays monthly benefits   12.____
    to current retirees and their families and to surviving spouses and children of
    workers who have died.
    A. 85%   B. 75%   C. 60%   D. 50%

13. _____ of Social Security tax goes to a trust fund that pays benefits to   13.____
    people with disabilities and their families.
    A. 50%   B. 25%   C. 40%   D. 15%

14. A person can earn a maximum of _____ credits per year for availing Social   14.____
    Security benefits.
    A. three   B. four   C. five   D. six

15. Full retirement age for people born in the year 1960 or later is _____ years. 15.____
    A. 60   B. 65   C. 67   D. 70

16. Current Social Security tax rate for self-employed people is   16.____
    A. 9.9%   B. 10.4%   C. 12.10%   D. 12.4%

17. Credits were previously known as   17.____
    A. points for social benefits   B. quarters of coverage
    C. work coverage   D. social points

18. Most people need _____ credits to qualify for Social Security benefits.   18.____
    A. 20   B. 30   C. 40   D. 50

19. What are the "computational years"?   19.____
    Computational years are the years
    A. when people serve the U.S. government
    B. with highest earnings selected from the "base years"
    C. when SSA is evaluating the case of an applicant
    D. when the applicant is receiving Social Security benefits

20. The term CPI stands for _____ in the Social Security Administration (SSA). 20._____
    A. Consumer Price Index   B. Cost Performance Index
    C. Crisis Prevention Index   D. Composite Performance Index

21. The MINIMUM age to become eligible for widow benefits is _____ years. 21._____
    A. 45   B. 50   C. 55   D. 60

22. A person who earns Social Security credits while working for wages or   22._____
    self-employment income is called a
    A. wage earner   B. number holder
    C. worker   D. all of the above

23. The Social Security Administration (SSA) considers _____ of the self-   23._____
    employed people to evaluate their Social Security benefits.
    A. Annual Investment   B. Capital Gains
    C. Net Earnings   D. Government Benefits

24. The Social Security number is a _____ digit code.   24._____
    A. 10   B. 9   C. 8   D. 7

25. The Social Security Administration accepts _____ if the applicant does not 25._____
    have a birth certificate.
    A. religious record of birth   B. U.S. hospital record of your birth
    C. passport   D. all of the above

KEY (CORRECT ANSWERS)

1.	A	11.	B
2.	D	12.	A
3.	D	13.	D
4.	A	14.	B
5.	C	15.	C
6.	D	16.	D
7.	A	17.	B
8.	D	18.	C
9.	B	19.	B
10.	C	20.	A

21. D
22. D
23. C
24. B
25. D

EXAMINATION SECTION
TEST 1

DIRECTIONS: Each question or incomplete statement is followed by several suggested answers or completions. Select the one that BEST answers the question or completes the statement. *PRINT THE LETTER OF THE CORRECT ANSWER IN THE SPACE AT THE RIGHT.*

Questions 1-10.

DIRECTIONS: For each of the sentences given below, numbered 1 through 10, select from the following choices the MOST correct choice and print your choice in the space at the right. Select as your answer:
  A – if the statement contains an unnecessary word of expression
  B – if the statement contains a slang term or expression ordinarily not acceptable in government report writing
  C – if the statement contains an old-fashioned word or expression, where a concrete, plain term would be more useful
  D – if the statement contains no major faults

1. Every one of us should try harder.   1._____

2. Yours of the first instant has been received.   2._____

3. We will have to do a real snow job on him.   3._____

4. I shall contact him next Thursday.   4._____

5. None of us were invited to the meeting with the community.   5._____

6. We got this here job to do.   6._____

7. She could not help but see the mistake in the checkbook.   7._____

8. Don't bug the Director about the report.   8._____

9. I beg to inform you that your letter has been received.   9._____

10. This project is all screwed up.   10._____

Questions 11-15.

DIRECTIONS: Read the following Inter-office Memo. Then answer Questions 11 through 15 based ONLY on the memo.

INTER-OFFICE MEMORANDUM

To: Alma Robinson, Human Resources Aide
From: Frank Shields, Social Worker

I would like to have you help Mr. Edward Tunney who is trying to raise his two children by himself. He needs to learn to improve the physical care of his children and especially of his daughter Helen, age 9. She is avoided and ridiculed at school because her hair is uncombed, her teeth not properly cleaned, her clothing torn, wrinkled and dirty, as well as shabby and poorly fitted. The teachers and school officials have contacted the Department and the social worker for two years about Helen. She is not able to make friends because of these problems. I have talked to Mr. Tunney about improvements for the child's clothing, hair, and hygiene. He tends to deny these things are problems, but is cooperative, and a second person showing him the importance of better physical care for Helen would be helpful.

Perhaps you could teach Helen how to fix her own hair. She has all the materials. I would also like you to form your own opinion of the sanitary conditions in the home and how they could be improved.

Mr. Tunney is expecting your visit and is willing to talk with you about ways he can help with these problems.

11. In the above memorandum, the Human Resources Aide is being asked to help Mr. Tunney to

    A.   improve the learning habits of his children
    B.   enable his children to make friends at school
    C.   take responsibility for the upbringing of his children
    D.   give attention to the grooming and cleanliness of his children

11.____

12. This case was brought to the attention of the social worker by

    A.   government officials
    B.   teachers and school officials
    C.   the Department
    D.   Mr. Tunney

12.____

13. In general, Mr. Tunney's attitude with regard to his children could BEST be described as

    A.   interested in correcting the obvious problems, but unable to do so alone
    B.   unwilling to follow the advice of those who are trying to help
    C.   concerned, but unaware of the seriousness of these problems
    D.   interested in helping them, but afraid of taking the advice of the social worker

13.____

14. Which of the following actions has NOT been suggested as a possible step for the Human Resources Aide to take?

    A.   Help Helen to learn to care for herself by teaching her grooming skills
    B.   Determine ways of improvement through information gathered on a home visit
    C.   Discuss her own views on Helen's problems with school officials
    D.   Ask Mr. Tunney in what ways he believes the physical care may be improved

14.____

15. According to the memo, the Human Resources Aide is ESPECIALLY being asked to observe and form her own opinions about 　　15.____

    A.   the relationship between Mr. Tunney and the school officials
    B.   Helen's attitude toward her classmates and teacher
    C.   the sanitary conditions in the home
    D.   the reasons Mr. Tunney is not cooperative with the agency

16. In one day, an aide receives 18 inquiries by phone and 27 inquiries in person. What percentage of the inquiries received that day were by phone? 　　16.____

    A. 33%   B. 40%   C. 45%   D. 60%

17. If the weekly pay checks for 5 part-time employees are: $129.32, $162.74, $143.67, $135.75, and $156.56, then the combined weekly income for the 5 employees is 　　17.____

    A. $727.84   B. $728.04   C. $730.84   D. $737.04

18. Suppose that there are 17 aides working in an office where many community complaints are received by telephone. In one ten-day period, 4250 calls were received.
If the same number of calls were received each day, and the aides divided the work load equally, about how many calls did each aide respond to daily? 　　18.____

    A. 25   B. 35   C. 75   D. 250

19. Suppose that an assignment was divided among 5 aides. If the first aide spent 67 hours on the assignment, the second aide spent 95 hours, the third aide spent 52 hours, the fourth aide spent 78 hours, and the fifth aide spent 103 hours, what was the AVERAGE amount of time spent by each aide on the assignment? 　　19.____
_____ hours.

    A. 71   B. 75   C. 79   D. 83

20. If there are 240 employees in a center and 1/3 are absent on the day of a bad snow-storm, how many employees were at work in the center on that day? 　　20.____

    A. 80   B. 120   C. 160   D. 200

KEY (CORRECT ANSWERS)

1.	D	11.	D
2.	C	12.	B
3.	B	13.	C
4.	D	14.	C
5.	D	15.	C
6.	B	16.	B
7.	D	17.	B
8.	B	18.	A
9.	C	19.	C
10.	B	20.	C

TEST 2

DIRECTIONS: Each question or incomplete statement is followed by several suggested answers or completions. Select the one that BEST answers the question or completes the statement. *PRINT THE LETTER OF THE CORRECT ANSWER IN THE SPACE AT THE RIGHT.*

1. Suppose that an aide takes 25 minutes to prepare a letter to a client. If the aide is assigned to prepare 9 letters on a certain day, how much time should she set aside for this task? _____ hours.

    A. 3 3/4   B. 4 1/4   C. 4 3/4   D. 5 1/4

1.____

2. Suppose that a certain center uses both Form A and Form B in the course of its daily work, and that Form A is used 4 times as often as Form B. If the total number of both forms used in one week is 750, how many times was Form A used?

    A. 100   B. 200   C. 400   D. 600

2.____

3. Suppose a center has a budget of $1092.70 from which 8 desks costing $78.05 apiece must be bought? How many ADDITIONAL desks can be ordered from this budget after the 8 desks have been purchased?

    A. 4   B. 6   C. 9   D. 14

3.____

4. When researching a particular case, a team of 16 aides was asked to check through 234 folders to obtain the necessary information. If half the aides worked twice as fast as the other half, and the slow group checked through 12 folders each hour, about how long would it take to complete the assignment? _____ hours.

    A. $4\frac{1}{4}$ B. 5   C. 6   D. $6\frac{1}{2}$

4.____

5. The difference in the cost of two printers is $28.32. If the less expensive printer costs $153.61, what is the cost of the other printer?

    A. $171.93   B. $172.03   C. $181.93   D. $182.03

5.____

Questions 6-8.

DIRECTIONS: Questions 6 through 8 are to be answered on the basis of the following information contained on a sample page of a payroll book.

Emp. No.	Name of Employee	M	T	W	Th	F	Total Hours Worked	Pay PerHour	Total Wages
1	James Smith	8	8	8	8	8			$480.00
2	Gloria Jones	8	7 3/4	7		7 1/2		$16.00	$560.00
3	Robert Adams	6	6	71/2	71/2	8 3/4		$18.28	

6. The pay per hour of Employee No. 1 is   6.____

    A. $12.00   B. $13.72   C. $15.00   D. $19.20

7. The number of hours that Employee No. 2 worked on Friday is   7.____

    A. 4   B. 5 1/2   C. 4.63   D. 4 3/4

8. The total wages for Employee No. 3 is   8.____

    A. $636.92   B. $648.94   C. $661.04   D. $672.96

9. As a rule, the FIRST step in writing a check should be to   9.____

    A. number the check
    B. write in the payee's name
    C. tear out the check stub
    D. write the purpose of the check in the space provided at the bottom

10. If an error is made when writing a check, the MOST widely accepted procedure is to   10.____

    A. draw a line through the error and initial it
    B. destroy both the check and check stub by tearing into small pieces
    C. erase the error if it does not occur in the amount of the check
    D. write *Void* across both the check and check stub and save them

11. The check that is MOST easily cashed is one that is   11.____

    A. not signed   B. made payable to *Cash*
    C. post-dated   D. endorsed in part

12.   12.____

No. *103*	$ *142. 77*
May 14	
To *Alan Jacobs*	
For *Wages (5/6-5/10)*	
Bal. Bro't For'd	2340. 63
Amt. Deposited	205. 24
Total	
Amt. This Check	142. 77
Bal. Car'd For'd	

The balance to be carried forward on the check stub above is
    A. $2,278.16   B. $1,992.62   C. $2,688.64   D. $2,403.10

13. The procedure for reconciling a bank statement consists of _____ the bank balance and _____ the checkbook balance.   13.____

    A. *adding* outstanding checks to; *subtracting* the service and check charges from
    B. *subtracting* the service charge from; *subtracting* outstanding checks from
    C. *subtracting* the service charge from; *adding* outstanding checks to
    D. *subtracting* outstanding checks from; *subtracting* the service and check charges from

14. An employee makes $15.70 an hour and receives time-and-a-half in overtime pay for every hour more than 40 in a given week. If the employee works 47 hours, the employee's total wages for that week would be   14.____

    A. $792.85   B. $837.90   C. $875.25   D. $1,106.85

15. A high-speed copier can make 25,000 copies before periodic service is required. Before this service is necessary, _____ copies of a 137-page document can be printed.   15.____

    A. 211   B. 204   C. 190   D. 178

16. An aide is typing a letter to the James Weldon Johnson Head Start Center. To be sure that a Mr. Joseph Maxwell reads it, an attention line is typed below the inside address. The salutation should, therefore, read: 16.____

    A. To Whom It May Concern: B. Dear Mr. Maxwell:
    C. Gentlemen: D. Dear Joseph:

17. When describing the advantages of the numeric filing system, it is NOT true that it   17.____

    A. is the most accurate of all methods
    B. allows for unlimited expansion according to the needs of the agency
    C. is a system useful for filing letters directly according to name or subject
    D. allows for cross-referencing

18. In writing a letter for your Center, the PURPOSE of the letter should usually be stated in   18.____

    A. the first paragraph. This assists the reader in making more sense of the letter.
    B. the second paragraph. The first paragraph should be used to confirm receipt of the letter being answered
    C. the last paragraph. The first paragraphs should be used to build up to the purpose of the letter.
    D. any paragraph. Each letter has a different purpose and the letter should conform to that purpose.

19. If you open a personal letter addressed to another aide by mistake, the one of the following actions which it would generally be BEST for you to take is to   19.____

    A. reseal the envelope or place the contents in another envelope and pass it on to the employee
    B. place the letter inside the envelope, indicate under your initials that it was opened in error and give it to the employee
    C. personally give the employee the letter without any explanation
    D. ignore your error, attach the envelope to the letter, and give it out in the usual manner

20. Of the following, the MAIN purpose of the head start program is to   20.____

    A. provide programs for pre-school development of children
    B. provide children between the ages of 6 and 12 with after-school activity
    C. establish a system for providing care for teenage youngsters with working parents
    D. supervise centers providing 24-hour child care

KEY (CORRECT ANSWERS)

1.	A		11.	B
2.	D		12.	D
3.	B		13.	D
4.	D		14.	A
5.	C		15.	D
6.	A		16.	C
7.	D		17.	C
8.	B		18.	A
9.	A		19.	B
10.	D		20.	A

———

EXAMINATION SECTION
TEST 1

DIRECTIONS : Each question or incomplete statement is followed by several suggested answers or completions. Select the one that BEST answers the question or completes the statement. *PRINT THE LETTER OF THE CORRECT ANSWER IN THE SPACE AT THE RIGHT.*

1. One day an elderly man asks you if he can apply for Social Security at the welfare office. Your response should be to
    1.____

    A. tell him that it is foolish to think he can apply for Social Security at the welfare office
    B. take him back to his apartment because he is too old to be roaming the streets asking questions
    C. explain that Social Security is a federal program and direct him to the nearest Social Security office
    D. call his daughter and tell her that the family should take better care of their father

2. One of your duties is to occasionally visit clients. On one occasion, you visit Mrs. B., who needs assistance in referral of her children for day care so that she may enter a job training program. She has postponed completing the referral.
What should you do in this situation?
    2.____

    A. Tell her that if she doesn't hurry there will be no room at the day care center and the training program will be closed.
    B. Make the arrangements and tell Mrs. B. that she should do what you say.
    C. Remember that all people who ask for help are not always ready to receive it and continue to allow Mrs. B. time to complete the referral by herself.
    D. The next time Mrs. B. asks for help, see that she gets it as slowly as possible.

3. Assume that you are trying to contact a community group to offer to meet with their representative to explain a new agency policy about intake procedures.
In order to "get your message across," you should
    3.____

    A. write a short concise letter explaining why you want to meet with them and when you will be available
    B. write a short letter stating only that it is important that they contact you in order to arrange a meeting
    C. ask a secretary to help you because you do not really like to write to groups
    D. call the agency rather than write since you know someone there

4. It is necessary for you to call the director of a head start center in order to discuss a training program for teaching aides. The operator asks who you are and what you wish to discuss with the director.
Your response should be to
    4.____

    A. tell her that you would rather explain to the director and you want to speak to her immediately
    B. identify yourself, your department and the nature of your business with the director
    C. hang up and try to call again when another operator is on duty
    D. tell your supervisor that the operator at the head start center is rude and you would rather not be asked to call there again

5. Mrs. A. wants her children to go to summer camp. She has received the request forms, but does not understand all of the questions and you are asked to help her complete them. She comes to the office at the appointed time.
   Of the following, the action you should take is to

    A. tell her she has taken so long that maybe the children will not go to camp
    B. see her as quickly as possible, explain the questions to her and help her in completing the forms
    C. help her, but tell her she will have to learn to read better and refer her to an evening school
    D. fill out the forms for her by yourself

5.____

6. Mrs. B. needs a referral to the cancer clinic. You contact the clinic and make arrangements for her visit. You go to her home to inform her about the time because she has no phone. She thanks you for your help and then offers you a piece of jewelry that appears to be rather expensive. Of the following, the action you should take is to

    A. take the gift because you don't want to hurt her feelings
    B. tell her that she is foolish and should spend her money on herself
    C. explain to her that you are pleased with her thoughtfulness, but you are unable to accept the gift
    D. refuse the gift and get someone else to make referrals in the future because she is trying to pay you for your help

6.____

7. Mrs. C., a seemingly healthy, intelligent woman whose husband is disabled, and who works part time, asks for help in getting homemaker services.
   Of the following, the action you should take is to

    A. give Mrs. C. the necessary information and help her get the services
    B. tell Mrs. C. that you do not feel she needs these services since her husband is capable of helping
    C. make note of her request since you do not feel it is urgent
    D. refer her to a caseworker since she obviously needs help in defining her role as a woman

7.____

8. When you are interviewing clients, it is important to notice and record how they say what they say - angrily, nervously, or with "body English" - because these signs may

    A. tell you that the client's words are the opposite of what the client feels and you may need to dig to find out what those feelings are
    B. be the prelude to violent behavior which no aide is prepared to handle
    C. show that the client does not really deserve serious consideration
    D. be important later should you be asked to defend what you did for the client

8.____

9. You are recording a visit you have made with a client who was angry and abusive to you during the interview. At one point you lost your temper and said some things that you immediately regretted. You are embarrassed to record that you lost your temper. However, it would be desirable to record this MAINLY because

    A. you would feel guilty if you did not record it
    B. your supervisor might hear about it from the client, so it would be better to have it written down from your point of view
    C. your supervisor can use the information to help you to improve your skills
    D. it is agency policy to write down everything

9.____

10. Through one of your clients you learn that a day care program's hours have been extended. You confirm this information with the day care center.
It is then MOST important for you to

    10._____

    A. make a note of this fact, since it will mean you have to change your schedule in working with the client
    B. add this information to your personal resource file so that you can refer other clients to the day care program
    C. inform your supervisor of the new information so that it can be added to the central resource file
    D. ignore the information, since your client does not need to have her child in day care for any extra hours

11. You are sent to a meeting of day-care parents to explain the programs of your agency. One of the parents becomes very angry, saying that welfare departments treat people like animals.
You should remain as calm as possible and say to the parent that

    11._____

    A. he is right, but you have no control over what your agency does
    B. he is disrupting the meeting and you have come to explain a program, not to listen to complaints
    C. you understand his feelings and that sometimes clients do not get the services they wish as quickly as possible; however, you will do whatever you can to assist him
    D. he should call your supervisor tomorrow and make an appointment to discuss his feelings

12. Assume that you receive a telephone call from a very angry father. His daughter took money from his wallet, and he wants the caseworker to control the daughter. He yells, screams and swears at you.
What is the BEST way for you to respond?

    12._____

    A. Hang up because you are not responsible for his daughter's actions. He shouldn't scream and swear at you.
    B. Remember to be courteous and polite at all times, never losing your temper despite the circumstances. Listen to him and assure him that the caseworker will receive his message.
    C. Transfer the call to the supervisor because you are concerned about the father's unreasonableness and do not want the responsibility of dealing with him.
    D. Tell him that behavior such as he is demonstrating is the reason his daughter steals from him.

13. Mrs. D.'s son, aged 12, has been getting into difficulty in the neighborhood. At a community meeting, she asks your help in finding worthwhile activities for him.
It is *appropriate* for you to respond to her because

    13._____

    A. you should have knowledge of the social services available in the neighborhood and the activities they offer
    B. you have known Mrs. D. and her family for several years and know how much trouble she has had with her son
    C. it is your job to do what the caseworker assigns to you without question
    D. you are concerned about impressing Mrs. D. with your knowledge

14. Several clients live in your neighborhood. They know that you work for the human
resources administration. One day one of them tells you that there is a rumor that
another client is pregnant and asks if this is true. You know from a past discussion with
the caseworker that this client is pregnant.
The BEST answer for you to give would be to

    A. tell her it is none of her business and if she wants to know, she should ask the
caseworker
    B. ask her who told her that this client is pregnant
    C. explain that anything told to the agency is held in confidence and will not be shared
with anyone else
    D. tell her you don't know, but will ask when you get back to the office and let her
know later

15. The area senior-citizens group asks for an agency representative to discuss old-age
assistance and new SSI regulations. Your supervisor asks you to attend this meeting;
however, you do not wish to go because you really do not feel that you work well with
older people. In fact, you don't like them very much.
What should be your response?

    A. Tell the supervisor that you cannot go because you have an appointment with the
doctor that day
    B. Get another worker to go for you and assume his task while he is gone
    C. Explain to your supervisor what problems you have in working with old-age clients
    D. Go, because you should do the tasks that are assigned to you according to your
job description

16. At a center where you are distributing literature about agency programs, a citizen comes
up to you and begins to complain loudly about agency programs.
What should be your response?

    A. Call the police and have the complainer removed from the center
    B. Tell him that you do not make policy; suggest that he go to the office and complain
    C. Remain as calm as possible and ask that he discuss the complaints with you
calmly. If necessary, make an appointment with him
    D. Yell at him since this seems to be the way he relates to agency people

17. A community group is having a training program. You are sent to explain agency policy
and answer questions. Providing this type of contact between the agency and community
groups is *proper* because

    A. you like people and are a good public speaker
    B. it is the responsibility of the agency to cooperate with community groups in order to
help the public to be well informed about agency policy
    C. you were once in the same training program and understand the kind of people
who are being trained
    D. once in a while everyone should have the opportunity to speak to a community
group

14.____
15.____
16.____
17.____

18. While you are assisting in the intake area, a young man who is applying is cooperative but begins to ask you personal questions: your age, where you live, whether you have children and other similar questions.
You are disturbed by these questions, so you should

    A. tell him that agency policy does not allow you to answer personal questions and send him to another intake worker
    B. tell him it is your responsibility to ask questions, not his
    C. tell your supervisor that you do not want to work in intake because clients can get too nosy and you get nervous
    D. avoid answering personal questions and try to get him to return to the purpose of the interview

18.____

19. You are assigned to the reception area for the day. A mother arrives in the office with three small children. In a rage, she says that she does not have enough money to feed the children and demands that you find a home for them.
The BEST action for you to take should be to

    A. call a security officer and have him remove her and the children from the office
    B. attempt to calm her down by listening to her, attend to the children's needs and call for a supervisor
    C. take the children from her and ask her to leave at once
    D. call the supervisor and security because it is their job to take care of abusive clients

19.____

20. Assume that you are interviewing a young unwed mother who has recently arrived in the city from Alabama. She is a likable girl and is very cooperative. However, it is difficult to understand the meaning of her conversation, due to her accent and different use of words.
You would like to establish a good relationship with her, so you should FIRST

    A. suggest that she go to evening school so that she can learn to speak like other people in the city
    B. tell her that you don't understand her sometimes and you would appreciate it if she would explain what she means
    C. take another worker with you on visits to help you in the interview
    D. try to find a worker in the agency who has a similar background and have the case handled by the worker

20.____

21. A man being interviewed is entitled to Medicaid, but he refuses to sign up for it because he says he cannot accept any form of welfare. Of the following, the BEST course of action for an aide to take FIRST is to

    A. try to discover the reason for his feeling this way
    B. tell him that he should be glad financial help is available
    C. explain that others cannot help him if he will not help himself
    D. suggest that he speak to someone who is already on Medicaid

21.____

22. Of the following, the outcome of an interview by an aide depends MOST heavily on the

    A. personality of the interviewee
    B. personality of the aide

22.____

C. subject matter of the questions asked
D. interaction between aide and interviewee

23. Some patients being interviewed are primarily interested in making a favorable impres-   23.____
sion. The aide should be aware of the fact that such patients are more likely than other
patients to

A. try to anticipate the answers the interviewer is looking for
B. answer all questions openly and frankly
C. try to assume the role of interviewer
D. be anxious to get the interview over as quickly as possible

24. The type of interview which an aide usually conducts is substantially different from most   24.____
interviewing situations in all of the following aspects EXCEPT the

A. setting   B. kinds of clients
C. techniques employed   D. kinds of problems

25. During an interview, an aide uses a "leading question." This type of question is so-called   25.____
because it generally

A. starts a series of questions about one topic
B. suggests the answer which the aide wants
C. forms the basis for a following "trick" question
D. sets, at the beginning, the tone of the interview

───────────

KEY(CORRECT ANSWERS)

1.	C		11.	C
2.	C		12.	B
3.	A		13.	A
4.	B		14.	C
5.	B		15.	C
6.	C		16.	C
7.	A		17.	B
8.	A		18.	D
9.	C		19.	B
10.	C		20.	B

21.	A
22.	D
23.	A
24.	C
25.	B

───────────

TEST 2

DIRECTIONS : Each question or incomplete statement is followed by several suggested answers or completions. Select the one that BEST answers the question or completes the statement. *PRINT THE LETTER OF THE CORRECT ANSWER IN THE SPACE AT THE RIGHT.*

1. Miss Lally is an old-age assistance recipient. Her health is not good and it is important that she have three good meals each day. She follows these instructions except on Friday she refuses to eat meat because of her religious beliefs. She will not even substitute fish.
You are very concerned about this, so you should

    1.____

    A. tell your supervisor so that she will go to see Miss Lally and make her eat nourishing meals on Friday
    B. call her doctor and tell him so that he will see her and explain to her that fasting is not good for her health
    C. attempt to understand her value system and accept that it is possible that she is acting in good faith with her own values even though they may be harmful to her health
    D. explain to her how important it is that she eat meat each day in order to be in good health and enjoy the remaining years of her life

2. Theodore is a junkie. Every cent he can get his hands on legally or illegally is used to supply his habit. You are angry because the junkie is destroying himself and his family. You feel that the courts should punish him for his illegal acts.
Of the following, the BEST action for you to take is to

    2.____

    A. suggest to your supervisor that the income maintenance center reduce the family grant, taking out his portion
    B. help his wife to find another apartment for her and the children away from him
    C. call the local police to find out why they are doing nothing about this man's activities in the community
    D. reconsider your ideas about punishment, remembering that punishment *alone* will not help the man to change his behavior

3. You are regularly assigned to taking Sarah Jones and her young son to the clinic. She is a very warm, friendly woman and your relationship with her is good. However, she invited you to come for dinner on Sunday and to go to a school play with her. You would like to accept the invitations because you need weekend activities and you like her. What should be your PRIMARY consideration in coming to a decision?

    3.____

    A. You need friends just as she does, so you should accept the invitations
    B. You are a worker and should not be seen with a client in public places
    C. Decide whether accepting the invitation will help to meet agency needs or will hamper the relationship you are expected to establish
    D. Tell her "no" because it is not a good policy to be on such friendly terms with clients

4. Martha's husband has been arrested in a drug raid and she is extremely anxious. Your   4.____
    supervisor asks that you visit her to determine ways in which the agency may help her.
    You visit and find her weeping; the house and the children have obviously been
    neglected.
    The BEST thing for you to do is to

    A. tell her to stop crying and help her to clean the apartment and the children
    B. remind her that her husband has been warned and now has to pay for not listening
    C. listen to her, allowing her to express her feelings of fear, loss and grief, and reas-
        sure her of your concern
    D. listen to her but caution her that she is neglecting the home and children because
        of her anxiety and you may have to ask your supervisor to remove the children if
        she doesn't get any better

5. Mrs. Dwight's landlord is very slow in making repairs in her apartment. Each time you   5.____
    see her, she complains about this over and over again, calling her landlord names and
    threatening to report him to the city. She complains to any agency person she meets.
    Realizing that these complaints are not getting any action, you should

    A. avoid meeting with her because she is annoying
    B. suggest that she see a doctor because she is irrational and should get some help
    C. ask her what she would like to do about the problem and assist her in carrying out
        her plans
    D. ask the supervisor to see her because you do not have the skills to help her

6. In the day-to-day operations of the human resources administration, which of the follow-   6.____
    ing would you consider to be the PRIMARY function of the agency?

    A. Getting work done to meet city and federal deadlines
    B. Being sure that all of the clients who come to the agency are seen before closing
        time
    C. Delivering services to those persons who are eligible for assistance
    D. Making sure everyone gets his check on time

7. During the course of an interview you find it is necessary to arrange a special appoint-   7.____
    ment for the client to return for a further interview. After checking your calendar, you tell
    the client the date she is to come back. The client, however, says she cannot see you on
    that date because she is to attend a rally at a community center in her neighborhood.
    Of the following, your BEST action should be to

    A. let her know that any other day is an inconvenience to you and remind her that the
        appointment is for her benefit
    B. forget about the special appointment and try to get along with the information you
        have
    C. explain to her the need for the appointment and ask when she can meet with you
    D. tell her that since the community center is not city-operated, she must keep her
        appointment with you

8. In working with community groups, it is important that you be able to define what a com-   8.____
    munity is.
    Of the following definitions, which is the *most appropriate*?
    A community

A.   consists of a group of people living fairly close together in a more or less compact territory, who come together in their chief concerns
B.   is a particular section of a city designated on a census tract
C.   is that portion of a city which constitutes an election district
D.   is a section of a city or town in which a particular ethnic group conducts its social, business and religious life

9.   The agency has implemented a new policy regarding the intake procedure. You wish to explain and discuss this policy with as many community groups as possible. You make an initial contact by mail.
In order to get your message across well, your letter should be

   9._____

A.   short and as concise as possible explaining why you want to meet with them, and offer several possible times that you will be available
B.   short, explaining only that it is important that the groups contact you in order to arrange a meeting
C.   drafted by the center's secretary and sent to the usual groups
D.   put in the usual announcement form in the center's newsletter

10.   A group of young welfare mothers want to form an organization that will provide baby-sitting services for mothers of children who are too young to enroll in a day care center. What should be your answer to them?

   10._____

A.   Tell them to try to get the center to change its policy to include young children
B.   Arrange the time to meet with them to offer as much advice and support as possible, since most communities do need this service
C.   Suggest that it may be better that they spend their time taking care of their own children
D.   Ask a social worker to survey the community to determine if such a service is really needed at this time

11.   New regulations have removed the disabled, blind and old age assistance cases from the public assistance caseload. Assistance in these categories is given directly by the federal government. A former client has not received his check. The chairman of the senior citizens committee calls and angrily demands that your agency do something in this man's behalf.
In response you should

   11._____

A.   answer politely, explaining that your agency is not concerned about OAA clients
B.   arrange to meet with him in order to discuss the new policy
C.   refer him to the Social Security office covering the area where the client lives
D.   ask that he call again when he is calmer so that you may discuss this matter with him

12.   A high school student from the community comes to see you about a homework assignment to write a report on your center.
The BEST way to help him is to

   12._____

A.   refer him to a social worker who has daily contact with clients in their homes
B.   contact the boy's teacher and find out why you were not warned of his coming
C.   explain your center's program and answer as many of his questions as you can
D.   give him literature about the welfare system in the city and state

13. Assume that the women's group of the Community Baptist Church has invited you to a   13._____
Sunday afternoon service to celebrate the tenth anniversary of the pastor. The agency's
relationship with the women is good in that they often offer their homes as emergency
homes for adult clients. What should you do about the invitation?

    A. Do not attend but send them a note congratulating the pastor and explaining that
agency personnel do not work on Sundays
    B. Ask a social worker who lives close to the church to go
    C. Accept the invitation if at all possible, attend the service and whatever social hour
they may have afterwards
    D. Ignore the invitation since this function has little relationship to your job

14. Suppose that a person you are interviewing becomes angry at some of the questions   14._____
you have asked, calls you meddlesome and nosy, and states that she will not answer
those questions.
Of the following, which is the BEST action for you to take?

    A. Explain the reasons the questions are asked and the importance of the answers
    B. Inform the interviewee that you are only doing your job and advise her that she
should answer your questions or leave your office
    C. Report to your supervisor what the interviewee called you and refuse to continue
the interview
    D. End the interview and tell the interviewee she will not be serviced by your depart-
ment

15. Suppose that during the course of an interview the interviewee demands in a very rude   15._____
way that she be permitted to talk to your supervisor or someone in charge.
Which of the following is probably the BEST way to handle this situation?

    A. Inform your supervisor of the demand and ask her to speak to the interviewee
    B. Pay no attention to the demands of the interviewee and continue the interview
    C. Report to your supervisor and tell her to get another interviewer for this interviewee
    D. Tell her you are the one "in charge" and that she should talk to you

16. Suppose that a worker asks a client to answer several required but rather personal ques-   16._____
tions about the family's health history. The client delays and seems embarrassed about
giving the answers.
Of the following, the MOST reasonable response to the client is one which

    A. shows an awareness of the client's efforts to hide something
    B. demonstrates the worker's qualifications for asking such questions
    C. allows this client to be excused from answering the questions
    D. convinces the client that his uneasiness in the situation is understood

17. A representative from a planned parenthood group comes to see you to get information   17._____
for a community education program.
You should

    A. check out this group to make sure it is not promoting zero population growth for
minority groups
    B. develop a good relationship with him so as to provide better service to clients
    C. make sure they will not encourage unnecessary abortions
    D. refuse to see him

18. A member of a clerical training program is continually late to classes. He explains to you that he has a hard time getting up and asks that you report him on time because he needs to train for a job.
What should your response be?

    A. Tell him that you get there on time and so should he
    B. Tell him that you do not lie for anyone
    C. Explain that it is your duty to keep accurate records and refer him to a counselor
    D. Tell him that you will cooperate with him but he has to try to do better

18.____

19. In a community meeting to explain a new agency policy, you find that the audience has no questions about the policy or your explanations.
What would be the *most appropriate* response to the silence?

    A. Leave right away before they think of questions
    B. Thank the audience for their attention and assure them that you will be available if there are any questions later
    C. Ask several members in the audience if they understand the new policy
    D. Explain that the audience could not possibly understand all of the policy and they must have questions

19.____

20. Assume that you are confronted by an angry member of the public who has not been able to obtain the information he needs from your office. You do not know the answer to his question.
The BEST thing for you to do would be to

    A. tell him to come back another time, after you have looked up the information
    B. check with your supervisor to find the correct answer
    C. tell him to ask in another office, so that you will not lose time looking for the information
    D. make up an answer to keep the man satisfied until the right answer is found

20.____

KEY (CORRECT ANSWERS)

1. C		11. C
2. D		12. C
3. C		13. C
4. C		14. A
5. C		15. A
6. C		16. D
7. C		17. B
8. A		18. C
9. A		19. B
10. B		20. B

EXAMINATION SECTION
TEST 1

DIRECTIONS: Each question or incomplete statement is followed by several suggested answers or completions. Select the one that BEST answers the question or completes the statement. *PRINT THE LETTER OF THE CORRECT ANSWER IN THE SPACE AT THE RIGHT.*

1. You are visiting a patient for the first time to determine whether she is eligible for health care benefits.
   Of the following, the MOST appropriate way for you to begin the interview is by saying:
   Good morning,

   A. it is important that you answer my questions honestly because the information you give will have to be verified
   B. I'm sorry to learn of your illness; let's hope your health insurance will pay for your hospital bill
   C. I am going to ask you some questions to help determine what financial resources and programs can be used to pay your hospital bill
   D. if you cooperate in answering my questions, you will have nothing to worry about

   1.____

2. You are interviewing a patient to determine whether she is eligible for medical assistance. Of the many questions that you have to ask her, some are routine questions that patients tend to answer willingly and easily. Other questions are more personal and some patients tend to resent being asked them and avoid answering them directly.
   For you to begin the interview with the more personal questions would be

   A. *desirable,* because the end of the interview will go smoothly and the patient will be left with a warm feeling
   B. *undesirable,* because the patient might not know the answers to the questions
   C. *desirable,* because you will be able to return to these questions later to verify the accuracy of the responses
   D. *undesirable,* because you might antagonize the patient before you have had a chance to establish rapport

   2.____

3. Assume that you have been asking a patient questions to fill out the forms needed to process his application for Medicaid. Although the questions you are asking are the ones you usually ask patients, he refuses to answer them, claiming that the information is none of your business. You have already explained, to the best of your ability, that he will require outside financial resources to help pay his hospital bill, that the questions must be answered in order to process his application for Medicaid, and that applying for Medicaid is no reason to be embarrased or ashamed. The patient still maintains that he has no intention of answering your *prying* questions regardless of the consequences.
   The one of the following which is the MOST appropriate course of action for you to take is to

   A. advise the patient that you intend to continue the interview until you have obtained all the necessary information
   B. end the interview and ask your supervisor for suggestions in handling the situation
   C. advise the patient that he seems to be too excited to continue with the interview and ask him to contact you when he is ready to answer the questions
   D. end the interview and contact a member of his family to discuss possible causes for the patient's irrational behavior

   3.____

35

4. Which one of the following is the most important purpose for using a direct approach such as *how many children do you have?* rather than a less direct approach such as *tell me about your children* in interviewing a patient for medical assistance?
To

    A. establish the patient's confidence in the investigator's objectivity
    B. discourage the patient from trying to withhold information from the investigator
    C. encourage the patient to speak freely about matters which are important to him
    D. elicit from the patient specific information the investigator is seeking

4.____

5. Of the following, the BEST time to write up the information you have obtained from and given to the patient in your initial interview is

    A. shortly after the interview is completed to avoid forgetting the information
    B. after a day or two when you have had time to digest the information you have gathered
    C. during the interview in order to save time that you can devote to interviewing other patients
    D. as soon as you have verified all the statements that the patient made during the interview

5.____

6. The patient you are interviewing states that he has never been hospitalized. However, his wife previously told you that he had been a patient in the same hospital about six months before.
Of the following, the BEST way for you to handle this situation is to

    A. inform the patient that you know that he had previously been a patient in the hospital
    B. tell the patient that his wife has revealed that he was previously a patient in the hospital
    C. advise the patient to reconsider his statement because you have reason to believe that he is not telling you the truth
    D. check hospital records to determine whether he was previously a patient in the hospital

6.____

7. The one of the following which is the BEST reason NOT to ask the patient questions such as, *you have never been in this hospital before, right?* is that they

    A. suggest that the interviewer is uninformed
    B. require lengthy explanations by the patient
    C. suggest a specific desired response
    D. require the interviewer to exercise great care in formulating them

7.____

8. You have just completed an interview during which the patient displayed hostility toward you and was uncooperative in his responses. Recently, patients have reacted to you in this manner with increasing frequency.
Of the following, what would be MOST appropriate for you to do FIRST in handling this situation?

8.____

A. Develop a forceful approach that you can use in counteracting anticipated incidents of patient hostility
B. Assess your own behavior during these interviews to determine whether you contributed toward patient hostility
C. Accept these incidents as being atypical in the light of your many successful interviews
D. Ask your supervisor to make a more equitable distribution of the difficult cases as you seem to be getting a disproportionate share of them

9. You are interviewing a patient to obtain information to be used in filling out the forms required to determine his eligibility for medical assistance. He doesn't seem to understand some technical terms you are using, such as *real property, assets,* and *disability.* Of the following, the BEST way to convey the meanings of the terms to the patient is for you to   9.____

A. define each of the terms and then illustrate each one by giving examples
B. repeat the terms often throughout the interview so that the patient will be able to learn their meanings by the way they are being used
C. ask a patient in a nearby bed to help explain the terms to the patient being interviewed
D. write down the terms so that the patient can see them as well as hear them

10. During an interview with a patient, you realize that he bears a strong physical resemblance to Mr. Fisher, a patient you have interviewed previously. Mr. Fisher was difficult to work with and uncooperative in answering your questions.
Of the following, the MOST appropriate action for you to take is to   10.____

A. try to determine if there are similarities in the patients' personalities as well as in their physical appearances
B. convey to the patient your hope that he will be cooperative and easy to deal with
C. maintain your ability to obtain accurate information from the patient
D. recognize that it will not be easy to continue the interview and ask your supervisor to assign the case to another investigator

11. To verify the amount a patient receives in Social Security disability benefits, which one of the following sources would be LEAST appropriate?   11.____

A. The patient's Social Security Medicare identification card
B. The notice the patient received from the Social Security Administration indicating the amount awarded for disability
C. The patient's monthly Social Security disability benefits check
D. A statement from the Social Security Administration attesting to the amount of the patient's disability benefits check

12. To verify the amount earned by a married female patient who is currently employed, which one of the following sources would be LEAST appropriate?   12.____

A. The patient's most recent W-2 form
B. A written statement from her employer specifying the amount she earns
C. Several of the patient's most recent pay stubs
D. A written statement from her husband specifying the amount she earns

13. Of the following, the MOST important reason for verifying that a female patient is married to a veteran with a service-connected total disability is that she may be

13.____

    A. receiving a dependent's disability allowance from the Veterans Administration
    B. eligible for benefits under a medical insurance program as the spouse of a veteran with a total service-connected disability
    C. eligible for a discount on her hospital bill as the dependent of a disabled veteran
    D. receiving a pension from the Veterans Administration that should be considered income

14. You are interviewing a patient who complains that he does not want to answer any more questions right now because he is tired. You agree to return the next day. As you are leaving, he mentions something that seems to supplement a previous response.
For you to consider this additional information to be of value would be

14.____

    A. *advisable,* because it is still part of the interview and should be considered with the rest of the information the patient provided
    B. *inadvisable,* because the patient had told you he was too tired to continue with the interview and might not know what he is saying
    C. *advisable,* because information that is volunteered is more important than information obtained in response to a direct question
    D. *inadvisable,* because the patient did not offer the information in response to a direct question

15. You have interviewed a patient to fill out an application for medical assistance. While verifying the information the patient provided, you find discrepancies in important areas, such as sources of income.
Of the following, the MOST appropriate approach for you to take is to

15.____

    A. process the application with a notation that the patient had submitted fraudulent information
    B. inform the patient that you have uncovered fraudulent information and advise her of the consequence
    C. set up a second interview with the patient to discuss the conflicting information
    D. assume the patient was confused and process the application routinely

16. For you to use responses such as *That's interesting, Uh-huh,* and *Good* during an interview with a patient is

16.____

    A. *desirable,* because they indicate that the investigator is attentive
    B. *undesirable,* because they are meaningless to the patient
    C. *desirable,* because the investigator is not supposed to talk excessively
    D. *undesirable,* because they tend to encourage the patient to speak freely

17. During an interview, a patient repeatedly complains that her doctor does not discuss her medical condition with her. She fears that she has a very serious illness.
Of the following, the MOST appropriate way for you to handle this situation is to

17.____

    A. reassure the patient by telling her that you know that the diagnosis is not serious and proceed with the interview
    B. suggest to the patient that her doctor probably has good reasons for not discussing her condition with her
    C. refrain from responding to the patient's complaints and proceed with the interview

D. indicate to the patient that you understand her concern about her medical condition and proceed with the interview

18. The patient you are interviewing is reticent and guarded in responding to your questions. He is not providing the information needed to complete his application for medical assistance.
In this situation, the one of the following which is the most appropriate course of action for you to take FIRST is to

    A. end the interview and ask him to contact you when he is ready to answer your questions
    B. advise the patient that you cannot end the interview until he has provided all the information you need to complete the application
    C. emphasize to the patient the importance of the questions and the need to answer them in order to complete the application
    D. advise the patient that if he answers your questions the interview will be easier for both of you

18.____

19. At the end of an interview with a patient, he describes a problem he is having with his teenage son, who is often truant and may be using narcotics. The patient asks you for advice in handling his son.
Of the following, the MOST appropriate action for you to take is to

    A. make an appointment to see the patient and his son together
    B. give the patient a list of drug counseling programs to which he may refer his son
    C. suggest to the patient that his immediate concern should be his own hospitalization rather than his son's problem
    D. tell the patient that you are not qualified to assist him but will attempt to find out who can

19.____

20. In response to a question about his employment history, a patient you are interviewing rambles and talks about unrelated matters.
Of the following, the MOST appropriate course of action for you to take FIRST is to

    A. ask questions to direct the patient hack to his employment history
    B. advise him to concentrate on your questions and not to discuss irrelevant information
    C. ask him why he is resisting a discussion of his employment history
    D. advise him that if you cannot get the information you need, he will not be eligible for medical assistance

20.____

21. A patient whom you are interviewing has not clearly answered one of your questions. You have asked him to restate his answer and you still are not certain of what he is saying.
Of the following, the MOST effective method of ensuring you understand what the patient has said is to

    A. ask him to continue to respond to the question until you are sure you understand
    B. rephrase his response in your own words and ask him if that is what he meant
    C. write down word-for-word what he is saying and try to analyze what he said after you have left him
    D. advise the patient that it is his responsibility to make himself clear to you in order for you to help him

21.____

22. Which one of the following questions would it be LEAST appropriate for you to use in obtaining accurate information from an adult patient?

    A. Have you ever been hospitalized previously?
    B. You have been in the hospital for how long?
    C. Do you have any children?
    D. You don't have any savings, do you?

22.____

23. You are interviewing an elderly married patient who is having trouble supplying you with the information needed to determine if she is eligible for medical assistance. She appears to be forgetful and confused.
Of the following approaches, the one which would be LEAST appropriate in obtaining information about this patient is to

    A. contact her husband to ask him to provide the needed information
    B. check whether she has a previous medical record on file in the hospital
    C. ask her to get the necessary information and to contact you after she has obtained it
    D. check whether the social services department of the hospital has the information that you need

23.____

24. While interviewing a patient about her family composition, the patient asks you whether you are married.
Of the following, the MOST appropriate way for you to handle this situation is to

    A. answer the question briefly and redirect her back to the topic under discussion
    B. refrain from answering the question and proceed with the interview
    C. advise the patient that it is more important that she answer your questions than that you answer hers, and proceed with the interview
    D. promise the patient that you will answer her question later, in the hope that she will forget, and redirect her back to the topic under discussion

24.____

25. The one of the following which is the LEAST acceptable way to bring to a close the first of several interviews with a patient is to

    A. tell the patient that you look forward to seeing him at the next interview
    B. assure the patient that you know that he will be well soon
    C. discuss with the patient an appropriate time for the next interview
    D. review briefly the important points covered in the interview

25.____

KEY (CORRECT ANSWERS)

1.	C		11.	A
2.	D		12.	D
3.	B		13.	B
4.	D		14.	A
5.	A		15.	C
6.	D		16.	A
7.	C		17.	D
8.	B		18.	C
9.	A		19.	D
10.	C		20.	A

21.	B
22.	D
23.	C
24.	A
25.	B

———

EXAMINATION SECTION

TEST 1

DIRECTIONS: Each question or incomplete statement is followed by several suggested answers or completions. Select the one that BEST answers the question or completes the statement. *PRINT THE LETTER OF THE CORRECT ANSWER IN THE SPACE AT THE RIGHT.*

Questions 1-4.

DIRECTIONS: Questions 1 through 4 are to be answered SOLELY on the basis of the information and the American Hospitalization Claim Form given below. Assume that the word *patient* refers ONLY to Karen Drew.

Karen Drew was born on May 3, 1981 in Selma, Alabama. At the time of her admission to City Hospital, 128 Front Street, she was residing with her husband, James Drew, and her father-in-law, Harold Drew, at 208 Second Avenue. She has been living there since her marriage on April 15, 2012. She was admitted to City Hospital on April 24, 2014 at 8 P.M. It was the first time that she had ever been hospitalized. The attending physician was John Wilson, whose office is located on the ground floor of his residence at 231 Lincoln Avenue, Manhattan. Karen gave birth by means of a classic cesarean section, to a six-pound daughter, Sharon Ann, on April 25, 2014 at 10 P.M. On May 2, 2014, James Drew was informed that his wife and daughter were to be discharged from the hospital at 10 A.M. that morning. He took that day off from his job as an ambulance driver with the Metropolitan Ambulance Company, located at 311 Elm Avenue, Manhattan, and took his wife and daughter home. The hospital charges were paid, in part, by the American Hospitalization contract, Certificate Number 372-71-7100, held by James Drew.

AMERICAN HOSPITALIZATION CLAIM FORM			
PATIENT'S NAME (LAST)	(FIRST)		(MIDDLE INITIAL)
ADDRESS (NO.) (STREET)	(CITY)	(STATE) (ZIP)	
PATIENT'S BIRTHDATE MO. DAY YEAR	PATIENT'S EMPLOYER		
NAME OF CONTRACT HOLDER	CONTRACT HOLDER'S EMPLOYER (IF CONTRACT HOLDER ISN'T PATIENT)		
PAT'S RELATIONSHIP TO CONT. HLDR. SEL SPOUSE □ DAUGHTER □ SON □ F □	NAME AND ADDRESS OF PHYSICIAN		
DATE ADMITTED MO. DAY YEAR	HOUR ADMITTED AM PM	ADMITTING DIAGNOSIS(ES)	
DATE DISCHARGED	CURRENT OR FINAL DIAGNOSIS(ES)		IF SURGERY WAS PERFORMED, GIVE PROCEDURES AND DATES
CHECK IF □ DIED □ STILL INSURED	WAS PREGNANCY TERMINATED □ NO □ YES		
CHART NO.	HOSPITAL NAME AND ADDRESS		CODE NO.

1. Which one of the following boxes should be checked in the space on the American Hospitalization Claim Form labeled PAT'S RELATIONSHIP TO CONT. HLDR?
    A. Self   B. Spouse   C. Daughter   D. Son

1.____

2. Which one of the following should be entered in the space on the American Hospitalization Claim Form labeled HOSPITAL NAME AND ADDRESS?
    A. 128 Front Street   B. 208 Second Avenue
    C. 231 Lincoln Avenue   D. 311 Elm Avenue

2.____

3. Which one of the following spaces on the American Hospitalization Claim Form could NOT be completed based solely on the information given above?
    A. Hour Admitted   B. Patient's Birthdate
    C. Patient's Employer   D. Name of Contract Holder

3.____

4. Which one of the following dates should be entered in the space on the American Hospitalization Claim Form labeled DATE DISCHARGED?
    A. April 24, 2014   B. April 25, 2014
    C. May 2, 2014   D. May 3, 2014

4.____

Questions 5-10.

DIRECTIONS: Questions 5 through 10 are to be answered SOLELY on the basis of the information obtained in the patient interview and from the previous Admission given below.

PATIENT INTERVIEW

You have interviewed a patient, William J. Marcy, who was admitted to the hospital with a bleeding ulcer on April 15, 2014 by his physician, Henry Sampson. The patient has told you that he resides at 74-21 134th Street, Flushing, Queens, New York, with his wife, Denise, and her two daughters by a previous marriage. Their home phone number is (718) 842-1987. His next of kin is his daughter, Diane James, who resides at 2904 River Street, Bronx, New York. He is employed by the New York Realty Corporation, 25 East 34th Street, Brooklyn, New York, as an elevator starter and has been in their employ for twenty years. His only health insurance coverage is that provided by Blue Cross/Blue Shield, Certificate Number 436-81-2942.

At the end of the interview, he tells you that he had previously been admitted to this hospital on February 11, 2013. Based on this information, you obtain a copy of his previous admission record, which follows.

3 (#1)

ADMISSION RECORD
(previous)

LINE NO.		
1	PATIENT'S NAME (LAST, FIRST, MIDDLE INITIAL) Marcy, William J.	PATIENT'S SOCIAL SECURITY NO. 436-81-2942
2	PATIENT'S ADDRESS 74-21 134th Street, Flushing, Queens, New York	PATIENT'S PHONE NO. (HOME) (718) 842-1987
3	PATIENT'S DATE OF BIRTH AGE 56 4.5.56	SEX MARITAL STATUS (Check One) M ☐ Single ☐ Married ☐ Divorced ☒ Widowed ☐ Other
4	NAME AND ADDRESS OF NEXT OF KIN Diane James, 2904 River Street, Bronx, New York	RELATIONSHIP OF NEXT OF KIN TO PATIENT Daughter

5	PATIENT'S OCCUPATION Window Cleaner	NAME & ADDRESS OF PATIENT'S EMPLOYER New York Realty Corp. 25 E. 34th St., Bklyn, NY	NAME & TITLE OF PATIENT'S SUPERVISOR George Grant Window Cleaning Foreman

6	DATE OF ADMISSION 2.11.13	TIME OF ADMISSION 3:00 PM	DATE OF DISCHARGE 2.24.13	TIME OF DISCHARGE 10:00 AM	LENGTH OF STAY 13 days

7	NAME OF ATTENDING PHYSICIAN Sam Henry	REASON FOR ADMISSION Concussion and broken ribs

8	TYPE(S) OF INSURANCE COVERAGE (IF ANY) Blue Cross/Blue Shield	CERT. NO. 436-81-2942	INJURED/SICK ON JOB ☒ YES ☐ NO

Questions 5 through 10 refer to entries that would be made on the current Admission Record shown below. These entries are to be based SOLELY on the information obtained from the patient interview and the previous Admission Record given above.

ADMISSION RECORD
(current)

LINE NO.					
1	DATE OF ADMISSION	TIME OF ADMISSION	DATE OF DISCHARGE	LENGTH OF STAY	DATE(S) OF PRIOR ADMISSION(S) TO THIS HOSPITAL
2	PATIENT'S NAME (LAST, FIRST, MIDDLE INITIAL)		PATIENT'S ADDRESS		PATIENT'S PHONE NO. (Home)
3	PATIENT'S AGE	DATE OF BIRTH	SEX	MARITAL STATUS (Check One) ☐ Single ☐ Married ☐Divorced ☐ Widowed ☐ Other	
4	PATIENT'S OCCUPATION	NAME AND ADDRESS OF PATIENT'S EMPLOYER		PATIENT'S PHONE NO. (Work)	
5	NAME AND TITLE OF PATIENT'S SUPERVISOR		PATIENT'S SOCIAL SECURITY NO.	INJURED/SICK ON JOB ☐ Yes ☐ No	
6	NAME OF ATTENDING PHYSICIAN		REASON FOR ADMISSION		
7	NAME, ADDRESS, & TELEPHONE NO. OF NEXT OF KIN		RELATIONSHIP OF NEXT OF KIN TO PATIENT		
8	TYPES OF INSURANCE COVERAGE (IF ANY)		CERTIFICATE NO.		

5. Which one of the following entries should NOT be made on Line 3 of the
   current Admission Record?
   A. 5-4-56   B. 58   C. [x] Married   D. M

   5.____

6. Which one of the following entries would be the SAME on both admission
   records?
   A. 13 days   B. Window Cleaner
   C. Sam Henry   D. Blue Cross/Blue Shield

   6.____

7. Which one of the following lines on the current Admission Record could NOT
   be completed based solely on the information given in the patient interview and
   on the previous Admission Record?
   A. 7   B. 6   C. 3   D. 2

   7.____

8. Which one of the following lines on the current Admission Record could be
   completed based SOLELY on the information given in the patient interview and
   on the previous Admission Record?
   A. 1   B. 4   C. 5   D. 8

   8.____

9. In which one of the following spaces on the current Admission Record could
   an entry be made based SOLELY on the information obtained from the patient
   interview and from the previous Admission Record?
   A. Patient's Age
   B. Injured/Sick On Job
   C. Name, Address, and Telephone of Next of Kin
   D. Date of Discharge

   9.____

10. Which one of the following entries made on the previous Admission Record
    should NOT be transferred to the current Admission Record?
    A. 74-21 134th Street, Flushing, Queens, New York
    B. Concussion and broken ribs
    C. New York Realty Corp., 25 E. 34th St., Brooklyn, NY
    D. 436-81-2942

    10.____

11. Which of the following medical insurance programs utilizes a means test
    in determining a person's eligibility for the program?
    A. Medicare   B. Group Health Incorporated
    C. Blue Cross   D. Medicaid

    11.____

12. Which one of the following combinations MOST fully describes the sources
    of funding for the Medicaid program in the city? _____ tax funds.
    A. Federal, State, and City B. State and City
    C. Federal and City   D. Federal and State

    12.____

13. It would be MOST appropriate for a person wishing to enroll in Medicare to contact which one of the following organizations? The

    A. City Department of Social Services
    B. State Department of Health
    C. United States Social Security Administration
    D. State Department of Social Services

13.____

14. Assume that a hospital patient claims she has medical insurance under Medicare. The one of the following which would indicate whether the patient has such insurance is the patient's

    A. Medicare health insurance card
    B. Social Security card
    C. most recent Federal income tax return
    D. most recent W-2 form

14.____

15. The one of the following benefits which is NOT provided for a worker covered by State Worker's Compensation is

    A. payment of weekly cash benefits if he is disabled as a result of an occupational disease
    B. medical care he requires as a result of an accidental injury on his job
    C. payment of weekly cash benefits to his widow if he dies as a result of an accident on the job
    D. medical care for his widow and minor children if he dies as a result of an occupational disease

15.____

16. A 40-year-old woman is legally responsible to contribute, if able, to the support of which one of the following recipients of Medicaid? Her

    A. 22-year-old daughter   B. 65-year-old father
    C. 45-year-old husband   D. 30-year-old sister

16.____

Questions 17-19.

DIRECTIONS: Questions 17 through 19 are to be answered on the basis of the following information.

    A patient who is enrolled in the hospital insurance part of Medicare is entitled to receive covered services as a bed patient in a hospital participating in the Medicare program and to receive such services in a skilled nursing facility participating in the program. In a benefit period, Medicare will help to pay for a maximum number of hospital days in such hospital and for a maximum number of extended care days in a skilled nursing facility. A patient is also entitled to a specific number of hospital days for which he is covered in a benefit period.

    In each question, assume that the patient has not previously had any covered services.

17. The MAXIMUM number of hospital days in a benefit period that Medicare will help to pay for the patient is

    A. 100   B. 90   C. 60   D. 30

17.____

18. The MAXIMUM number of extended care days in a benefit period that Medicare will help to pay for the patient is   18.____
    A. 120   B. 100   C. 90   D. 60

19. The MAXIMUM number of lifetime reserve hospital days to which the patient is entitled is   19.____
    A. 120   B. 90   C. 60   D. 30

20. The one of the following persons who is automatically eligible for Medicaid in the city is anyone who is   20.____
    A. eligible for Medicare
    B. receiving public assistance from an income maintenance center
    C. eligible for Group Health Incorporated
    D. receiving disability insurance benefits from the state

21. The one of the following statements which BEST describes the term *Senior Care* as it is used in the Blue Cross Plan is that *Senior Care*   21.____
    A. is a substitute for the Medicare program
    B. provides custodial care benefits for senior citizens
    C. is a substitute for the Medicaid program
    D. supplements the benefits provided by the Medicare program

22. Assume that a patient who is eligible for benefits under the hospital insurance part of Medicare has never used these benefits. Payment CANNOT be made under the hospital insurance part of Medicare if the patient's *primary* need is for   22.____
    A. regular nursing care provided in a skilled nursing facility
    B. custodial care provided in a skilled nursing facility
    C. intensive care provided in a hospital
    D. medical social services provided in a hospital

23. Which one of the following children is NOT protected by a parent's family membership in the 120-day hospital program of Blue Cross/Blue Shield?   23.____
    A. Unemployed, married 17-year-old child
    B. Newborn child
    C. Employed, unmarried 18-year-old child
    D. Adopted 12-year-old child

24. Which one of the following statements BEST describes the term *catastrophic illness* as it is used in the Medicaid program? An illness which   24.____
    A. reduces a person's life expectancy to less than 6 months
    B. is the result of a natural disaster, such as an earthquake
    C. results in 60 or more consecutive days of hospital care
    D. results in hospital costs that exceed 25 percent of a person's annual net income

25. Which one of the following types of medical insurance covering a patient   25.____
    would NOT reimburse the patient directly but would reimburse only the provider
    of medical services?

    A. Medicare   B. Blue Shield
    C. Medicaid   D. State No-Fault Auto Insurance

_____

KEY (CORRECT ANSWERS)

1.	B		11.	D
2.	A		12.	A
3.	C		13.	C
4.	C		14.	A
5.	A		15.	D
6.	D		16.	C
7.	A		17.	B
8.	D		18.	B
9.	A		19.	C
10.	B		20.	B

21.	D
22.	B
23.	A
24.	D
25.	C

_____

TEST 2

DIRECTIONS: Each question or incomplete statement is followed by several suggested answers or completions. Select the one that BEST answers the question or completes the statement. *PRINT THE LETTER OF THE CORRECT ANSWER IN THE SPACE AT THE RIGHT.*

1. A patient spent two days in a municipal hospital for a leg injury after being struck in the city by a car registered and insured in the state. His hospital bill for this injury was $4,500. The patient was not eligible either for Workmen's Compensation or for Social Security disability benefits. The patient admitted that the accident was his fault as he was walking across the street against the traffic light. The patient owns a car which is also registered and insured in the state.
The one of the following that would contribute toward the payment of the patient's hospital bill is the
   A. patient, since the accident was his own fault
   B. company insuring the car that struck the patient
   C. company insuring the patient's car
   D. municipal hospital, since its medical services are free

1.____

2. Hospital patients eligible for the hospital insurance part of Medicare currently have the responsibility for paying the first part of their hospital expenses in each benefit period. According to the law establishing Medicare, this amount for which patients are responsible must be adjusted if annual review shows a significant change in
   A. hospital costs   B. the Social Security tax
   C. the consumer price index   D. patients' incomes

2.____

3. To which one of the following benefits is a subscriber of the 120-day hospital program of Blue Cross/Blue Shield entitled?
   A. Payment in full of the hospital charges for a private room
   B. Ambulance service
   C. Payment in full of the hospital charges for normal delivery of a baby
   D. Anesthesia supplies and use of anesthesia equipment

3.____

4. The one of the following owned by a patient which is considered to be an asset in determining his eligibility for Medicaid is his
   A. common stock holdings   B. automobile
   C. term insurance policy   D. color television set

4.____

5. Which one of the following categories of workers is NOT covered by Workmen's Compensation in the state?
   A. Public school aides
   B. Employees of the Federal government
   C. Private chauffeurs
   D. Employees of the state

5.____

6. A hospital's daily rate is $615. This rate includes all hospital services with   6.____
    the exception of blood for which the hospital charges an additional $10 per pint.
    If a patient was charged for 12 days of hospitalization and the total hospital bill,
    including blood, was $8,010, how many pints of blood did the patient receive?
       A. 5   B. 6   C. 7   D. 8

Questions 7-11.

DIRECTIONS: Questions 7 through 11 are to be answered SOLELY on the basis of the
information contained in the following passage.

The payment for medical services covered under the Outpatient Medical Insurance Plan
(OMI) may be made, by OMI, directly to a physician or to the OMI patient. If the physician and
the patient agree that the physician is to receive payment directly from OMI, the payment will be
officially assigned to the physician; this is the assignment method. If payment is not assigned,
the patient receives payment directly from OMI based on an itemized bill he submits, regardless
of whether or not he has already paid his physician.

When a physician accepts assignment of the payment for medical services, he agrees that
total charges will not be more than the allowed charge determined by the OMI carrier
administering the program. In such cases, the OMI patient pays any unmet part of the $85
annual deductible, plus 10 percent of the remaining charges to the physician. In unassigned
claims, the patient is responsible for the total amount charged by the physician. The patient will
then be reimbursed by the program 990 percent of the allowed charges in excess of the annual
deductible.

The rates of acceptance of assignments provide a measure of how many OMI patients are
spared *administrative participation* in the program. Because physicians are free to accept or
reject assignments, the rate in which assignments are made provide a general indication of the
medical community's satisfaction with the OMI program, especially with the level of amounts
paid by the program for specific services and the promptness of payment.

7. According to the above passage, in order for a physician to receive payment   7.____
    directly from OMI for medical services to an OMI patient, the physician would
    have to accept the assignment of payment, to have the consent of the patient,
    and to
       A. submit to OMI a paid itemized bill
       B. collect from the patient 90% of the total bill
       C. collect from the patient the total amount of the charges for his services, a
          portion of which he will later reimburse the patient
       D. agree that his charges for services to the patient will not exceed the
          amount allowed by the program

8. According to the above passage, if a physician accepts assignment of   8.____
    payment, the patient pays
       A. the total amount charged by the physician and is reimbursed by the
          program for 90 percent of the allowed charges in excess of the applicable
          deductible
       B. any unmet part of the $85 annual deductible, plus 90 percent of the
          remaining charges

C. the total amount charged by the physician and is reimbursed by the program for 10 percent of the allowed charges in excess of the $85 annual deductible

D. any unmet part of the $85 annual deductible, plus 10 percent of the remaining charges

9. A physician has accepted the assignment of payment for charges to an OMI patient. The physician's charges, all of which are allowed under OMI, amount to $115. This is the first time the patient has been eligible for OMI benefits and the first time the patient has received services from this physician.
According to the above passage, the patient must pay the physician
    A. $27   B. $76.50   C. $88   D. $103.50

9.____

10. In an unassigned claim, a physician's charges, all of which are allowed under OMI, amount to $165. The patient paid the physician the full amount of the bill. If this is the first time the patient has been eligible for OMI benefits, he will received from OMI a reimbursement of
    A. $72   B. $80   C. $85   D. $93

10.____

11. According to the above passage, if the rate of acceptance of assignments by physicians is high, it is LEAST appropriate to conclude that the medical community is generally satisfied with the
    A. supplementary medical insurance program
    B. levels of amounts paid to physicians by the program
    C. number of OMI patients being spared administrative participation in the program
    D. promptness of the program in making payment for services

11.____

Questions 12-15.

DIRECTIONS: Questions 12 through 15 are to be answered SOLELY on the basis of the information contained in the following passage.

One fundamental difference between the United States health care system and the health care systems of some European countries is the way that hospital charges for long-term illnesses affect their citizens.

In European countries, such as England, Sweden, and Germany, citizens can face, without fear, hospital charges due to prolonged illness, no matter how substantial they may be. Citizens of these nations are required to pay nothing when they are hospitalized, for they have prepaid their treatment as taxpayers when they were well and were earning incomes.

On the other hand, the United States citizen, in spite of the growth of payments by third parties which include private insurance carriers as well as public resources, has still to shoulder 40 percent of hospital care costs, while his private insurance contributes only 25 percent and public resources the remaining 35 percent. Despite expansion of private health insurance and social legislation in the United States, out-of-pocket payments for hospital care by individuals have steadily increased. Such payments, currently totaling $23 billion, are nearly twice as high as ten years ago.

Reform is inevitable and, when it comes, will have to reconcile sharply conflicting interests. Hospital staffs are demanding higher and higher wages. Hospitals are under pressure by citizens who, as patients, demand more and better services but who, as taxpayers, or as subscribers to hospital insurance plans, are reluctant to pay the higher cost of improved care. An acceptable reconciliation of these interests has so far eluded legislators and health administrators sin the United States.

12. According to the above passage, the one of the following which is an ADVANTAGE that citizens of England, Sweden, and Germany have over United States citizens is that when faced with long-term illness   12.____
    A. the amount of out-of-pocket payments made by these European citizens is small when compared to out-of-pocket payments made by United States citizens
    B. European citizens have no fear of hospital costs no matter how great they may be
    C. more efficient and reliable hospitals are available to the European citizens than is available to the United States citizens
    D. a greater range of specialized hospital care is available to the European citizens than is available to the United States citizens

13. According to the above passage, reform of the United States system of health care must reconcile all of the following EXCEPT   13.____
    A. attempts by health administrators to provide improved hospital care
    B. taxpayers' reluctance to pay for the cost of more and better hospital services
    C. demands by hospital personnel for higher wages
    D. insurance subscribers' reluctance to pay the higher costs of improved hospital care

14. According to the above passage, the out-of-pocket payments for hospital care that individuals made ten years ago was APPROXIMATELY _____ billion.   14.____
    A. $32   B. $23   C. $12   D. $3

15. According to the above passage, the GREATEST share of the costs of hospital care in the United States is paid by   15.____
    A. United States citizens   B. private insurance carriers
    C. public resources   D. third parties

Questions 16-19.

DIRECTIONS: Questions 16 through 19 are to be answered SOLELY on the basis of the information contained in the following passage.

Effective cost controls have been difficult to establish in most hospitals in the United States. Ways must be found to operate hospitals with reasonable efficiency without sacrificing quality and in a manner that will reduce the amount of personal income now being spent on health care and the enormous drain on national resources. We must adopt a new public objective of providing higher quality health care at significantly lower cost. One step that can be taken to achieve this goal is to carefully control capital expenditures for hospital construction and expansion. Perhaps the way to start is to declare a moratorium on all hospital construction and to determine the factors that should be considered in deciding whether a hospital should be built. Such factors might include population growth, distance to the nearest hospital, availability of medical personnel, and hospital bed shortage.

A second step to achieve the new objective is to increase the ratio of out-of-hospital patient to in-hospital patient care. This can be done by using separate health care facilities other than hospitals to attract patients who have increasingly been going to hospital clinics and overcrowding them. Patients should instead identify with a separate health care facility to keep them out of hospitals.

A third step is to require better hospital operating rules and controls. This step might include the review of a doctor's performance by other doctors, outside professional evaluations of medical practice, and required refresher courses and re-examinations for doctors. Other measures might include obtaining mandatory second opinions on the need for surgery in order to avoid unnecessary surgery, and outside review of work rules and procedures to eliminate unnecessary testing of patients.

A fourth step is to halt the construction and public subsidizing of new medical schools and to fill whatever needs exist in professional coverage by emphasizing the medical training of physicians with specialties that are in short supply and by providing a better geographic distribution of physicians and surgeons.

16. According to the above passage, providing higher quality health care at lower   16.____
cost can be achieved by the
    A. greater use of out-of-hospital facilities
    B. application of more effective cost controls on doctors' fees
    C. expansion of improved in-hospital patient care services at hospital clinics
    D. development of more effective training programs in hospital
       administration

17. According to the above passage, the one of the following which should be   17.____
taken into account in determining if a hospital should be constructed is the
    A. number of out-of-hospital health care facilities
    B. availability of public funds to subsidize construction
    C. number of hospitals under construction
    D. availability of medical personnel

18. According to the above passage, it is IMPORTANT to operate hospitals   18.____
efficiently because
    A. they are currently in serious financial difficulties
    B. of the need to reduce the amount of personal income going to health care
    C. the quality of health care services has deteriorated
    D. of the need to increase productivity goals to take care of the growing
       population in the United States

19. According to the above passage, which one of the following approaches is   19.____
MOST likely to result in better operating rules and controls in hospitals?
    A. Allocating doctors to health care facilities on the basis of patient
       population
    B. Equalizing the workloads of doctors
    C. Establishing a physician review board to evaluate the performance of
       other physicians
    D. Eliminating unnecessary outside review of patient testing

Questions 20-25.

DIRECTIONS: Questions 20 through 25 are to be answered SOLELY on the basis
              of the information given in the following passage.

The United States today is the only major industrial nation in the world without a system of
national health insurance or a national health service. Instead, we have placed our prime
reliance on private enterprise and private health insurance to meet the need. Yet in a recent
year, of the 180 million Americans under 65 years of age, 34 million had no hospital insurance;
38 million had no surgical insurance; 63 million had no outpatient x-ray and laboratory
insurance; 94 million had no insurance for prescription drugs; and 103 million had no insurance
for physician office visits or home visits. Some 35 million Americans under the age of 65 had no
health insurance whatsoever. Some 64 million additional Americans under age 65 had health
insurance coverage that was less than that provided to the aged under Medicare.
Despite more than three decades of enormous growth, the private health insurance
industry today pays benefits equal to only one-third of the total cost of private health care,
leaving the rest to be borne by the patient - essentially the same ratio which held true a decade
ago. Moreover, nearly all private health insurance is limited; it provides partial benefits, not
comprehensive benefits; acute care, not preventive care; it siphons off the young and healthy,
and ignores the poor and medically indigent. The typical private carrier usually pays only the
cost of hospital care, forcing physicians and patients alike to resort to wasteful and inefficient
use of hospital facilities, thereby giving further impetus to the already soaring costs of hospital
care. Valuable hospital beds are used for routine tests and examinations. Unnecessary
hospitalization, unnecessary surgery, and unnecessarily extended hospital stays are
encouraged. These problems are exacerbated by the fact that administrative costs of
commercial carriers are substantially higher than they are for Blue Shield, Blue Cross, or
Medicare.

20. According to the above passage, the PROPORTION of total private health care   20.____
costs paid by private health insurance companies today as compared to ten
years ago, has
    A. increased by approximately one-third
    B. remained practically the same
    C. increased by approximately two-thirds
    D. decreased by approximately one-third

21. According to the above passage, the one of the following which has   21.____
contributed MOST to wasteful use of hospital facilities is the
    A. increased emphasis on preventive health care
    B. practice of private carriers of providing comprehensive health care
       benefits
    C. increased hospitalization of the elderly and the poor
    D. practice of a number of private carriers of paying only for hospital care
       costs

22. Based on the information in the above passage, which one of the following   22.____
patients would be LEAST likely to receive benefits from a typical private health
insurance plan? A
    A. young patient who must undergo an emergency appendectomy
    B. middle-aged patient who needs a costly series of x-ray and laboratory
       tests for diagnosis of gastrointestinal complaints
    C. young patient who must visit his physician weekly for treatment of a
       chronic skin disease
    D. middle-aged patient who requires extensive cancer surgery

23. Which one of the following is the MOST accurate inference that can be   23.____
drawn from the above passage?
    A. Private health insurance has failed to fully meet the health care needs of
       Americans.
    B. Most Americans under age 65 have health insurance coverage better
       than that provided to the elderly under Medicare.
    C. Countries with a national health service are likely to provide poorer health
       care for their citizens than do countries that rely primarily on private
       health insurance.
    D. Hospital facilities in the United States are inadequate to meet the nation's
       health care needs.

24. Of the total number of Americans under age 65, what percentage belonged   24.____
in the combined category of persons with no health insurance or health
insurance less than that provided to the aged under Medicare?
    A. 19%   B. 36%   C. 55%   D. 65%

25. According to the above passage, the one of the following types of health   25.____
insurance which covered the SMALLEST number of Americans under age 65
was
    A. hospital insurance
    B. surgical insurance
    C. insurance for prescription drugs
    D. insurance for physician office or home visits

_____

KEY (CORRECT ANSWERS)

1.	B		11.	C
2.	A		12.	B
3.	D		13.	A
4.	A		14.	C
5.	B		15.	D
6.	B		16.	A
7.	D		17.	D
8.	D		18.	B
9.	C		19.	C
10.	A		20.	B

21.	D
22.	C
23.	A
24.	C
25.	D

TEST 3

DIRECTIONS: Each question or incomplete statement is followed by several suggested answers or completions. Select the one that BEST answers the question or completes the statement. *PRINT THE LETTER OF THE CORRECT ANSWER IN THE SPACE AT THE RIGHT.*

Questions 1-3.

DIRECTIONS: Questions 1 through 3 are to be answered SOLELY on the basis of the information contained in the following passage.

Statistical studies have demonstrated that disease and mortality rates are higher among the poor than among the more affluent members of our society. Periodic surveys conducted by the United States Public Health Service continue to document a higher prevalence of infectious and chronic diseases within low income families. While the basic lifestyle and living conditions of the poor are to a considerable extent responsible for this less favorable health status, there are indications that the kind of health care received by the poor also plays a significant role. The poor are less likely to be aware of the concepts and practices of scientific medicine and less likely to seek health care when they need it. Moreover, they are discouraged from seeking adequate health care by the depersonalization, disorganization, and inadequate emphasis on preventive care which characterizes the health care most often provided for them.

To achieve the objective of better health care for the poor, the following approaches have been suggested: encouraging the poor to seek preventive care as well as care for acute illness and to establish a lasting one-to-one relationship with a single physician who can treat the poor patient as a whole individual; sufficient financial subsidy to put the poor on an equal footing with *paying patients*, thereby giving them the opportunity to choose from among available health service providers; inducements to health service providers to establish public clinics in poverty areas; and legislation to provide for health education, earlier detection of disease and coordinated health care.

1. According to the above passage, the one of the following which is a function of the United States Public Health Service is
   A. gathering data on the incidence of infectious diseases
   B. operating public health clinics in poverty areas lacking private physicians
   C. recommending legislation for the improvement of health care in the United States
   D. encouraging the poor to participate in programs aimed at the prevention of illness.

1.____

2. According to the above passage, the one of the following which is MOST characteristic of the health care currently provided for the poor is that it
   A. aims at establishing clinics in poverty areas
   B. enables the poor to select the health care they want through the use of financial subsidies
   C. places insufficient stress on preventive health care
   D. over-emphasizes the establishment of a one-to-one relationship between physician and patient

2.____

3.   The above passage implies that the poor lack the financial resources to   3._____
     A. obtain adequate health insurance coverage
     B. select from among existing health services
     C. participate in health education programs
     D. lobby for legislation aimed at improving their health care

Questions 4-6.

DIRECTIONS: Questions 4 through 6 are to be answered SOLELY on the basis of the
              information contained in the following passage.

The concept of *affiliation*, developed more than ten years ago, grew out of a series of studies which found evidence of faulty care, surgery of *questionable* value and other undesirable conditions in the city's municipal hospitals. The affiliation agreements signed shortly thereafter were designed to correct these deficiencies by assuring high quality medical care. In general, the agreements provided the staff and expertise of a voluntary hospital – sometimes connected with a medical school – to operate various services or, in some cases, all of the professional divisions of a specific municipal hospital. The municipal hospitals have paid for these services, which last year cost the city $200 million, the largest single expenditure of the Health and Hospitals Corporation. In addition, the municipal hospitals have provided to the voluntary hospitals such facilities as free space for laboratories and research. While some experts agree that affiliation has resulted in improvements in some hospital care, they contend that many conditions that affiliation was meant to correct still exist. In addition, accountability procedures between the Corporation and voluntary hospitals are said to be so inadequate that audits of affiliation contracts of the past five years revealed that there may be more than $200 million in charges for services by the voluntary hospitals which have not been fully substantiated. Consequently, the Corporation has proposed that future agreements provide accountability in terms of funds, services supplied, and use of facilities by the voluntary hospitals.

4.   According to the above passage, *affiliation* may BEST be defined as an   4._____
     agreement whereby
     A. voluntary hospitals pay for the use of municipal hospital facilities
     B. voluntary and municipal hospitals work to eliminate duplication of services
     C. municipal hospitals pay voluntary hospitals for services performed
     D. voluntary and municipal hospitals transfer patients to take advantage of
         specialized services

5.   According to the above passage, the MAIN purpose for setting up the   5._____
     affiliation agreement was to
     A. supplement the revenues of municipal hospitals
     B. improve the quality of medical care in municipal hospitals
     C. reduce operating costs in municipal hospitals
     D. increase the amount of space available to municipal hospitals

6. According to the above passage, inadequate accountability procedures have   6.____
    resulted in
    A. unsubstantiated charges for services by the voluntary hospitals
    B. emphasis on research rather than on patient care in municipal hospitals
    C. unsubstantiated charges for services by the municipal hospitals
    D. economic losses to voluntary hospitals

Questions 7-9.

DIRECTIONS: Questions 7 through 9 are to be answered SOLELY on the basis of the
               following hypothetical medical insurance plan schedule of allowances for in-
               hospital medical services which gives the amounts of money patients are
               allowed toward payment of their hospital bills.

SCHEDULE OF ALLOWANCES FOR IN-HOSPITAL MEDICAL SERVICES

Routine Care	Allowance Per Day
1st day...	$1500
2nd through 365th day...	$700

Intensive Care
When an illness is of such a critical nature as to require repeated or prolonged
attendance by a physician, an additional allowance of $150 per day for a maximum of 5
days during the period of hospitalization will be provided.

Nervous and Mental Conditions Pulmonary Tuberculosis Physical Therapy and Rehabilitation	Allowance Per Day
1st day...	$1500
2nd through 30th day..	$700

Consultations	Allowance
For a consultation requiring a complete physical examination with a written report..	$350
For a consultation requiring less than a complete physical examination..	$250

Premature Infants	Allowance Per Week
4 pounds or less at birth	
1st week..	$5000
2nd through 4th week...	$2500
5 pounds or less but more than 4 pounds at birth....................	$2500

THE MAXIMUM ALLOWANCE FOR PREMATURE INFANTS IS $1,250

7. According to the Schedule of Allowances for In-Hospital Medical Services   7.____
above, a patient hospitalized for 10 days, 2 days of which required intensive
care, would be entitled to a total allowance of MOST NEARLY
   A. $780   B. $940   C. $1080   D. $1500

8. Assume that a patient is hospitalized for 21 days. During her stay, she   8.____
received intensive care for 8 days and a consultation requiring a complete
physical examination with a written report. According to the Schedule of
Allowances for In-Hospital Medical Services above, this patient would be
entitled to a total allowance of MOST NEARLY
   A. $2300   B. $2560   C. $2650   D. $3100

9. According to the Schedule of Allowances for In-Hospital Medical Services   9.____
above, a premature infant, weighing 3 pounds, 14 ounces at birth, who has
been hospitalized since birth for a period of five weeks, would be entitled to a
total allowance of MOST NEARLY
   A. $1500   B. $1250   C. $1000   D. $750

Questions 10-11.

DIRECTIONS: Questions 10 and 11 are to be answered SOLELY on the basis of
the information show below which indicates the charges for hospital
services and physician services given in a hospital and a patient's
annual income for each of our consecutive years.

Year	Patient's Annual Income	Charges for Hospital Services and Physician Services Given in a Hospital
2009	$30,000	$7,400
2010	$31,000	$7,980
2011	$43,000	$10,820
2012	$47,000	$11,550

10. A hospitalized patient may qualify for Medicaid benefits when the charges   10.____
for hospital services and for physician services given in the hospital exceed 25
percent of the patient's annual income. According to the information shown
above, the one of the following that indicates ONLY those years in which the
patient qualifies for Medicaid benefits is
   A. 2010, 2011   B. 2009, 2010, 2012
   C. 2010, 2012   D. 2010, 2011, 2012

11. The one of the following that is the patient's average annual income for the   11.____
entire four-year period shown above is MOST NEARLY
   A. $32,250   B. $32,750   C. $37,350   D. $37,750

Questions 12-13.

DIRECTIONS: Questions 12 and 13 are to be answered SOLELY on the basis of the following passage.

In calculating a patient's ability to pay hospital charges, a certain insurance plan allows an exemption of family savings equal to $5,000 for each member of the patient's family up to a maximum family savings of $20,000. In addition, exemption of savings equal to one-half of the family's annual net income is allowed. A patient with savings greater than the allowable exemptions will be required to use these non-exempted savings toward payment of a hospital bill assuming no other sources of payment are available.

12.   A family of six with an annual net income of $64,000 would be allowed a   12.____
      savings exemption of MOST NEARLY
      A. $62,000   B. $52,000   C. $30,000   D. $20,000

13.   Mr. Brown has savings totaling $84,000 and is the sole source of income of a   13.____
      family of three. Mr. Brown's annual net income is $72,000. Assume Mr. Brown
      has no other sources of payment for his hospital bill. The percentage of Mr.
      Brown's savings that he will be required to use to pay his hospital bill is MOST
      NEARLY
      A. 29%   B. 39%   C. 43%   D. 61%

Questions 14-15.

DIRECTIONS: Questions 14 and 15 are to be answered SOLELY on the basis of the information shown below, which gives the hospital bill and the amount paid by an insurance plan for each of four patients.

Patient's Name	Hospital Bill	Amount Paid by the Insurance Plan Toward Hospital Bill
Mr. D. Harris	$8,753	$5,952
Mr. W. Smith	$4,504	$3,285
Mr. T. Jones	$7,211	$5,048
Mr. M. White	$12,255	$8,712

14.   According to the information given above, which patient, when compared   14.____
      with the other three patients, had the HIGHEST percentage of his bill paid by
      the Insurance Plan?
      A. Mr. W. Smith   B. Mr. D. Harris
      C. Mr. T. Jones   D. Mr. M. White

15.   The average amount paid by the Insurance Plan toward the hospital bills of   15.____
      the four patients shown above is MOST NEARLY
      A. $5,269   B. $5,499   C. $5,749   D. $5,766

Questions 16-18.

DIRECTIONS: Questions 16 through 18 are to be answered SOLELY on the basis of the
following information.

A medical insurance plan will reimburse a patient covered by such insurance for 80% of
charges for outpatient services in a hospital in any given calendar year provided that the patient
has paid the first $600 of such charges in that year.

16.   Ms. Miller received treatment in the outpatient clinic of a hospital in January   16.____
of 2009. She paid the hospital the $1100 she was charged for this treatment.
This was the first time she received treatment within this year. The one of the
following that MOST NEARLY indicates how much Ms. Miller will be
reimbursed by the plan is
   A. $400   B. $480   C. $600   D. $700

17.   Mr. Franklin received treatment in the outpatient clinic of a hospital only in   17.____
November 2013 and February 2014. He paid the hospital the $780 he was
charged for the services he received in November and also paid the $480 he
was charged for the services he received in February. The one of the following
that MOST NEARLY indicates how much Mr. Franklin will be reimbursed by the
plan is
   A. $144   B. $488   C. $574   D. $968

18.   In 2014, Ms. Green received outpatient services at a hospital only in February   18.____
and September. She paid the hospital the $500 she was charged for the
services she received in February and also paid the $200 she was charged for
the services she received in September. The one of the following that MOST
NEARLY indicates how much Ms. Green will be reimbursed by the plan is
   A. $20   B. $80   C. $100   D. $120

Questions 19-21.

DIRECTIONS: Questions 19 through 21 are to be answered SOLELY on the basis of the
following information.

For the first 21 days of a subscriber's hospitalization in any participating hospital, a
medical plan provides covered-in-full benefits. Should the subscriber remain hospitalized or be
re-admitted for hospitalization, the next 180 days are discount days, with the subscriber paying
50% of the hospital charges, and the plan paying the other 50%.
A new benefit period of 21 days covered-in-full and 180 discount days would begin 90
days after completion of a previous hospital stay, or after 12 continuous months of
hospitalization. Should a subscriber use up all the covered-in-full and discount days without
qualifying under the terms described above for a new benefit period, the subscriber would pay
100% of the hospital charges.

The patients in the following questions are subscribers to the medical plan described above and have had hospital stays at the same participating hospital. The all-inclusive charge for services at this hospital is $200 per day. In computing the length of a patient's hospital stay, include the date the patient was admitted but do NOT include the date the patient was discharged.

The calendar shown below may be used in answering the following questions.

JANUARY

		1	2	3	4	5
6	7	8	9	10	11	12
13	14	15	16	17	18	19
20	21	22	23	24	25	26
27	28	29	30	31		

FEBRUARY

					1	2
3	4	5	6	7	8	9
10	11	12	13	14	15	16
17	18	19	20	21	22	23
24	25	26	27	28		

MARCH

					1	2
3	4	5	6	7	8	9
10	11	12	13	14	15	16
17	18	19	20	21	22	23
24	25	26	27	28	29	30
31						

APRIL

	1	2	3	4	5	6
7	8	9	10	11	12	13
14	15	16	17	18	19	20
21	22	23	24	25	26	27
28	29	30				

MAY

			1	2	3	4
5	6	7	8	9	10	11
12	13	14	15	16	17	18
19	20	21	22	23	24	25
26	27	28	29	30	31	

JUNE

						1
2	3	4	5	6	7	8
9	10	11	12	13	14	15
16	17	18	19	20	21	22
23	24	25	26	27	28	29
30						

JULY

	1	2	3	4	5	6
7	8	9	10	11	12	13
14	15	16	17	18	19	20
21	22	23	24	25	26	27
28	29	30	31			

AUGUST

				1	2	3
4	5	6	7	8	9	10
11	12	13	14	15	16	17
18	19	20	21	22	23	24
25	26	27	28	29	30	31

SEPTEMBER

1	2	3	4	5	6	7
8	9	10	11	12	13	14
15	16	17	18	19	20	21
22	23	24	25	26	27	28
29	30					

OCTOBER

		1	2	3	4	5
6	7	8	9	10	11	12
13	14	15	16	17	18	19
20	21	22	23	24	25	26
27	28	29	30	31		

NOVEMBER

					1	2
3	4	5	6	7	8	9
10	11	12	13	14	15	16
17	18	19	20	21	22	23
24	25	26	27	28	29	30

DECEMBER

1	2	3	4	5	6	7
8	9	10	11	12	13	14
15	16	17	18	19	20	21
22	23	24	25	26	27	28
29	30	31				

19. Patient A was admitted to the hospital on January 14 and discharged on March 19. The patient was then re-admitted on April 21 and discharged on May 15. The total amount that the patient must pay the hospital for both stays is MOST NEARLY

    A. $4,300   B. $4,600   C. $6,400   D. $6,700

19._____

20. Patient B was admitted to the hospital on April 2 and discharged on May 13. She was re-admitted on September 12 and discharged on October 13. The total amount that the patient must pay the hospital for both stays is MOST NEARLY

    A. $3,000   B. $4,100   C. $5,100   D. $7,200

20._____

21. Patient C was admitted to the hospital on September 6 last year and discharged November 13 this year, having been continuously hospitalized for a period of 433 days. Assume that there are 365 days in a year and that Patient C receives, at the completion of her hospital stay, one bill that includes the charges for her total hospitalization. The amount Patient C must pay the hospital is MOST NEARLY

    A. $22,700   B. $41,200   C. $55,500   D. $57,600

21.____

22. A patient's hospital bill is $24,600. The patient has three different medical insurance plans, each of which will make partial payment toward his bill. One plan will pay $6,500 of the patient's bill, another will pay $7,300 of the bill, and the third will pay $8,832 of the bill. The percentage of the bill that the patient's three insurance plans combined do NOT pay for is MOST NEARLY

    A. 5%   B. 8%   C. 10%   D. 20%

22.____

23. A patient has stayed at a hospital for which the all-inclusive daily rate is $205.00. The patient was hospitalized for 27 days. The patient is covered by a private insurance plan that will pay the hospital 2/3 of the patient's total hospital bill. The one of the following that MOST NEARLY indicates how much of the patient's hospital bill would NOT be covered by this insurance plan is

    A. $1,845   B. $2,078   C. $3,690   D. $4,156

23.____

24. A hospital charges a flat daily rate for all hospital services. In February 2007 the hospital charged a patient $2,772 for 14 days of hospitalization. In April 2009 the same patient was charged for 16 days of hospitalization at the same hospital. If the daily rate charged by the hospital increased by $7.00 between the patient's 2007 hospitalization and his 2009 hospitalization, the total amount that the patient must pay for the 2009 hospitalization is MOST NEARLY

    A. $3,296   B. $3,280   C. $3,264   D. $3,248

24.____

25. A hospital insurance plan that previously covered 3/5 of the total hospital charges for its subscribers, has recently been improved and coverage for total hospital charges has been increased by 25% of the previous rate. A subscriber to this plan has just completed a hospital stay and has received a bill for total hospital charges of $6,200. Assuming that the hospital stay is covered by the recently improved plan, the one of the following that MOST NEARLY indicates how much the plan now provides the patient toward the payment of the hospital bill is

    A. $1,500   B. $3,720   C. $4,650   D. $5,270

25.____

KEY (CORRECT ANSWERS)

1.	A		11.	D
2.	C		12.	B
3.	B		13.	B
4.	C		14.	A
5.	B		15.	C
6.	A		16.	A
7.	C		17.	A
8.	C		18.	B
9.	B		19.	D
10.	A		20.	A

21.	C
22.	B
23.	A
24.	B
25.	C

EXAMINATION SECTION
TEST 1

DIRECTIONS: Each question or incomplete statement is followed by several suggested answers or completions. Select the one that *BEST* answers the question or completes the statement. *PRINT THE LETTER OF THE CORRECT ANSWER IN THE SPACE AT THE RIGHT.*

1. You are interviewing a patient who is evasive and unresponsive to your questions. When you ask about his hospital coverage, he tells you about his life insurance. In order to obtain specific answers from this patient, of the following, your *MOST* effective approach would be to   1.____

    A. allow the patient to ramble, since he will eventually answer your questions
    B. ask direct, pointed questions which require short, simple answers
    C. tell him that if he does not answer your questions, he will have to pay the bill himself
    D. ask a nurse to be present during the interview as a witness to the patient's refusal to cooperate

2. An insurance carrier calls you to request information from a medical record for a patient who has made application for life insurance. Generally, the *proper* way for you to handle this request would be to   2.____

    A. give the carrier the information, since the patient cannot obtain life insurance until the medical information is released
    B. advise the carrier that you cannot give out any medical information whatever
    C. advise the carrier that the information is privileged and confidential, and can be released only with the patient's authorization
    D. send a copy of the medical record to the patient and have him forward it to the carrier so he can obtain his life insurance

3. All of the following statements are in accord with the goals or benefits of the Medicaid program *EXCEPT:*   3.____

    A. Medicaid eligibles have the right to avail themselves of the services of any institution, agency or person qualified to participate in the Medicaid program
    B. High-quality medical care will be made available to everyone regardless of race, age, national origin or economic standing
    C. Hospitals must provide the same standard of medical care and health services to Medicaid eligibles as to any self-paying patient
    D. Medicaid benefits will be terminated when the cost of the patient's care exceeds a predetermined amount

4. As an investigator, you may be required to provide concrete services for some patients, when necessary. According to accepted terminology, which one of the following would be an example of a concrete service?   4.____

    A. Assuring a patient that "everything will be all right"
    B. Referring a patient to the department of social services for emergency assistance
    C. Obtaining a special favor for a patient such as a between-meal snack
    D. Moving a patient to a more pleasant ward in another part of the hospital

5. Which one of the following statements represents a *BASIC* similarity between Medicare and Medicaid?   5.____

    A. Persons over 65 can qualify under both programs
    B. Both have the same minimum income requirements
    C. Both require a means test for determining eligibility
    D. Both have the same residency requirements

6. Of the following, the usual manner of payment for an eligible Medicaid patient utilizing health and hospitals services is from the   6.____

    A. government to the patient
    B. government to the hospital
    C. government to the attending physician
    D. patient to the hospital

7. Which one of the following groups is **AUTOMATICALLY** eligible for Medicaid, according to Federal requirements?   7.____

    A. Medically indigent persons, regardless of eligibility under any other public assistance program
    B. Medically indigent children under 21, regardless of the family's eligibility for categorical assistance
    C. Persons receiving all or part of their basic living expenses from public assistance
    D. Medically indigent persons who meet all but the income requirements for categorical assistance

8. The agency responsible for administration of payment for hospital services under the Medicaid program is the   8.____

    A. City Department of Social Services
    B. City Department of Health
    C. City Health and Hospitals Corporation
    D. U. S. Department of Health, Education and Welfare

9. Of the following, a *distinction* between the Medicaid and Medicare programs is in the   9.____

    A. clientele services   B. source of funding
    C. authorizing legislation
    D. types of services reimbursed

10. The one of the following health plans which is *NOT* paid for by the patient or a group is   10.____

    A. Medicare   B. Blue Cross
    C. Medicaid   D. Health Insurance Plan

Questions 11-13.

DIRECTIONS: Answer Questions 11 through 13 based *SOLELY* on the following passage.
    In the field of investigation, the terms "interview" and "interrogation" have different meanings. The interview is an informal questioning for the purpose of learning facts. The objective of the interrogation is to obtain an admission of guilt, preferably in the form of a signed statement.

Successful interviewing requires that the investigator be able to learn, through questioning, what the person being interviewed has learned, or has observed through his sight, hearing, taste, smell, and touch. In order to gain the most benefit from an interview, the investigator must provide himself with a background of information before arranging the interview. Random questioning is seldom successful, and the investigator should be prepared to conduct the interview in a logical manner. Before opening an interview, the investigator must estimate what the interviewed person knows, or should know, about the subject of the investigation.

The investigator must always keep in mind that he has no power to force persons to give him information, and that he must often encourage the interviewee to cooperate. Many persons are unwilling to become involved, believing that any statement they give may involve them in future obligations. Obtaining a statement requires an acquaintance with psychological methods. Often an appeal to a person's sympathies will overcome his reluctance to become "involved."

11. According to the above passage, all of the following techniques should be employed by an investigator *EXCEPT*

    A. gaining a preliminary estimate of an interviewee's knowledge of the subject under investigation
    B. appealing to an interviewee's sympathies
    C. utilizing random questioning
    D. utilizing background information

11.____

12. According to the passage, the *MAIN* difference between an interrogation and an interview lies in the

    A. method by which information is obtained
    B. use to which the information is put
    C. type of person asking the questions
    D. background information needed before questioning begins

12.____

13. According to the passage, the interviewer should have a knowledge of psychological methods in order to

    A. obtain an admission of guilt
    B. force the interviewee to cooperate
    C. encourage persons to become involved
    D. make the person sympathetic to the interviewer

13.____

Questions 14-16.

DIRECTIONS: Questions 14 through 16 are to be answered *SOLELY* on the gasis of the following passage.

An important question which arises from the concept of the right to a minimum standard of health care for all persons concerns the viability of the means test, which is a part of the Medicaid program. If the financial barrier is to be removed for the medically indigent, it is necessary to define who the medically indigent are. Paradoxically, the means test necessary to define the medically indigent may itself prove to be a significant barrier to adequate health care. The attitude of the poor towards the means test may prvent their using available services. If this proves to be true, the government must remove the barrier if it is to protect the right of the individual to health care. This does not, however, automatically require removing the means test. The government would be faced with a choice: remove the means test or change the attitude of the people toward the test. In devising Medicare, a means test was considered to be degrading; there was to be nothing second-class about the elderly. Rather than trying to change the idea that a means test is degrading, all people beyond a certain age were made eligible.

14. The *MOST* appropriate of the following titles for this passage would be   14.____

    A.   THE CONCEPT OF THE MEANS TEST IN MEDICAID AND MEDICARE
    B.   HOW THE POOR VIEW THE MEANS TEST
    C.   VIEWS ON HEALTH CARE FOR THE POOR
    D.   THE MEANS TEST AS VIEWED BY THE ELDERLY

15. According to an implication made in the passage, in order for the poor to derive maxi-   15.____
mum benefit from the Medicaid program, which one of the following conditions must be met?

    A.   The means test must automatically be removed
    B.   All persons, young and elderly, should be made eligible
    C.   Public feeling about the means test should be changed
    D.   The requirements for Medicaid should be similar to those of Medicare

16. The paradox alluded to in the passage refers to the   16.____

    A.   reluctance of the poor to use Medicaid, which was developed as a means of pro-
viding health care for the poor
    B.   attitudes of the elderly, who considered the means test to be degrading, and, there-
fore, did not use Medicare
    C.   difficulty of administering the means test, which is a necessary component of any
program to define the medically indigent
    D.   the government's decision to remove the means test as a Medicare requirement
instead of changing the attitude of the elderly toward the test

Questions 17-20.

DIRECTIONS: Answer Questions 17 through 20 *SOLELY* on the basis of the information contained in the following passage.
    The Aid to the Blind program calls for determination of blindness and need, but in most other respects the statutory requirements for the state plan are similar to those for Old Age Assistance (OAA). Blindness need not be total to be considered qualifying for assistance. The usual test of whether a person is deemed to be blind relates to the ability to earn a liveli-hood, what is sometimes termed "economic blindness." Need is ascertained by determining whether there is a budget deficiency, as in OAA, except that the state may, in computing need, disregard the first $85 per month of earned income, plus one-half of earned income in excess of $85 per month; these sums are to be taken into account after $5 of any income. With respect to age, some states have no age limit, while others set 16, 18 or 21 years at the lower limit,and some set the upper age limit as under 65 years. It should be noted that, although some persons may meet the eligibility specifications of more than one category, it is possible to receive a monthly grant from only one of them. It is expected that every effort will be made to enable blind persons to become self-supporting in some measure. These include efforts by the recipients to cash grants to move from dependency to independency, as well as referrals to social service agencies in order to offer and facilitate rehabilitation opportunities.

17. As used in the above passage, the expression "economic blindness" refers to a blind per- 17.____
son's

    A. budget deficiency   B. capacity for self-support
    C. efforts toward rehabilitation
    D. eligibility specifications

18. According to the above passage, in computing the need for assistance, which one of the 18.____
following amounts is disregarded for a blind person earning $200 per month?

    A. $122.50   B. $127.50   C. $132.50   D. $147.50

19. The one of the following criteria which is NOT mentioned in the passage as a consider- 19.____
ation in determining elibility for aid is

    A. age   B. financial need
    C. degree of blindness   D. education

20. On the basis of the above passage, it can be concluded that an important aspect of the 20.____
Aid to the Blind Program is to

    A. assist blind persons until they can achieve some degree of economic self-suffi-
       ciency
    B. encourage blind persons to establish their right to financial assistance
    C. provide direct social service and rehabilitation assistance to blind persons
    D. establish categories of assistance on the basis of degree of blindness

----

KEY (CORRECT ANSWERS)

1.	B	11.	C
2.	C	12.	B
3.	D	13.	C
4.	B	14.	A
5.	A	15.	C
6.	B	16.	A
7.	C	17.	B
8.	A	18.	D
9.	B	19.	D
10.	C	20.	A

TEST 2

DIRECTIONS: Each question or incomplete statement is followed by several suggested answers or completions. Select the one that *BEST* answers the question or completes the statement. *PRINT THE LETTER OF THE CORRECT ANSWER IN THE SPACE AT THE RIGHT.*

Questions 1-4.

DIRECTIONS: Answer Questions 1 through 4 based *SOLELY* on the information on the Hospital Care Authorization and Claim Form given below.

Paul Forand was born on January 12, 1941 in Miami, Florida. His Medicare number is 064-26-3000A. At the time of his admission to Bell View Hospital, 100 First Ave., Manhattan, he was living with his wife, Mary Forand, and daughter, Debbie Forand, at 200 Second Avenue, Manhattan. He was admitted on April 10, 2015. The attending physician was John Smith. This was the second time he had ever been hospitalized. He was previously hospitalized on April 21, 2011 in Lexington Hill Hospital for a gall bladder operation.

On April 12, 2015 it was decided to transfer Paul Forand to Bleakman Midtown Hospital, 102 E. 29th Street, Manhattan, because his primary admitting diagnosis could be treated better at this facility. His attending physician at Bleakman Midtown Hospital was Richard Jones. On April 14, 2015, Mary Forand was informed that her husband would be discharged from the hospital at 4 p.m. that afternoon. She planned to leave early from her job as Securities Analyst with the firm of Farrell Winch to take her husband home.

Mary Forand is the head of the household. Her social security number is 624-60-0030.

HOSPITAL CARE AUTHORIZATION and CLAIM

DATE SUBMITTED	HOSPITAL NAME Bell View Hospital		☐ OUT OF STATE HOSPITAL	HOSPITAL NO	HOSPITAL ADMITTING NO

PATIENT'S NAME	LAST	FIRST	AGE	RACE	SEX	BIRTH DATE	CATEGORY	MEDICAID NO	SUFFIX	CENTER

PATIENT'S ADDRESS	NO. & STREET	TELEPHONE NO.	NAME ON MEDICAID CARD, OR HEAD OF HOUSEHOLD

CITY (BOROUGH)	STATE	ZIP CODE	EXPIRATION DATE MO YR.	D.S.S. 515A ☐ ATTACHED ☐	DATE ORIGINAL SUBMITTED
13		14	26		27

PATIENT'S RELATIONSHIP TO HEAD OF HOUSEHOLD					PREFIX	MEDICARE NO.	SUFFIX
☐ SELF ☐ SPOUSE ☐ DAUGHTER ☐ SON ☐ OTHER: _____ 15					28		

RESPONSIBLE PHYSICIAN	FULL NAME	SOCIAL SECURITY NUMBER	NAME ON CUBAN REFUGEE CARD / CUBAN REFUGEE NO
16		17	29

PREVIOUS CARE - HOSPITAL NAME	NAME OF FAMILY MEMBER	DATE ADMITTED	DATE DISCHARGED	WORKMAN'S COMP	DISABILITY FORM ATTACHED
18	19	20	21	☐ YES ☐ NO 30	☐ AWARD LETTER ☐ D.S.S. 486 ☐ D.S 115 31

DATE ADMITTED 32	HOUR A.M. P.M. 33	PRIMARY ADMITTING DIAGNOSIS 34	CODE 35	ACCOM. 36	TYPE OF ADMISSION ☐ ELECT ☐ ER ☐ OBS ☐ ACUTE TRANS ☐ OTH TRA 37

DATE FIRST SURGERY 38	FIRST MAJOR SURGERY 39	CODE 40	SECONDARY DISCHARGE DIAGNOSIS 45	CODE 46

DATE DISCHARGED 41	HOUR A.M. P.M. 42	PRIMARY DISCHARGE DIAGNOSIS 43	CODE 44	TERTIARY DISCHARGE DIAGNOSIS 47	CODE 48

STATUS CIRCLE ONE 49	DISCHARGED 1	STILL IN 2	DIED 3	TRANSFERRED TO 4	SPECIAL PROGRAM IF APPLICABLE CIRCLE ONE 50	PHC 1	PREM 2	NARC 3	SFP 4	T.B. INEL 5	DIAL PT B 6	FAM PLAN 7	SC 8	IND REF 9

TYPE OF CARE CIRCLE ONE 51	MED. SURG. A	MATERNITY B	ABORTION C	NEW BORN D	BOARDER BABY E	PSYCH FULL TIME F	PSYCH DAY G	CHRONIC J	PHIC K	ECF L	T.B. M	ALC. REH N	DIALYSIS P	HFT REH R	SPC

PATIENT STATES ACCIDENT CASE 52	☐ YES	DATE OF INJURY 53	HOUR A.M. P.M. 54	HOW INJURY SUSTAINED 55	POLICE SHIELD NO. 56	PRECINCT 57
	☐ NO	NAME, ADDRESS, LICENSE NO. ETC. OF PERSON ALLEGEDLY AT FAULT 58				

1. Which box should be checked in the space on the Hospital Care Authorization and Claim   1._____
    Form labeled "Patient's Relationship to Head of Household?"

    A. Daughter   B. Self   C. Spouse   D. Other

2. Which box should be circled in the space on the Hospital Care Authorization and Claim   2._____
    Form labeled "Status Circle One?"

    A. 1   B. 2   C. 3   D. 4

3. Which one of the following spaces on the Hospital Care Authorization and Claim Form   3._____
    can *NOT* be completed based *solely* on the information given above?

    A. Medicare No.   B. Patient's Address
    C. Responsible Physician   D. Primary Admitting Diagnosis

4. Which one of the following dates should be entered in the box labeled "Date Admitted"   4._____
    (box 20) on the Hospital Care Authorization and Claim Form?

    A. April 21, 2011   B. April 10, 2015
    C. April 12, 2015   D. April 14, 2015

Questions 5-8.

DIRECTIONS: Answer Questions 5 through 8 *SOLELY* on the basis of the information
               obtained in the patient interview and from the previous admission record given
               below.

PATIENT INTERVIEW

As a Hospital Care Investigator, you have interviewed a patient, Giselle Krebs, who was
admitted to the hospital with a fractured hip on March 12, 2015, by her physician, Jane Kelly.
The patient has told you that she resides at 2801 Roger Avenue, Brooklyn, N. Y. with her
retired husband, Sandor, and their daughter and son-in-law. Her next of kin is her eldest
daughter, Julie Cohen, who resides at 5025 Van Buren Street, Miami, Florida. Mrs. Krebs is
employed by Green View Gardens, 2802 Holbrook Boulevard, Brooklyn, New York, as a part-
time saleslady and has been in their employ for 3 years. Her only health insurance coverage
is that provided by Green Cross/ Green Shield, certificate number 707-36-5491.

At the end of the interview Mrs. Krebs tells you that she had previously been admitted to
this hospital on July 12, 2011. Based on this information you obtain a copy of her previous
Notice of Admission, which is given on the following page.

NOTICE OF ADMISSION (PREVIOUS)

Admitting No.	Date 7/17/15	Hosp. Empl. Initials	Soc. Sec. Number 707-36-5194	Suffix G		Case No. C-77-23071
1		Is patient Medicare eligible?				

2	Patient's Name and Address (Last) Krebs (First) Giselle (Middle Initial)	Age 70	Patient's Birthdate 2/22/45	Sex F	Patient's Employer Green View Gardens

3	(No.) 1301 Ave R (Street)	Name of Contract Holder S Krebs	Contract Holder's Employer Sandor's Nursery

4	(City) Brooklyn (State) New York	Pat's relationship: Contract Holder Self ☐ Spouse ☒ Dghtr ☐ Son ☐	Priv ☐ Sem Priv ☒ Priv ☐ ICu ☐

5	Full Name and Address of Physician Maurice J. Kellert 1844-48 Street, Bklyn. N.Y.	Was admission a result of auto accident? ☐ Yes ☒ No

6	Date Admitted Mo 7 Day 12 Year 15	Hour A.M. P.M. 7:15	Admitting Diagnosis Stroke	Name and address of next of kin Julie Cohen 5625 Van Buren St Miami, Florida

7	Date Discharged CHECK ☐ Died ☒ Still in	Current or final diagnosis Stroke Was pregnancy terminated? ☐ No ☐ Yes	Chart No. 414	Hospital Name Brooklyn Hospital	Relationship of next of kin to patient Daughter	Hospital Code 8	Check Digit 14

Questions 5 through 8 refer to entries that would be made on the current Notice of Admission shown on the next page. These entries are to be based *SOLELY* on the information obtained from the patient interview and the previous Notice of Admission given above.

NOTICE OF ADMISSION (CURRENT)

Admitting No.	Date	Hosp. Empl. Initials	Soc. Sec. Number	Suffix	Case No. C-

1 — Is patient Medicare eligible?

2 Patient's Name and Address (Last) (First) (Middle Initial) | Age | Patient's Birthdate | Sex | Patient's Employer

3 (No) (Street) | Name of Contract Holder | Contract Holder's Employer

4 (City) (State) | Pat's. Relationship to Contract Holder: Self ☐ Spouse ☐ Dghtr ☐ Son ☐ | Semi Priv. ☐ Priv. ☐ Ward ☐ ICU ☐

5 Full Name and Address of Physician | Was admission a result of auto accident? ☐ Yes ☐ No

6 Date Admitted Mo. DAY YEAR | AM Hour P.M. | Admitting Diagnosis | Name and address of next of kin

7 Date Discharged | Current or final diagnosis | Relationship of next of kin to patient
CHECF ☐ Died ☐ Still in | Was pregnancy terminated? ☐ No ☐ Yes | Chart No. | Hospital Name | Hospital Code | Check Digit

5. Which one of the following lines on the current Notice of Admission could be completed based SOLELY on the information given in the Patient Interview on the previous Notice of Admission? (Assume that, unless otherwise specified, the information contained in the 2015 record remains the same.)

A. 4   B. 3   C. 5   D. 7

6. Which one of the following entries made on the previous Notice of Admission should NOT be transferred to the current Notice of Admission?

A. 1301 Avenue R, Brooklyn, New York
B. 5025 Van Buren Street, Miami, Florida
C. 2/22/45
D. 707-36-5491

7. Which one of the following entries would be the same on both Notices of Admission?

A. Sandor's Nursery   B. Stroke
C. 7/12/08   D. Brooklyn Hospital

8. Which one of the following entries should NOT be made on Line 2 of the current Notice of Admission?

A. Green View Gardens   B. F
C. 70   D. 2/22/45

75

9. A patient's hospital bill is $27,200. The patient has two different medical insurance plans,   9.____
each of which will make partial payment toward her bill. One plan will pay the first
$10,000 of the patient's bill, and the other will pay 50% of the remaining part of the bill
not paid for by any other plan.
The percentage of the entire bill paid for by the two plans is, most nearly,

   A. 64%   B. 66%   C. 68%   D. 70%

10. A hospital's daily rate is $285. This rate includes all hospital services with the exception   10.____
of blood, for which the hospital charges an additional $55 per pint. If a patient was
charged for 17 days of hospitalization and the total hospital bill, including blood, was
$5,285, *how many* pints of blood did the patient receive?

   A. 8   B. 9   C. 10   D. 11

Questions 11-12.

DIRECTIONS: Questions 11 and 12 are to be answered *SOLELY* on the basis of the information shown below which indicates the charges for hospital services and physician services given in a hospital and a patient's annual income for each of four
consecutive years,

YEAR	PATIENT'S ANNUAL INCOME	CHARGES FOR HOSPITAL SERVICES AND PHYSICIAN SERVICES GIVEN IN A HOSPITAL
2011	$14,000	$3,600
2012	$17,500	$4,250
2013	$18,600	$5,200
2014	$19,200	$5,850

11. A hospitalized patient may qualify for Medicaid benefits when the charges for hospital   11.____
services and for physician services given in the hospital exceed 30% of the patient's
annual income.
According to the information shown above, the one of the following that indicates *only*
those years in which the patient qualifies for Medicaid benefits is

   A. 2013, 2014   B. 2011, 2013   C. 2012   D. 2014

12. The one of the following that is the patient's *average* annual income for the entire four-   12.____
year period shown above is

   A. $17,200   B. $17,300   C. $17,325   D. $17,525

Questions 13-14.

DIRECTIONS: Questions 13 and 14 are to be answered on the basis of the information shown
below, which gives the hospital bill and the amount paid by an Insurance Plan
for each of four patients.

PATIENT'S NAME	HOSPITAL BILL	AMOUNT PAID BY INSURANCE PLAN TOWARD HOSPITAL BILL
Mr. C. Minsky	$2,089	$1,890
Mr. S. Obrow	$6,823	$5,318
Ms. B. Kaet	$9,182	$8,000
Ms. D. Frieda	$7,633	$5,575

13. According to the information given above, which patient, when compared with the other three patients, had the LOWEST percentage of his bill paid by the Insurance Plan?　13.____

   A. Mr. C. Minsky　　　　　　B. Mr. S. Obrow
   C. Ms. B. Kaet　　　　　　　D. Ms. D. Frieda

14. The average amount of the hospital bills of the four patients shown above is, most nearly,　14.____

   A. $6,334　　　B. $6,431　　　C. $6,481　　　D. $6,841

15. According to the provisions of the public health law, rate schedules for city hospital services are based on　15.____

   A. per capita income of residents living in the area serviced by the hospital
   B. cost to the hospital of providing such services
   C. each patient's ability to pay
   D. gross family income of residents living in the area serviced by the hospital.

16. Which one of the following statements best describes the "no-fault" provisions of the State insurance law?　16.____

   A. No one person is truly to blame for any auto accident
   B. Regardless of fault in an auto accident, some insurance will be provided to cover medical costs
   C. Passing a red light is not necessarily the fault of the driver
   D. If a pedestrian slips in front of a store, the store owner is not legally liable and is not to be held at fault

17. Assume that one of your cases has been in the hospital for about six weeks due to an on-the-job injury. Which one of the following agencies should be PRIMARILY billed for his hospital stay?　17.____

   A. Bureau of Medical Assistance
   B. Crime Victims Compensation Board
   C. State Unemployment Bureau
   D. Workmen's Compensation Board

Questions 18-20.

DIRECTIONS:　Questions 18 through 20 are to be answered SOLELY on the basis of the following information.

The White Cross Medical Plan provides covered-in-full benefits for the first 24 days in any participating hospital. If a policy-holder remains hospitalized or is readmitted for hospitalization, the next 150 days are discount days, with the policyholder paying 40% of the hospital charges and the plan paying 60%.

A new benefit period of 24 days covered-in-full and 150 discount days begins 60 days after completion of a previous hospital stay, or after 270 continuous days of hospitalization. If the policyholder uses up the entire covered-in-full and discount days without qualifying under the terms described above for a new benefit period, the policyholder pays 100% of the hospital charges.

In the following questions, the patients are policyholders in the medical plan described above and have had hospital stays at the same participating hospital. The all-inclusive rate for services at this hospital is $255 per day. In computing the length of a patient's hospital stay, include the date the patient was admitted but do *NOT* include the date the patient was discharged.

The calendar which follows should be used in answering the following questions.

2015

```
        JANUARY                      MAY                      SEPTEMBER
S  M  T  W  T  F  S         S  M  T  W  T  F  S         S  M  T  W  T  F  S
         1  2  3  4                     1  2  3            1  2  3  4  5  6
5  6  7  8  9 10 11         4  5  6  7  8  9 10         7  8  9 10 11 12 13
12 13 14 15 16 17 18       11 12 13 14 15 16 17        14 15 16 17 18 19 20
19 20 21 22 23 24 25       18 19 20 21 22 23 24        21 22 23 24 25 26 27
26 27 28 29 30 31          25 26 27 28 29 30 31        28 29 30

       FEBRUARY                      JUNE                      OCTOBER
S  M  T  W  T  F  S         S  M  T  W  T  F  S         S  M  T  W  T  F  S
                  1         1  2  3  4  5  6  7                     1  2  3  4
2  3  4  5  6  7  8         8  9 10 11 12 13 14         5  6  7  8  9 10 11
9 10 11 12 13 14 15       15 16 17 18 19 20 21        12 13 14 15 16 17 18
16 17 18 19 20 21 22       22 23 24 25 26 27 28        19 20 21 22 23 24 25
23 24 25 26 27 28          29 30                       26 27 28 29 30 31

        MARCH                        JULY                     NOVEMBER
S  M  T  W  T  F  S         S  M  T  W  T  F  S         S  M  T  W  T  F  S
                  1            1  2  3  4  5                            1
2  3  4  5  6  7  8         6  7  8  9 10 11 12         2  3  4  5  6  7  8
9 10 11 12 13 14 15       13 14 15 16 17 18 19         9 10 11 12 13 14 15
16 17 18 19 20 21 22       20 21 22 23 24 25 26        16 17 18 19 20 21 22
23 24 25 26 27 28 29       27 28 29 30 31              23 24 25 26 27 28 29
30 31                                                  30

        APRIL                       AUGUST                    DECEMBER
      1  2  3  4  5                        1  2            1  2  3  4  5  6
6  7  8  9 10 11 12         3  4  5  6  7  8  9         7  8  9 10 11 12 13
13 14 15 16 17 18 19       10 11 12 13 14 15 16        14 15 16 17 18 19 20
20 21 22 23 24 25 26       17 18 19 20 21 22 23        21 22 23 24 25 26 27
27 28 29 30                24 25 26 27 28 29 30        28 29 30 31
                           31
```

18. Mrs. Foley was admitted to the hospital on March 15, 2015 and discharged on May 22, 2015. She was readmitted on July 17, 2015 and discharged on July 26, 2015. The total amount Mrs. Foley should pay for *BOTH* hospital stays is, most nearly,

    A. $4,488   B. $5,046   C. $5,406   D. $5,610   18.____

19. Mr. Crane was admitted to the hospital on January 12, 2015 and discharged on February 5, 2015. He was then readmitted on June 5, 2015 and discharged on August 9, 2015. The total amount Mr. Crane should pay for *BOTH* hospital stays is, most nearly,

    A. $4,182   B. $6,273   C. $9,078   D. $10,455   19.____

20. Mr. Hayes was admitted to the hospital on October 20, 2014 and discharged on December 4, 2015, having been continuously hospitalized for a period of 410 days. Assume that there are 365 days in a year and that Mr. Hayes receives, at the completion of his hospital stay, one bill that includes the charges for his total hospitalization.
The amount that Mr. Hayes must pay the hospital is, most nearly,

    A. $24,480   B. $39,780   C. $44,513   D. $51,612

20._____

KEY (CORRECT ANSWERS)

1.	C	11.	D
2.	D	12.	C
3.	D	13.	D
4.	B	14.	B
5.	B	15.	B
6.	A	16.	B
7.	D	17.	D
8.	C	18.	C
9.	C	19.	A
10.	A	20.	D

EXAMINATION SECTION
TEST 1

DIRECTIONS: Each question or incomplete statement is followed by several suggested answers or completions. Select the one that BEST answers the question or completes the statement. *PRINT THE LETTER OF THE CORRECT ANSWER IN THE SPACE AT THE RIGHT.*

1. A specialist is meeting with a panel of local community leaders to determine their perceptions about the effectiveness of a recent outreach program. The leaders seem unresponsive to the specialist's questions, looking at the floor or each other without directly answering the specialist's questions. One strategy that might work to elicit the desired information would be to

    A. try to discern the hidden meaning of their silence
    B. adopt a mildly confrontational tone and remind them of what's at stake in the community
    C. keep asking open-ended questions and wait patiently for responses
    D. tell them to come back when they're ready to tell you their opinions

1.____

2. Each of the following statements about maintaining a community's attention is true, EXCEPT

    A. The more challenging it is to pay attention to a message, the more likely it is that it will be attended to.
    B. Listeners will be more motivated to pay attention if a speech is personally meaningful.
    C. People will be more likely to attend if a speaker pauses to suggest natural transitions in a speech.
    D. Listeners will attend to messages that stand out.

2.____

3. Each of the following is a key strategy to integrative bargaining among community members in conflict, EXCEPT

    A. focusing on positions, rather than interests
    B. separating the people from the problem
    C. aiming for an outcome based on an objectively identified standard
    D. using active listening skills, such as rephrasing and questioning

3.____

4. Which of the following is NOT one of the major variables to take into account when considering a community-needs assessment?

    A. State of program development
    B. Resources available
    C. Demographics
    D. Community attitudes

4.____

5. Which of the following groups would probably be formed specifically for, or be involved in, the purpose of addressing a specific unmet community need?

    A. An existing consumer group
    B. A council of community representatives
    C. A committee
    D. An existing community organization

5.____

6. If a public outreach campaign designed to mobilize a community fails, the most likely rea-   6.____
son for this failure is that the campaign

    A. was not specific about what it wanted people to do
    B. was overly serious and did not appeal to people's sense of humor
    C. offered no incentive for the audience to make a change
    D. did not use language that appealed to the audience's emotions

7. Nationwide, the rate of involvement of elderly people in community-based programs   7.____
demonstrates that they are

    A. underserved when compared to other age groups
    B. served at about the same rate as other age groups
    C. over-served when compared to other age groups
    D. hardly served at all

8. In projecting the likelihood of an education program's success, a domestic violence spe-   8.____
cialist identifies every single event that must occur to complete the project. The specialist
then arranges these events in sequential order and allocates time requirements for each.
Finally, the total time is calculated and a model showing all their events and timelines is
charted. The specialist has used

    A. a PERT chart
    B. a simulation
    C. a Markov model
    D. the critical path method

9. When working with members of a predominantly African-American community, special-   9.____
ists from other cultural backgrounds should be aware that African Americans tend to
express thoughts and feelings through descriptions of

    A. physically tangible sensations
    B. problems to be analyzed
    C. corresponding analogies
    D. spiritual issues

10. Local nonprofessionals should be considered useful to a specialist who is looking to   10.____
undertake a community outreach or educational initiative. Which of the following is
LEAST likely to be a characteristic or role demonstrated by these community members?

    A. Undertaking support functions at the agency
    B. Serving as a communication channel between the agency and clients
    C. Encouraging greater agency acceptance and credibility within the community
    D. Helping the agency to accomplish meaningful change

11. In working with Native American groups or clients, it is important to recognize that the   11.____
greatest health problem facing their communities today is

    A. domestic violence   B. depression and suicide
    C. alcoholism   D. tuberculosis

12. A specialist is facilitating a cooperative conflict resolution session between community members who have different opinions about what kinds of intervention services should be offered by the local adult protective services agency. Which of the following is NOT a guideline that should be followed in this process?

    A. Early in the negotiations, ask each party to name the issues on which they will positively not yield.
    B. Try to get the parties to view the issue from other points of view, beside the two or three conflicting ones.
    C. Have each side volunteer what it would be willing to do to resolve the conflict.
    D. At the end of the session, draw up a formal agreement with agreed-upon actions for both parties.

12.____

13. A specialist wants to evaluate the effectiveness of a local women's shelter. The shelter has suffered from lax participation, given the number of women who have been abused in the surrounding area. The specialist wants to speak with the women in the community who did not follow up on referrals to the shelter, and begins by visiting some of these women. After gaining the trust of these women, the specialist asks for the names of women they know who might be in need of help with a domestic violence situation. The specialist's approach in this case is _____ sampling.

    A. maximum variation   B. snowball
    C. convenience   D. typical case

13.____

14. When it comes to perceiving messages, people typically DON'T

    A. tend to simplify causal connections and sometimes even seek a single cause to explain what may be a highly complex effect
    B. tend to perceive messages independently of a categorical framework, especially if the message may be distorted by such an interpretation
    C. have a predisposition toward accepting any pattern that a speaker offers to explain seemingly unconnected facts
    D. tend to interpret things in the way they are viewed by their reference group

14.____

15. The elder members of Native American communities, regardless of kinship, are most commonly referred to as

    A. the ancients   B. father or mother
    C. grandfather or grandmother   D. chiefs

15.____

16. Each of the following is typically an objective of community mobilization, EXCEPT

    A. To convince existing community resources to alter their services or work together to address an unmet need
    B. To gather and distribute information to consumers and agencies about unmet needs
    C. To publicize existing community resources and make them more accessible
    D. To bring an unmet community need to public attention in order to achieve acceptance of and support for fulfilling the need

16.____

17. Research in community outreach shows that women often build friendships through shared positive feelings, whereas men often build friendships through

    A. metacommunication
    B. catharsis
    C. impression management
    D. shared activities

18. Typically, the FIRST step in a community-needs assessment is to

    A. identify community's strengths
    B. explore the nature of the neighborhood
    C. get to know the area and its residents
    D. talk to people in the community

19. Most public relations experts agree that _____ exposure(s) to a message is the minimum just to get the message noticed. If the aim of a public outreach campaign is action or a change in behavior, the agency budget must plan for more exposures.

    A. one   B. two   C. three   D. four

20. In the program development/community liaison model of community work and public outreach, the primary constituency is considered to be

    A. community representatives and the service agency board or administrators
    B. elected officials, social agencies, and interagency organizations
    C. marginalized or oppressed population groups in a city or region
    D. residents of a neighborhood, parish or rural county

21. Social or interpersonal problems in many African American communities have their roots in

    A. personality deficits
    B. unresolved family conflicts
    C. poor communication
    D. external stressors

22. A public outreach campaign should
    I. focus on short-term, measurable goals, rather than ultimate outcomes
    II. try to alter entrenched attitudes within a short time, with powerfully worded messages
    III. proceed in steps or phases, each of which lays out a mechanism that leads to the desired effect
    IV. ignore causes that led to a problem, and instead focus on solutions

    A. I and II   B. II and III   C. III only   D. I, II, III and IV

23. Research findings indicate that in listing preferences for helping professional attributes, individuals from culturally diverse groups are MOST likely to consider _____ as more important than _____.

    A. personality similarity; either race/ethnic similarity or attitude similarity
    B. therapist experience; any kind of similarity
    C. race/ethnic similarity; attitude similarity
    D. attitude similarity; race/ethnic similarity

17.____
18.____
19.____
20.____
21.____
22.____
23.____

24. Each of the following is considered to be an objective of community organization, EXCEPT

    A. effecting changes in the distribution of decision-making power
    B. helping people develop and strengthen the traits of self-direction and cooperation
    C. effecting and maintaining the balance between needs and resources in a community
    D. helping people deal with their problems by developing alternative behaviors

24._____

25. A specialist is helping the adult protective services agency to design a public outreach campaign. The topic to be addressed is complex, public understanding is low, and most professionals at the agency feel that having more complete information might change the opinions of community members. Which method of pre-campaign research is probably most appropriate?

    A. Deliberative polling
    B. Attitude scales
    C. Surveys or questionnaires
    D. Focus groups

25._____

KEY (CORRECT ANSWERS)

1.	C		11.	C
2.	A		12.	A
3.	A		13.	B
4.	C		14.	B
5.	C		15.	C
6.	A		16.	B
7.	A		17.	D
8.	D		18.	B
9.	C		19.	C
10.	A		20.	A

21.	D
22.	C
23.	D
24.	D
25.	A

TEST 2

Each question or incomplete statement is followed by several suggested answers or completions. Select the one the BEST answers the question or completes the statement. *PRINT THE LETTER OF THE CORRECT ANSWER IN THE SPACE AT THE RIGHT.*

1. A specialist has been called in to resolve a dispute between two community leaders who have been arguing about the level of service needed within the community. The discussion has been going on for several hours when the specialist arrives, and both people seem to be upset. After calming the two down and getting each of them to agree on a statement of the problem, the specialist should ask each person to

    1.____

    A. summarize his or her argument in three main points
    B. explain why he or she became so upset
    C. clearly state, in objective terms, the position of the other in a form that meets with the other's approval
    D. identify the best alternative outcome, other than their presumed ideal

2. In evaluating the impact of a public outreach campaign, the _____ model can be used early in the campaign to address first impressions.

    2.____

    A. exposure or advertising
    B. expert interview
    C. impact monitoring or process
    D. experimental or quasi-experimental

3. When trying to motivate an older population to take action on a community problem, it is helpful to remember that older people

    3.____

    A. are more self-reliant in their decision-making than other members of the same family
    B. often need more time to decide than younger people
    C. are more likely than younger people to view community problems self-referentially
    D. tend to take a pragmatic, rather than philosophical, view of life

4. The method of group or community decision-making that is normally most time-consuming is

    4.____

    A. majority opinion
    B. consensus
    C. expert opinion
    D. authority rule

5. A local adult protective services agency has identified one of the goals of its recent public outreach campaign to be the mobilization of activists. The campaign should probably

    5.____

    A. target neutral audiences
    B. home in on supporters
    C. stick to purely factual information
    D. try to persuade community fence-sitters

6. Research of Native American youths' perceptions of family concerns for their well-being has generally found that these youths

    A. have a high degree of uncertainty about their families' feelings toward them
    B. believe their families don't care about them
    C. believe that their mothers care a great deal about them, but their fathers don't
    D. believe their families care a great deal about them

6.____

7. A domestic violence specialist is developing a new outreach program for the local community. The specialist has defined the target problem, set program goals, and planned the actions that will take place as a result of the program. Most likely, the next step will be to

    A. evaluate the resources available to achieve program goals
    B. define and sequence the steps that will be taken to achieve program goals
    C. determine how the program will be evaluated
    D. decide how the program will operate

7.____

8. In the following exchange, what listening skill is evident in the underlined statement?

Elder:	*I'm so glad to have someone to talk to, someone who really understands my problem.*
Specialist:	*It is nice to be able to talk to someone who will listen.*
Elder:	That's for sure.

    A. verbatim response   B. paraphrasing
    C. advising   D. evaluation

8.____

9. Which of the following activities is involved in the specialist's task of mobilizing?

    A. Meeting individuals in the community with problems and assisting them in finding help
    B. Identifying unmet community needs
    C. Speaking out against an unjust policy or procedure
    D. Developing new services or linking presently available services to meet community needs

9.____

10. The preliminary research associated with a public outreach campaign should FIRST be aimed at determining

    A. the budget
    B. the message's ultimate audience
    C. what media to use
    D. the short-term behavioral goals of the campaign

10.____

11. A specialist in a low-income community wants to plan programs that will deal with the influence of unemployment on domestic disturbances. The specialist needs to know not only how many unemployed people are in the community now, but also how many people will be unemployed at any particular time in the future, and how those numbers will vary given certain conditions. Probably the best way to trace employment rates over time and within differing conditions is through the use of

11.____

A. the critical path method
B. linear programming
C. difference equations
D. the Markov model

12. Generally, public outreach programs–whatever their stated goal–should　　　　12.____
      I. create a sense of urgency about a problem
      II. decline to identify opponents of the issue or idea
      III. propose concrete, easily understandable solutions
      IV. urge a specific action

    A. I only   B. I, III and IV   C. II and III   D. I, II, III and IV

13. Which of the following methods of community needs assessment relies to the greatest   13.____
degree on existing public records?

    A. Social indicators
    C. Rates-under treatment
    B. Field study
    D. Key informant

14. During an interview with a Native American client, a specialist is careful to maintain close   14.____
and nearly constant eye contact. The client is most likely to interpret this as

    A. a show of high concern
    B. a sign of disrespect
    C. an uncomfortable assumption of intimacy
    D. an attempt to intimidate

15. The best strategy for addressing an audience that is known to be captive, or even hostile,   15.____
is to

    A. refer to experiences in common
    B. flatter the audience
    C. joke about things in or near the audience
    D. plead for fairness

16. Integrative conflict resolution is characterized by   16.____

    A. an overriding concern to maximize joint outcomes
    B. one side's interests opposing the other's
    C. a fixed and limited amount of resources to be divided, so that the more one group
       gets, the less another gets
    D. manipulation and withholding information as negotiation strategies

17. A specialist wants to learn how to interact with the members of a largely Latino commu-   17.____
nity in a more culturally sensitive way. Which of the following is NOT a guideline for inter-
acting with members of a Latino community?

    A. Efforts to foster independence and self-reliance may be interpreted by many Lati-
       nos as a lack of concern for others.
    B. Efforts to deal one-on-one with an adolescent client may serve to alienate the par-
       ents, especially the mother.
    C. A nonverbal gesture such as lowering the eyes is interpreted by many Latinos as a
       sign of respect and deference to authority.
    D. In much of Latino culture, the locus of control for problems tends to be much more
       external than internal.

18. Each of the following is a supporting assumption of community organization, EXCEPT   18._____

    A. democracy requires cooperative participation
    B. in order for communities to change, it is necessary for each individual in the community to be willing to change
    C. communities often need help with organization and planning
    D. holistic approaches work better than fragmented or ad-hoc programs

19. Helping professionals often have difficulty to bring community resources together to fulfill unmet community needs. Which of the following is NOT usually a reason for this?   19._____

    A. Some community groups resist assistance when it is offered.
    B. Few community groups make their needs known.
    C. Community resources frequently change the type of services they offer.
    D. Often, community resources prefer to work alone

20. When dealing with groups or populations of elderly clients, specialists should be mindful that about _____ of the nation's elderly suffer from mental health problems.   20._____

    A. a tenth   B. a quarter   C. a third   D. half

21. In an African American community, a specialist from another culture should recognize that church participation, for most African Americans, is viewed as a   21._____

    A. method for maintaining control and communicating competency
    B. way of depersonalizing problems or troubles
    C. way to divert attention away from problems
    D. means of cathartic emotional release

22. Adult protective service programs supported by state statutes protect elderly people from abuse and neglect under the doctrine of   22._____

    A. parens patriae   B. habeas corpus
    C. in loco parentis   D. volenti non fit injuria

23. In terms of public outreach, which of the following statements about an audience is NOT generally true?   23._____

    A. The more heterogeneous the audience, the more necessary it will be to use specific examples and appeals to certain types of people
    B. The smaller the audience, the more likely that its members will share assumptions and values
    C. When the speaker does not know the status of an audience, it is best to assume that they are captive rather than voluntary
    D. The larger an audience, the more formal a presentation is likely to be

24. A specialist often spends time in the places frequented by community residents. She lis-   24.___
tens carefully to what residents seem most concerned about, and engages many in conversations, asking them how they see the problems in the community. During these
conversations, she makes mental notes about whether the statements of the problems
are the same things that are mentioned in their conversations. From these conversations,
the worker determines what she thinks the unmet needs of the community are. Which of
the key issues in identifying unmet needs has the worker neglected to address?

   A. The different points of view regarding the issues, and whether there is any com-
      mon ground.
   B. Whether the stated problems and the conversations with community residents
      reflect the same concerns.
   C. How community residents define the issues.
   D. What the residents talk about with one another in a community.

25. Which of the following political styles should be used to promote an issue that could   25.___
become controversial if it is perceived to involve major reforms?

   A. High-conflict, polarized
   B. High-conflict, consensual
   C. Moderate conflict, compromise-oriented
   D. Low-conflict, technical

KEY (CORRECT ANSWERS)

1.	C		11.	D
2.	A		12.	B
3.	B		13.	A
4.	B		14.	B
5.	B		15.	A
6.	D		16.	A
7.	A		17.	D
8.	B		18.	B
9.	D		19.	C
10.	B		20.	B

21.	D
22.	A
23.	A
24.	A
25.	D

COMMUNICATION
EXAMINATION SECTION
TEST 1

DIRECTIONS: Each question or incomplete statement is followed by several suggested answers or completions. Select the one that BEST answers the question or completes the statement. *PRINT THE LETTER OF THE CORRECT ANSWER IN THE SPACE AT THE RIGHT.*

1. In some agencies the counsel to the agency head is given the right to bypass the chain of command and issue orders directly to the staff concerning matters that involve certain specific processes and practices.
   This situation *most nearly* illustrates the PRINCIPLE of   1.____

   A. the acceptance theory of authority   B. multiple - linear authority
   C. splintered authority   D. functional authority

2. It is commonly understood that communication is an important part of the administrative process.
   Which of the following is NOT a valid principle of the communication process in adminis-tration?   2.____

   A. The channels of communication should be spontaneous
   B. The lines of communication should be as direct and as short as possible
   C. Communications should be authenticated
   D. The persons serving in communications centers should be competent

3. Of the following, the *one* factor which is generally considered LEAST essential to suc-cessful committee operations is   3.____

   A. stating a clear definition of the authority and scope of the committee
   B. selecting the committee chairman carefully
   C. limiting the size of the committee to four persons
   D. limiting the subject matter to that which can be handled in group discussion

4. Of the following, the failure by line managers to accept and appreciate the benefits and limitations of a new program or system *very frequently* can be traced to the   4.____

   A. budgetary problems involved
   B. resultant need to reduce staff
   C. lack of controls it engenders
   D. failure of top management to support its implementation

5. If a manager were thinking about using a committee of subordinates to solve an operat-ing problem, which of the following would generally NOT be an *advantage* of such use of the committee approach?   5.____

   A. Improved coordination   B. Low cost
   C. Increased motivation   D. Integrated judgment

6. Every supervisor has many occasions to lead a conference or participate in a conference   6.___
of some sort.
Of the following statements that pertain to conferences and conference leadership, which
is generally considered to be MOST valid?

   A. Since World War II, the trend has been toward fewer shared decisions and more
      conferences.
   B. The most important part of a conference leader's job is to direct discussion.
   C. In providing opportunities for group interaction, management should avoid consid-
      eration of its past management philosophy.
   D. A good administrator cannot lead a good conference if he is a poor public speaker.

7. Of the following, it is usually LEAST desirable for a conference leader to   7.___

   A. call the name of a person after asking a question
   B. summarize proceedings periodically
   C. make a practice of repeating questions
   D. ask a question without indicating who is to reply

8. Assume that, in a certain organization, a situation has developed in which there is little   8.___
difference in status or authority between individuals.
Which of the following would be the *most likely* result with regard to communication
in this organization?

   A. Both the accuracy and flow of communication will be improved.
   B. Both the accuracy and flow of communication will substantially decrease.
   C. Employees will seek more formal lines of communication.
   D. Neither the flow nor the accuracy of communication will be improved over the
      former hierarchical structure.

9. The main function of many agency administrative officers is "information management."   9.___
Information that is received by an administrative officer may be classified as active or
passive, depending upon whether or not it requires the recipient to take some action.
Of the following, the item received which is *clearly* the MOST active information is

   A. an appointment of a new staff member
   B. a payment voucher for a new desk
   C. a press release concerning a past event
   D. the minutes of a staff meeting

10. Of the following, the one LEAST considered to be a communication barrier is   10.___

   A. group feedback   B. charged words
   C. selective perception   D. symbolic meanings

11. Management studies support the hypothesis that, in spite of the tendency of employees   11.___
to censor the information communicated to their supervisor, subordinates are *more likely*
to communicate problem-oriented information UPWARD when they have a

   A. long period of service in the organization
   B. high degree of trust in the supervisor
   C. high educational level
   D. low status on the organizational ladder

12. Electronic data processing equipment can produce more information faster than can be generated by any other means. In view of this, the MOST important problem faced by management at present is to   12._____

    A. keep computers fully occupied
    B. find enough computer personnel
    C. assimilate and properly evaluate the information
    D. obtain funds to establish appropriate information systems

13. A well-designed management information system *essentially* provides each executive and manager the information he needs for   13._____

    A. determining computer time requirements
    B. planning and measuring results
    C. drawing a new organization chart
    D. developing a new office layout

14. It is generally agreed that management policies should be periodically reappraised and restated in accordance with current conditions.
Of the following, the approach which would be MOST effective in determining whether a policy should be revised is to   14._____

    A. conduct interviews with staff members at all levels in order to ascertain the relationship between the policy and actual practice
    B. make proposed revisions in the policy and apply it to current problems
    C. make up hypothetical situations using both the old policy and a revised version in order to make comparisons
    D. call a meeting of top level staff in order to discuss ways of revising the policy

15. Your superior has asked you to notify division employees of an important change in one of the operating procedures described in the division manual. Every employee presently has a copy of this manual.
Which of the following is normally the MOST practical way to get the employees to understand such a change?   15._____

    A. Notify each employee individually of the change and answer any questions he might have
    B. Send a written notice to key personnel, directing them to inform the people under them
    C. Call a general meeting, distribute a corrected page for the manual, and discuss the change
    D. Send a memo to employees describing the change in general terms and asking them to make the necessary corrections in their copies of the manual

16. Assume that the work in your department involves the use of many technical terms.
In such a situation, when you are answering inquiries from the general public, it would *usually* be BEST to   16._____

    A. use simple language and avoid the technical terms
    B. employ the technical terms whenever possible
    C. bandy technical terms freely, but explain each term in parentheses
    D. apologize if you are forced to use a technical term

17. Suppose that you receive a telephone call from someone identifying himself as an employee in another city department who asks to be given information which your own department regards as confidential.
    Which of the following is the BEST way of handling such a request?

    A. Give the information requested, since your caller has official standing
    B. Grant the request, provided the caller gives you a signed receipt
    C. Refuse the request, because you have no way of knowing whether the caller is really who he claims to be
    D. Explain that the information is confidential and inform the caller of the channels he must go through to have the information released to him

17.___

18. Studies show that office employees place high importance on the social and human aspects of the organization. What office employees like best about their jobs is the kind of people with whom they work. So strive hard to group people who are most likely to get along well together.
    Based on this information, it is *most reasonable* to assume that office workers are MOST pleased to work in a group which

    A. is congenial   B. has high productivity
    C. allows individual creativity
    D. is unlike other groups

18.___

19. A certain supervisor does not compliment members of his staff when they come up with good ideas. He feels that coming up with good ideas is part of the job and does not merit special attention.
    This supervisor's practice is

    A. *poor,* because recognition for good ideas is a good motivator
    B. *poor,* because the staff will suspect that the supervisor has no good ideas of his own
    C. *good,* because it is reasonable to assume that employees will tell their supervisor of ways to improve office practice
    D. *good,* because the other members of the staff are not made to seem inferior by comparison

19.___

20. Some employees of a department have sent an anonymous letter containing many complaints to the department head. Of the following, what is this *most likely* to show about the department?

    A. It is probably a good place to work.
    B. Communications are probably poor.
    C. The complaints are probably unjustified.
    D. These employees are probably untrustworthy.

20.___

21. Which of the following actions would usually be MOST appropriate for a supervisor to take *after* receiving an instruction sheet from his superior explaining a new procedure which is to be followed?

    A. Put the instruction sheet aside temporarily until he determines what is wrong with the old procedure
    B. Call his superior and ask whether the procedure is one he must implement immediately

21.___

C. Write a memorandum to the superior asking for more details
D. Try the new procedure and advise the superior of any problems or possible improvements

22. Of the following, which one is considered the PRIMARY advantage of using a committee to resolve a problem in an organization?   22.____

A. No one person will be held accountable for the decision since a group of people was involved
B. People with different backgrounds give attention to the problem
C. The decision will take considerable time so there is unlikely to be a decision that will later be regretted
D. One person cannot dominate the decision-making process

23. Employees in a certain office come to their supervisor with all their complaints about the office and the work. Almost every employee has had at least one minor complaint at some time.   23.____
The situation with respect to complaints in this office may BEST be described as *probably*

A. *good;* employees who complain care about their jobs and work hard
B. *good;* grievances brought out into the open can be corrected
C. *bad;* only serious complaints should be discussed
D. *bad;* it indicates the staff does not have confidence in the administration

24. The administrator who allows his staff to suggest ways to do their work will *usually* find that   24.____

A. this practice contributes to high productivity
B. the administrator's ideas produce greater output
C. clerical employees suggest inefficient work methods
D. subordinate employees resent performing a management function

25. The MAIN purpose for a supervisor's questioning the employees at a conference he is holding is to   25.____

A. stress those areas of information covered but not understood by the participants
B. encourage participants to think through the problem under discussion
C. catch those subordinates who are not paying attention
D. permit the more knowledgeable participants to display their grasp of the problems being discussed

KEYS (CORRECT ANSWERS)

1.	D		11.	B
2.	A		12.	C
3.	C		13.	B
4.	D		14.	A
5.	B		15.	C
6.	B		16.	A
7.	C		17.	D
8.	D		18.	A
9.	A		19.	A
10.	A		20.	B

21.	D
22.	B
23.	B
24.	A
25.	B

TEST 2

DIRECTIONS: Each question or incomplete statement is followed by several suggested answers or completions. Select the one that BEST answers the question or completes the statement. *PRINT THE LETTER OF THE CORRECT ANSWER IN THE SPACE AT THE RIGHT.*

1. For a superior to use *consultative supervision* with his subordinates effectively, it is ESSENTIAL that he

   A. accept the fact that his formal authority will be weakened by the procedure
   B. admit that he does not know more than all his men together and that his ideas are not always best
   C. utilize a committee system so that the procedure is orderly
   D. make sure that all subordinates are consulted so that no one feels left out

1.____

2. The "grapevine" is an informal means of communication in an organization. The attitude of a supervisor with respect to the grapevine should be to

   A. ignore it since it deals mainly with rumors and sensational information
   B. regard it as a serious danger which should be eliminated
   C. accept it as a real line of communication which should be listened to
   D. utilize it for most purposes instead of the official line of communication

2.____

3. The supervisor of an office that must deal with the public should realize that planning in this type of work situation

   A. is *useless* because he does not know how many people will request service or what service they will request
   B. *must be done at a higher level* but that he should be ready to implement the results of such planning
   C. is *useful* primarily for those activities that are not concerned with public contact
   D. is *useful* for all the activities of the office, including those that relate to public contact

3.____

4. Assume that it is your job to receive incoming telephone calls. Those calls which you cannot handle yourself have to be transferred to the appropriate office.
   If you receive an outside call for an extension line which is busy, the one of the following which you should do FIRST is to

   A. interrupt the person speaking on the extension and tell him a call is waiting
   B. tell the caller the line is busy and let him know every thirty seconds whether or not it is free
   C. leave the caller on "hold" until the extension is free
   D. tell the caller the line is busy and ask him if he wishes to wait

4.____

5. Your superior has subscribed to several publications directly related to your division's work, and he has asked you to see to it that the publications are circulated among the supervisory personnel in the division. There are eight supervisors involved.
   The BEST method of insuring that all eight see these publications is to

   A. place the publication in the division's general reference library as soon as it arrives
   B. inform each supervisor whenever a publication arrives and remind all of them that they are responsible for reading it

5.____

    C.   prepare a standard slip that can be stapled to each publication, listing the eight supervisors and saying, "Please read, initial your name, and pass along"

    D.   send a memo to the eight supervisors saying that they may wish to purchase individual subscriptions in their own names if they are interested in seeing each issue

6. Your superior has telephoned a number of key officials in your agency to ask whether they can meet at a certain time next month. He has found that they can all make it, and he has asked you to confirm the meeting.
Which of the following is the BEST way to confirm such a meeting?

    A.   Note the meeting on your superior's calendar

    B.   Post a notice of the meeting on the agency bulletin board

    C.   Call the officials on the day of the meeting to remind them of the meeting

    D.   Write a memo to each official involved, repeating the time and place of the meeting

6.____

7. Assume that a new city regulation requires that certain kinds of private organizations file information forms with your department. You have been asked to write the short explanatory message that will be printed on the front cover of the pamphlet containing the forms and instructions.
Which of the following would be the MOST appropriate way of beginning this message?

    A.   Get the readers' attention by emphasizing immediately that there are legal penalties for organizations that fail to file before a certain date

    B.   Briefly state the nature of the enclosed forms and the types of organizations that must file

    C.   Say that your department is very sorry to have to put organizations to such an inconvenience

    D.   Quote the entire regulation adopted by the city, even if it is quite long and is expressed in complicated legal language

7.____

8. Suppose that you have been told to make up the vacation schedule for the 18 employees in a particular unit. In order for the unit to operate effectively, only a few employees can be on vacation at the same time.
Which of the following is the MOST advisable approach in making up the schedule?

    A.   Draw up a schedule assigning vacations in alphabetical order

    B.   Find out when the supervisors want to take their vacations, and randomly assign whatever periods are left to the non-supervisory personnel

    C.   Assign the most desirable times to employees of longest standing and the least desirable times to the newest employees

    D.   Have all employees state their own preference, and then work out any conflicts in consultation with the people involved

8.____

9. Assume that you have been asked to prepare job descriptions for various positions in your department.
Which of the following are the basic points that should be covered in a *job description*?

    A.   General duties and responsibilities of the position, with examples of day-to-day tasks

    B.   Comments on the performances of present employees

9.____

C. Estimates of the number of openings that may be available in each category during the coming year
D. Instructions for carrying out the specific tasks assigned to your department

10. Of the following, the biggest DISADVANTAGE in allowing a free flow of communications in an agency is that such a free flow   10.____

    A. *decreases* creativity
    B. *increases* the use of the "grapevine"
    C. *lengthens* the chain of command
    D. *reduces* the executive's power to direct the flow of information

11. A downward flow of authority in an organization is one example of _____ communication.   11.____

    A. horizontal   B. informal   C. circular   D. vertical

12. Of the following, the one that would *most likely* block effective communication is   12.____

    A. concentration only on the issues at hand   B. lack of interest or commitment
    C. use of written reports   D. use of charts and graphs

13. An ADVANTAGE of the *lecture* as a teaching tool is that it   13.____

    A. enables a person to present his ideas to a large number of people
    B. allows the audience to retain a maximum of the information given
    C. holds the attention of the audience for the longest time
    D. enables the audience member to easily recall the main points

14. An ADVANTAGE of the *small-group* discussion as a teaching tool is that   14.____

    A. it always focuses attention on one person as the leader
    B. it places collective responsibility on the group as a whole
    C. its members gain experience by summarizing the ideas of others
    D. each member of the group acts as a member of a team

15. The one of the following that is an ADVANTAGE of a *large-group* discussion, when compared to a small-group discussion, is that the large-group discussion   15.____

    A. moves along more quickly than a small-group discussion
    B. allows its participants to feel more at ease, and speak out more freely
    C. gives the whole group a chance to exchange ideas on a certain subject at the same occasion
    D. allows its members to feel a greater sense of personal responsibility

KEYS (CORRECT ANSWERS)

1.	D		6.	D
2.	C		7.	B
3.	D		8.	D
4.	D		9.	A
5.	C		10.	D

11. D
12. B
13. A
14. D
15. C

——————

EXAMINATION SECTION

TEST 1

DIRECTIONS: Each question or incomplete statement is followed by several suggested answers or completions. Select the one that BEST answers the question or completes the statement. *PRINT THE LETTER OF THE CORRECT ANSWER IN THE SPACE AT THE RIGHT.*

1. Which one of the following is considered a word processor program?   1._____
    A. Microsoft Word   B. Microsoft Works
    C. Notepad   D. Both A and B

2. Default headings are available under the _____ tab.   2._____
    A. Insert   B. Home   C. File   D. View

3. _____ deals with font, alignment and margins.   3._____
    A. Selecting   B. Formatting   C. Composing   D. Pattern

4. Which one of the following is the BEST format for storing bit-mapped images   4._____
    on the computer?
    A. .JPG   B. .PNG   C. .GIF   D. .TIF

5. A header specifies an area in the _____ margins of every page.   5._____
    A. top   B. bottom   C. left   D. right

6. When an Excel file is inserted into a Word document, the data is   6._____
    A. hyperlinked   B. placed in a Word table
    C. linked   D. embedded

7. A workbook in Excel is defined as a file that   7._____
    A. holds text and data
    B. can be modified
    C. can contain many sheets, chart sheets and worksheets
    D. both A and B

8. Excel can produce chart types that include   8._____
    A. only line graphs
    B. bar charts, line graphs and pie charts
    C. line graphs and pie charts only
    D. bar charts and line graphs only

9. In PowerPoint, the motion path is a   9._____
    A. method of moving items on the slide
    B. method of advancing slides
    C. indentation
    D. type of animation

10. _____ replaces similar words in a document.   10._____
    A. Word Count   B. Thesaurus   C. Wrap Text   D. Format Printer

11. The MOST simple description of the Internet is   11._____
    A. a single network
    B. a huge collection of different networks
    C. collection of LAN
    D. single WAN

12. How can a computer be connected to the Internet?   12._____
    A. Through internet service provider   B. Internet society
    C. Internet architecture board   D. Local area network

13. A software program that is used to view web pages is known as a(n)   13._____
    A. Internet browser   B. interpreter
    C. operating system   D. website

14. Which of the following is used to search anything on the Internet?   14._____
    A. Search engines   B. Routers
    C. Social networks   D. Websites

15. When a website is accessed, its main page is called   15._____
    A. home page   B. back end page
    C. dead end   D. both A and B

16. Google Docs provides _____, which is a salient feature of Google Doc.   16._____
    A. image processing   B. synchronization
    C. both A and B   D. installation

17. Documents in Google Drive could be accessed from   17._____
    A. only a personal computer
    B. any computer that has Internet connection
    C. only that computer that has Google drive on hard disk
    D. both B and C

18. In an email address, for example test@gmail.com, "gmail" is known as   18._____
    A. domain
    B. host computer in commercial domain
    C. internet service provider
    D. URL

19. Which of the following is NOT a well-known domain?   19._____
    A. .edu   B. .com   C. .org   D. .army

20. Cyberspace is an alternative name used for   20._____
    A. Internet   B. information   C. virtual space   D. data space

21. Which one of the following is NOT an Internet browser?   21._____
    A. Chrome   B. Firefly   C. Firefox   D. Safari

22. Which of the following is NOT a past or current search engine? 22.____
    A. Apple   B. Lycos   C. Bing   D. Google

23. Document scanning could be done through 23.____
    A. OCR   B. OMR
    C. both A and B   D. dot-matrix printer

24. _____ are used to fill out empty fields in scanned images of data. 24.____
    A. Computerized optical scanners   B. OCR software
    C. Scanners   D. Laser printers

25. All of the following are examples of hardware for standard home use EXCEPT 25.____
    A. flash drives   B. inkjet printers
    C. servers   D. laser printers

KEY (CORRECT ANSWERS)

1.	D		11.	B
2.	B		12.	A
3.	B		13.	A
4.	D		14.	A
5.	A		15.	A
6.	B		16.	B
7.	C		17.	B
8.	B		18.	B
9.	A		19.	D
10.	B		20.	A

21.	B
22.	A
23.	C
24.	A
25.	C

TEST 2

DIRECTIONS: Each question or incomplete statement is followed by several suggested answers or completions. Select the one that BEST answers the question or completes the statement. *PRINT THE LETTER OF THE CORRECT ANSWER IN THE SPACE AT THE RIGHT.*

1. In a spreadsheet, data is organized in the form of
   A. lines and spaces
   B. rows and columns
   C. layers and planes
   D. height and width

   1.____

2. Which one of the following menus is used to protect a worksheet?
   A. Edit   B. Format   C. Data   D. Tools

   2.____

3. _____ corrects spelling mistakes automatically.
   A. Word wrap
   B. AutoCorrect
   C. Spell checker
   D. Thesaurus

   3.____

4. Which function is used to automatically align text?
   A. Justification
   B. Indentation
   C. Both A and B
   D. None of the above

   4.____

5. Orientation is the property of the _____ function.
   A. Print
   B. Design
   C. Image
   D. Both A and B

   5.____

6. Special effects that are used to present slides in a presentation are known as
   A. effects
   B. custom animation
   C. transition
   D. present animation

   6.____

7. Page setup and print functions can typically be found in the ____ menu.
   A. tools   B. format   C. file   D. edit

   7.____

8. Which one of the following is considered removable storage media?
   A. Scanner
   B. Flash drive
   C. External hard drive
   D. Both B and C

   8.____

9. Which component of the computer is called the brain of the computer?
   A. ALU   B. Memory   C. Control Unit   D. CPU

   9.____

10. .txt is a file that is named for _____ files.
    A. Notepad   B. Word   C. Paint   D. Excel

    10.____

11. Software programs that are automatically downloaded and work within a browser are known as
    A. plug-in   B. utilities   C. widgets   D. add-on

    11.____

12. _____ is a computer that requests data from other computers on the Internet.   12.____
    A. Client   B. Server
    C. Super computer   D. Personal computer

13. A wizard is considered as a _____ file with prompt display.   13.____
    A. system   B. program   C. help   D. application

14. E-mails from unknown senders go into the _____ folder.   14.____
    A. Spam   B. Trash   C. Drafts   D. Inbox

15. LAN is an abbreviation for _____ area network.   15.____
    A. line   B. local   C. large   D. limited

16. Which of the following is NOT an extension for an image file?   16.____
    A. .bmp   B. .jpg   C. .png   D. .xls

17. In the e-mail address *test@gmail.com*, "test" is the _____ name.   17.____
    A. domain   B. user   C. server   D. ISP

18. To e-mail multiple recipients while hiding the recipients from view, use the ___ function. 18.____
    A. BCC   B. CC   C. send   D. hide

19. The system that translates an IP address into a simple form that is easy to   19.____
    remember is
    A. domain name system   B. domain
    C. domain numbering system   D. server domain

20. Which one of the following is the CORRECT method to send a file through   20.____
    e-mail?
    A. CC   B. Attachment
    C. Embed through HTML   D. Both A and B

21. Inkjet printers are categorized as a(n) _____ printer.   21.____
    A. character   B. ink   C. line   D. band

22. Which one of the following is a storage medium that has a shape of a   22.____
    circular plate?
    A. Disk   B. CPU   C. ALU   D. Printer

23. Ctrl+P activates the _____ function.   23.____
    A. reboot   B. save   C. print   D. paint

24. The file extension .exe represents an _____ file.   24.____
    A. examination   B. extra   C. executable   D. extension

25. Which of the following is NOT considered an input device?   25.____
    A. OCR   B. Optical scanner
    C. Printer   D. Keyboard

_____

KEY (CORRECT ANSWERS)

1.	B		11.	B
2.	D		12.	A
3.	B		13.	C
4.	A		14.	A
5.	A		15.	B
6.	C		16.	D
7.	C		17.	B
8.	D		18.	A
9.	D		19.	A
10.	A		20.	B

21.	C
22.	A
23.	C
24.	C
25.	C

_____

TEST 3

DIRECTIONS: Each question or incomplete statement is followed by several suggested answers or completions. Select the one that BEST answers the question or completes the statement. *PRINT THE LETTER OF THE CORRECT ANSWER IN THE SPACE AT THE RIGHT.*

1. Excel is a _____ program.   1.____
    A. graphics   B. word processor
    C. spreadsheet   D. typewriter

2. Basically, a word processor program like Microsoft Word is a replacement for   2.____
    A. manual work   B. typewriters
    C. both A and B   D. graphical programs

3. Which one of the following could be added as a sound effect to a PowerPoint   3.____
    presentation?
    A. .wav files and.mid files   B. .wav files and .gif files
    C. .wave files and .jpg files   D. .jpg files and.gif files

4. Google Drive is an example of _____ software.   4.____
    A. system   B. application   C. database   D. firmware

5. PDF stands for _____ document format.   5.____
    A. portable   B. picture   C. plain   D. private

6. Which one of the following is an example of internal memory of a computer?   6.____
    A. Disks   B. Pen drive   C. RAM   D. CDs

7. A keyboard is an example of a(n) _____ device.   7.____
    A. input   B. output
    C. word processor   D. printing

8. Clip art is a collection of _____ that can be inserted into a document.   8.____
    A. text files   B. image files
    C. templates   D. audio files

9. _____ is a distinctive part of memory which holds the contents temporarily   9.____
    during cut or copy functions.
    A. Clipboard   B. Macro   C. Template   D. Clip art

10. _____ is a process to store files on a computer from the Internet.   10.____
    A. Uploading   B. Downloading
    C. Pulling   D. Transferring

11. "Cut and paste" refers to   11.____
    A. deleting and moving text   B. restoring and updating software
    C. cleaning images   D. replacing images

12. Which one of the following is a compressed format for images?   12.____
    A. GIF   B. JPGE   C. PNG   D. JPG

13. A computer stores information and data inside the   13.____
    A. hard drive   B. CPU   C. CD   D. monitor

14. WWW is an abbreviation of   14.____
    A. world wide web   B. wide world web
    C. web worldwide   D. world wide website

15. A _____ computer holds more than one processor.   15.____
    A. multithread   B. multi-unit
    C. multiprocessor   D. multiprogramming

16. Landscape and portrait are properties of   16.____
    A. page layout   B. design   C. formatting   D. text

17. _____ includes the company's name, address, phone number and e-mail   17.____
    address.
    A. Letterhead   B. Template   C. Visiting Card D. Brochure

18. _____ Server provides database services for other computers.   18.____
    A. Application   B. Web   C. Database   D. FTP

19. Which one of the following is responsible for storing movies, images and   19.____
    pictures?
    A. File server   B. Web server
    C. Database server   D. Application server

20. GUI stands for graphical   20.____
    A. user interface   B. unified instrument
    C. unified interface   D. user instrument

21. Scanner is an example of a(n) _____ device.   21.____
    A. output   B. input   C. printing   D. both A and B

22. Which one of the following is NOT an example of computer hardware?   22.____
    A. Printer   B. Scanner   C. Mouse   D. Antivirus

23. Which one of the following provides the BEST quality reproduction of   23.____
    graphics?
    A. Laser printer   B. Inkjet printer
    C. Dot-matrix printer   D. Plotter

24. If an e-mail sender is unknown, then do not download the _____ because   24.____
    it might contain a virus.
    A. attachment   B. email
    C. spam   D. both A and B

25. The BEST way to send identical emails to more than one person is to   25._____
    A. use the CC option   B. add email ID to address
    C. forward   D. both A and B

KEY (CORRECT ANSWERS)

1.	C		11.	A
2.	B		12.	A
3.	A		13.	A
4.	B		14.	A
5.	A		15.	C
6.	C		16.	A
7.	A		17.	A
8.	B		18.	C
9.	A		19.	A
10.	B		20.	A

21.	B
22.	D
23.	D
24.	A
25.	A

TEST 4

DIRECTIONS: Each question or incomplete statement is followed by several suggested answers or completions. Select the one that BEST answers the question or completes the statement. *PRINT THE LETTER OF THE CORRECT ANSWER IN THE SPACE AT THE RIGHT.*

1. A keyboard shortcut for saving files is   1.____
   A. Alt+S   B. Ctrl+S   C. Ctrl+SV   D. S+Enter

2. Which of the following is NOT a term relevant to Excel?   2.____
   A. slide   B. cell
   C. formula   D. column

3. A _____ background is a grainy and non-smooth surface.   3.____
   A. texture   B. gradient   C. solid   D. pattern

4. Word wrap forces all text to fit within the defined   4.____
   A. margin   B. indent   C. block   D. box

5. In Microsoft Word, overview of the prepared document could be better seen 5.____
   through
   A. Preview   B. Print Preview
   C. Review   D. both A and B

6. The amount of vertical space between text line in a document is known as   6.____
   A. double space   B. line spacing
   C. single space   D. vertical spacing

7. Which one of the following devices is required for Internet connection?   7.____
   A. Joy stick   B. Modem   C. NIC card   D. Optical drive

8. IBM is a short form used for   8.____
   A. Internal Business Management
   B. International Business Management
   C. Internal Business Machines
   D. International Business Machines

9. Which one of the following is static and non-volatile memory?   9.____
   A. RAM   B. ROM   C. BIOS   D. Cache

10. One disadvantage of Google Docs is   10.____
    A. less storage   B. compatibility
    C. needs connectivity to Internet   D. synchronization

11. WAN is an abbreviation of _____ area network.   11.____
    A. wide   B. wired   C. whole   D. while

12. Bibliography can be created through the _____ tab.　　　　　　　12.____
   　A. References　　　B. Design　　　C. Review　　　D. Insert

13. The _____ is MOST likely shared in a computer network.　　　　　13.____
   　A. keyboard　　　B. speaker　　　C. printer　　　D. scanner

14. A normal computer is not able to boot if it does not have a(n)　　　14.____
   　A. operating system　　　　　　B. complier
   　C. loader　　　　　　　　　　D. assembler

15. _____ is another name for junk e-mails.　　　　　　　　　　　15.____
   　A. Spam　　　B. Spoof　　　C. Spool　　　D. Sniffer scripts

16. A table of contents can be created automatically by using an option in　16.____
   　A. Page Layout　　B. Insert　　C. References　D. View

17. ALU stands for　　　　　　　　　　　　　　　　　　　　　　17.____
   　A. arithmetic logic unit　　　　B. array logic unit
   　C. application logic unit　　　　D. both A and B

18. Orientation is concerned with the _____ set-up of the page.　　　　18.____
   　A. horizontal　　B. vertical　　C. both A and B　D. spacing

19. _____ is a form of written communication within the same company which　19.____
   comprises guide words as heading.
   　A. Memorandum　　　　　　　B. Letterhead
   　C. Template　　　　　　　　　D. None of the above

20. Which one of the following is NOT a web browser?　　　　　　　　20.____
   　A. Chrome　　　B. Opera　　　C. Firefox　　　D. Drupal

21. .net domain is specifically used for　　　　　　　　　　　　　　21.____
   　A. international organization
   　B. internet infrastructure and service providers
   　C. educational institutes
   　D. commercial business

22. A modem is not required when the Internet is connected through　　　22.____
   　A. Wi-Fi　　　　　　　　　　B. LAN
   　C. dial-up phone　　　　　　　D. cable

23. Mail Merge uses _____ to create separate copies of a document for　　23.____
   multiple people in Microsoft Word.
   　A. primary document　　　　　B. data document
   　C. both A and B　　　　　　　D. web page

24. Linus is an example of　　　　　　　　　　　　　　　　　　　24.____
   　A. operating system　　　　　B. malware
   　C. firmware　　　　　　　　　D. application program

25. Which one of the following is a CORRECT format for a website address?   25.____
   A. www@com
   B. www.test.com
   C. www.test25A@com
   D. www#TeST.com

KEY (CORRECT ANSWERS)

1.	B		11.	A
2.	A		12.	A
3.	B		13.	C
4.	A		14.	A
5.	B		15.	A
6.	B		16.	C
7.	B		17.	A
8.	D		18.	C
9.	B		19.	A
10.	C		20.	D

21.	B
22.	A
23.	C
24.	A
25.	B

EXAMINATION SECTION

TEST 1

DIRECTIONS: Each question or incomplete statement is followed by several suggested answers or completions. Select the one that BEST answers the question or completes the statement. *PRINT THE LETTER OF THE CORRECT ANSWER IN THE SPACE AT THE RIGHT.*

1. Physical components of computers are known as
   A. software   B. hardware   C. firmware   D. human ware

   1.____

2. A touchscreen is considered a(n) _____ device.
   A. input   B. output   C. display   D. both A and B

   2.____

3. Keyboards and microphones are examples of computer
   A. peripherals   B. software   C. add-ons   D. uploads

   3.____

4. Unauthorized access to a computer is prevented through the use of
   A. passwords   B. user logins
   C. access control software   D. computer keys

   4.____

5. In order to establish an Internet connection, a modem is always connected to a
   A. keyboard   B. monitor
   C. telephone line   D. printer

   5.____

6. _____ does NOT hold data permanently.
   A. RAM   B. ROM   C. Hard drive   D. Flash drive

   6.____

7. Identification of a user who comes back to the same website is done through the use of
   A. scripts   B. plug-in   C. cookies   D. both A and B

   7.____

8. File _____ is the process of moving a file from one computer to another computer across the network.
   A. encryption   B. transfer   C. copying   D. updating

   8.____

9. _____ is a type of software that controls specific hardware.
   A. Driver   B. Browser   C. Plug-in   D. Control panel

   9.____

10. _____ is a downloadable program that is used for Internet surfing.
    A. Messenger   B. Firefox
    C. Windows Explorer   D. Internet

    10.____

11. In Microsoft Word, _____ is NOT a font style.
    A. Bold   B. Regular   C. Superscript   D. Italic

    11.____

12. Which of the following is NOT associated with page margins in a Word document?   12.____
    A. Top   B. Center   C. Left   D. Right

13. Microsoft Office is a type of _____ software.   13.____
    A. application   B. system   C. Internet   D. website

14. A function that is inside another function is known as a(n) _____ function.   14.____
    A. round   B. nested   C. sum   D. average

15. To write a formula in Microsoft Excel, a user would start by typing   15.____
    A. %   B. =   C. #   D. @

16. The individual boxes used for data entry in an Excel file are known as   16.____
    A. cells   B. data points
    C. formulas   D. squares

17. In PowerPoint, _____ do NOT show with the slide layout.   17.____
    A. titles   B. animations   C. lists   D. charts

18. _____ is a basic option when looking for colorful images or graphics to publish in a PowerPoint presentation.   18.____
    A. Clip art   B. Online search
    C. MS Paint   D. Drawing

19. In a web browser, the addresses of Internet pages are known as   19.____
    A. web pages   B. URLs   C. scripts   D. plug-in

20. A company that provides Internet services is called a(n)   20.____
    A. ISP   B. IBM   C. LAN   D. Both A and B

21. _____ is the process of copying a file from personal computer to a remote computer.   21.____
    A. Downloading   B. Uploading
    C. Updating   D. Modification

22. _____ is a text that opens another page when clicked.   22.____
    A. Link   B. Hyperlink
    C. Both A and B   D. Web page

23. Dots per inch is the measure of printing   23.____
    A. quality   B. type   C. time   D. layout

24. _____ is the collection of computers connected with each other.   24.____
    A. Group   B. Team   C. Network   D. Meeting

25. Which one of the following is considered a high-end printer?   25.____
    A. Dot matrix printer   B. Inkjet printer
    C. Laser   D. Thermal

KEY (CORRECT ANSWERS)

1.	B		11.	C
2.	D		12.	B
3.	A		13.	A
4.	A		14.	B
5.	C		15.	B
6.	A		16.	A
7.	C		17.	B
8.	B		18.	A
9.	A		19.	B
10.	B		20.	A

21.	B
22.	C
23.	A
24.	C
25.	C

TEST 2

DIRECTIONS: Each question or incomplete statement is followed by several suggested answers or completions. Select the one that BEST answers the question or completes the statement. *PRINT THE LETTER OF THE CORRECT ANSWER IN THE SPACE AT THE RIGHT.*

1. Which one of the following is a storage device?   1._____
   A. Printer   B. Hard drive
   C. Scanner   D. Motherboard

2. DVD is an example of a(n) _____ disk.   2._____
   A. hard   B. optical   C. magnetic   D. floppy

3. _____ computers provide resources to other computers across the network.   3._____
   A. Server   B. Client   C. Framework   D. Digital

4. Random access memory is considered _____ computer memory.   4._____
   A. non-volatile   B. volatile   C. cache   D. permanent

5. Which one of the following is NOT an operating system?   5._____
   A. Windows   B. IOS   C. Android   D. MS Office

6. A(n) _____ is a person who gets illegal access to a computer system and steals   6._____
   information.
   A. administrator   B. computer operator
   C. hacker   D. programmer

7. Which one of the following is NOT application software?   7._____
   A. MS Word   B. Media player
   C. Linux   D. MS Power Point

8. Which one of the following represents a domain name?   8._____
   A. .com   B. www   C. URL   D. HTTP

9. _____ is NOT an example of an Internet browser.   9._____
   A. Opera   B. Google
   C. Mozilla   D. Internet Explorer

10. Which one of the following is NOT a search engine?   10._____
    A. Altavista   B. Bing
    C. Yahoo   D. Facebook

11. E-mail is an abbreviation of   11._____
    A. electronic mail   B. easy mail
    C. electric email   D. both A and B

12. A(n) _____ is a person who takes care of websites for large companies.   12.____
    A. administrator   B. webmaster
    C. programmer   D. hacker

13. _____ connect web pages with each other.   13.____
    A. Connecters   B. Links   C. Hyperlinks   D. Browsers

14. _____ is a program that is harmful for computers.   14.____
    A. Spam   B. Virus
    C. Operating system   D. Plug-in

15. CC is an abbreviation of _____ in emails.   15.____
    A. core copy   B. copycat
    C. carbon copy   D. copy copy

16. Software most commonly used for basic personal computing is   16.____
    A. Excel   B. SPSS   C. Illustrator   D. Dreamweaver

17. _____ is an option to send the same letter to different persons.   17.____
    A. Template   B. Macros   C. Mail Merge   D. Layout

18. Which one of the following is a file extension for MS Word?   18.____
    A. .doc   B. .txt   C. .bmp   D. .pdf

19. _____ displays the number of words in a document.   19.____
    A. Character Count   B. Word Count   C. Word Wrap   D. Thesaurus

20. In an Excel sheet, an active cell is specified with   20.____
    A. dotted border   B. dark wide border
    C. italic text   D. a dotted border

21. A(n) _____ is a file that contains rows and columns.   21.____
    A. database   B. spreadsheet
    C. word   D. drawing

22. _____ are objects on the slides that hold text in a PowerPoint presentation.   22.____
    A. Placeholders   B. Text holders
    C. Auto layouts   D. Object holders

23. Which one of the following brings up the first slide in a PowerPoint presentation?   23.____
    A. Ctrl+End   B. Ctrl+Home
    C. Page up   D. Next slide button

24. Which one of the following sends printing commands to a printer?   24.____
    A. F5   B. Ctrl+P   C. Ctrl+S   D. F12

25. Scanners are used to capture _____ copy of documents.   25.____
    A. soft   B. hard   C. single   D. first

KEY (CORRECT ANSWERS)

1.	B		11.	A
2.	B		12.	B
3.	A		13.	C
4.	B		14.	B
5.	D		15.	C
6.	C		16.	A
7.	C		17.	C
8.	A		18.	A
9.	B		19.	B
10.	D		20.	B

21.	B
22.	A
23.	B
24.	B
25.	B

TEST 3

DIRECTIONS: Each question or incomplete statement is followed by several suggested answers or completions. Select the one that BEST answers the question or completes the statement. *PRINT THE LETTER OF THE CORRECT ANSWER IN THE SPACE AT THE RIGHT.*

1. Which one of the following is the MOST appropriate operation to move a text block in MS Word?
   A. Cut
   B. Save As
   C. Cut and Paste
   D. Copy and Paste

   1.____

2. The Navigation pane opens under the _____ tab.
   A. View
   B. Review
   C. Page Layout
   D. Mailings

   2.____

3. Ctrl+B makes selected test
   A. italic
   B. bold
   C. bigger
   D. uppercase

   3.____

4. _____ is NOT an acceptable formula in Excel.
   A. 10+50
   B. =10+50
   C. =B7+B8
   D. =B7*B8

   4.____

5. A worksheet usually contains _____ columns.
   A. 128
   B. 256
   C. 512
   D. 320

   5.____

6. _____ is the process of getting data from the cell that is located in different worksheets.
   A. Accessing
   B. Referencing
   C. Updating
   D. Functioning

   6.____

7. The shortcut _____ selects all PowerPoint slides at once.
   A. Ctrl+Home
   B. Ctrl+A
   C. Alt+Home
   D. Shift+A

   7.____

8. By pressing Ctrl+V in a Word document, the user
   A. pastes text
   B. cuts and pastes text
   C. adds a video box
   D. deletes a page

   8.____

9. Transitions are applicable only on
   A. Excel worksheets
   B. PowerPoint slides
   C. image files
   D. Word document

   9.____

10. In MS Word, the _____ tab has options for margin, orientation and spacing.
    A. Design
    B. Review
    C. Page Layout
    D. Insert

    10.____

11. Which one of the following is graphic software?
    A. MS Office
    B. Adobe Photoshop
    C. Firefox
    D. Notepad

    11.____

12. Which one of the following is a social networking website?
    A. Facebook
    B. Yahoo
    C. Google
    D. ASK

    12.____

13. A computer monitor is referred to as a(n) _____ device.   13.____
    A. output   B. input   C. sound   D. printing

14. _____ memory is another name for the main memory of the computer.   14.____
    A. Primary   B. Direct   C. Simple   D. Quick

15. An operating system is _____ software.   15.____
    A. application   B. system   C. editing   D. both A and C

16. Which one of the following pieces of equipment is necessary for video calls?   16.____
    A. Webcam   B. Mouse   C. Scanner   D. Printer

17. _____ is a primary input device that is used to enter text and numbers.   17.____
    A. Mouse   B. Keyboard   C. Joystick   D. Microphone

18. Of the following, which is NOT an example of a web browser?   18.____
    A. Firefox   B. Opera   C. Chrome   D. Google Talk

19. A _____ is a collection of many web pages that are related to each other. 19.____
    A. web browser   B. website
    C. search engine   D. Firefox

20. Which one of the following is considered a personal journal used for   20.____
    posts?
    A. Blog   B. E-mail   C. Chat   D. Messengers

21. Windows _____ provides security against external threats.   21.____
    A. antivirus   B. spyware   C. firmware   D. firewall

22. Desktop and laptop computers are different from each other in terms of   22.____
    _____ and cost.
    A. operating system   B. functions
    C. physical structure   D. application software

23. _____ is a process of stealing confidential information without permission 23.____
    of the user.
    A. Forwarding   B. Hacking   C. Searching   D. Complaining

24. RAM is located in the _____ board.   24.____
    A. extension   B. external   C. mother   D. chip

25. All files on the computer are stored in   25.____
    A. hard drive   B. RAM
    C. cache   D. associative memory

122

KEY (CORRECT ANSWERS)

1.	C		11.	B
2.	A		12.	A
3.	B		13.	A
4.	A		14.	A
5.	B		15.	B
6.	B		16.	A
7.	B		17.	B
8.	A		18.	D
9.	B		19.	B
10.	C		20.	A

21. D
22. C
23. B
24. C
25. A

TEST 4

DIRECTIONS: Each question or incomplete statement is followed by several suggested
answers or completions. Select the one that BEST answers the question or
completes the statement. *PRINT THE LETTER OF THE CORRECT ANSWER
IN THE SPACE AT THE RIGHT.*

1. Which one of the following functions are performed by RAM?   1._____
    A. Read and Write   B. Read
    C. Write   D. Update

2. _____ is an example of secondary storage.   2._____
    A. Diode   B. Hard disk   C. RAM   D. ROM

3. USB is a type of _____ storage.   3._____
    A. primary   B. secondary   C. tertiary   D. temporary

4. MPG file extension is used for _____ files.   4._____
    A. video   B. audio   C. image   D. flash

5. .exe is an extension for _____ files.   5._____
    A. saved   B. executable   C. system   D. software

6. Which one of the following is NOT a type of printer?   6._____
    A. Inkjet   B. Dot matrix   C. Laser   D. CRT

7. _____ sends digital data across a phone line.   7._____
    A. Flash   B. Modem   C. NIC card   D. Keyboard

8. _____ is a wireless technology used to transfer data among devices over   8._____
    short distances.
    A. USB   B. Modem   C. Wi-Fi   D. Bluetooth

9. A user is listening to a song on his computer's music player. He is most likely   9._____
    listening to a(n) _____ file.
    A. .exe   B. .mus   C. .wav   D. .mp3

10. PNG is an extension used for _____ files.   10._____
    A. audio   B. video   C. text   D. image

11. Cache memory is located in the   11._____
    A. monitor   B. CPU   C. DVD   D. hard drive

12. Computer resolution determines the number of   12._____
    A. colors   B. pixels   C. images   D. icons

13. _____ is an extension used for images.   13._____
    A. GIF   B. MP3   C. MPG   D. PPT

124

14. Which one of the following is NOT an e-mail server?   14.____
    A. Gmail   B. Yahoo   C. Chrome   D. Hotmail

15. _____ is an operating system developed by Apple.   15.____
    A. Mac IOS   B. Linux   C. Android   D. Windows

16. "What You See Is What You Get" (WYSIWYG) refers to   16.____
    A. editing text and graphics for web design
    B. buying a computer at a set price that can't be negotiated
    C. purchasing products as is on websites like Amazon and eBay
    D. printing web pages exactly as they appear on the screen

17. Which one of the following is the BEST option to add a new slide in an   17.____
    existing PowerPoint presentation?
    A. File, add a new slide   B. File, open
    C. Insert, new slide   D. File, new

18. _____ is the default setup for page orientation in PowerPoint.   18.____
    A. Horizontal   B. Vertical   C. Landscape   D. Portrait

19. Items in a list are typically shown by using   19.____
    A. graphics   B. bullets   C. icons   D. markers

20. In PowerPoint, _____ displays only text.   20.____
    A. outline view   B. slide show
    C. print view   D. slider sorter view

21. In Excel, a cell can be edited by use of   21.____
    A. a single click   B. a double click
    C. the format menu   D. formulas

22. Formulas are important features of Microsoft   22.____
    A. Word   B. PowerPoint   C. Excel   D. Publisher

23. In MS Word, which one of the following is used to underline a text?   23.____
    A. Ctrl+I   B. Ctrl+B   C. Ctrl+U   D. Ctrl+P

24. Page color option can be found under the _____ tab.   24.____
    A. Page Layout   B. Design   C. Insert   D. View

25. The F1 key typically displays a program's ____ menu.   25.____
    A. print   B. help
    C. tools   D. task manager

KEY (CORRECT ANSWERS)

1.	A		11.	B
2.	B		12.	B
3.	C		13.	A
4.	A		14.	C
5.	B		15.	A
6.	D		16.	A
7.	B		17.	C
8.	D		18.	C
9.	D		19.	B
10.	D		20.	A

21.	A
22.	C
23.	C
24.	B
25.	B

READING COMPREHENSION
UNDERSTANDING AND INTERPRETING WRITTEN MATERIAL

EXAMINATION SECTION
TEST 1

DIRECTIONS: Each question or incomplete statement is followed by several suggested answers or completions. Select the one that BEST answers the question or completes the statement. *PRINT THE LETTER OF THE CORRECT ANSWER IN THE SPACE AT THE RIGHT.*

Questions 1-4.

DIRECTIONS: Questions 1 through 4 are to be answered SOLELY on the basis of the information in the following paragraphs.

Some authorities have questioned whether the term *culture of poverty* should be used since *culture* means a design for living which is passed down from generation to generation. The culture of poverty is, however, a very useful concept if it is used with care, with recognition that poverty is a subculture, and with avoidance of the *cookie-cutter* approach. With regard to the individual, the cookie-cutter view assumes that all individuals in a culture turn out exactly alike, as if they were so many cookies. It overlooks the fact that, at least in our urban society, every individual is a member of more than one subculture; and which subculture most strongly influences his response in a given situation depends on the interaction of a great many factors, including his individual make-up and history, the specifics of the various subcultures to which he belongs, and the specifics of the given situation. It is always important to avoid the cookie-cutter view of culture, with regard to the individual and to the culture or subculture involved.

With regard to the culture as a whole, the cookie-cutter concept again assumes homogeneity and consistency. It forgets that within any one culture or subculture there are conflicts and contradictions, and that at any given moment an individual may have to choose, consciously, between conflicting values or patterns. Also, most individuals, in varying degrees, have a dual set of values—those by which they live and those they cherish as best. This point has been made and documented repeatedly about the culture of poverty.

1. The *cookie-cutter* approach assumes that

    A. members of the same *culture* are all alike
    B. *culture* stays the same from generation to generation
    C. the term *culture* should not be applied to groups who are poor
    D. there are value conflicts within most *cultures*

1.____

2. According to the above passage, every person in our cities

    A. is involved in the conflicts of urban culture
    B. recognizes that poverty is a subculture
    C. lives by those values to which he is exposed
    D. belongs to more than one subculture

2.____

3. The above passage emphasizes that a culture is likely to contain within it   3._____

    A.   one dominant set of values
    B.   a number of contradictions
    C.   one subculture to which everyone belongs
    D.   members who are exactly alike

4. According to the above passage, individuals are sometimes forced to choose BETWEEN   4._____

    A.   cultures
    B.   subcultures
    C.   different sets of values
    D.   a new culture and an old culture

Questions 5-8.

DIRECTIONS: Questions 5 through 8 are to be answered SOLELY on the basis of the following passage.

There are approximately 33 million poor people in the United States; 14.3 million of them are children, 5.3 million are old people, and the remainder are in other categories. Altogether, 6.5 million families live in poverty because the heads of the households cannot work; they are either too old or too sick or too severely handicapped, or they are widowed or deserted mothers of young children. There are the working poor: the low-paid workers, the workers in seasonal industries, and soldiers with no additional income who are heads of families. There are the underemployed: those who would like full-time jobs but cannot find them, those employees who would like year-round work but lack the opportunity, and those who are employed below their level of training. There are the non-working poor: the older men and women with small retirement incomes and those with no income, the disabled, the physically and mentally handicapped, and the chronically sick.

5. According to the above passage, approximately what percent of the poor people in the United States are children?   5._____

    A. 33   B. 16   C. 20   D. 44

6. According to the above passage, people who work in seasonal industries are LIKELY to be classified as   6._____

    A.   working poor   B.   underemployed
    C.   non-working poor   D.   low-paid workers

7. According to the above passage, the category of non-working poor includes people who   7._____

    A.   receive unemployment insurance
    B.   cannot find full-time work
    C.   are disabled or mentally handicapped
    D.   are soldiers with wives and children

8. According to the above passage, among the underemployed are those who   8._____

    A.   can find only part-time work
    B.   are looking for their first jobs
    C.   are inadequately trained
    D.   depend on insufficient retirement incomes

Questions 9-13.

DIRECTIONS: Read the Inter-office Memo below. Then answer Questions 9 through 13 SOLELY on the basis of the memo.

INTER-OFFICE MEMORANDUM

To: Alma Robinson, Human Resources Aide

From: Frank Shields, Social Worker

I would like to have you help Mr. Edward Tunney who is trying to raise his two children by himself. He needs to learn to improve the physical care of his children and especially of his daughter Helen, age 9. She is avoided and ridiculed at school because her hair is uncombed, her teeth not properly cleaned, her clothing torn, wrinkled and dirty, as well as shabby and poorly fitted. The teachers and school officials have contacted the Department and the social worker for two years about Helen. She is not able to make friends because of these problems. I have talked to Mr. Tunney about improvements for the child's clothing, hair, and hygiene. He tends to deny these things are problems, but is cooperative, and a second person showing him the importance of better physical care for Helen would be helpful.

Perhaps you could teach Helen how to fix her own hair. She has all the materials. I would also like you to form your own opinion of the sanitary conditions in the home and how they could be improved.

Mr. Tunney is expecting your visit and is willing to talk with you about ways he can help with these problems.

9.   In the above memorandum, the Human Resources Aide is being asked to help Mr. Tunney to   9.____

   A.   improve the learning habits of his children
   B.   enable his children to make friends at school
   C.   take responsibility for the upbringing of his children
   D.   give attention to the grooming and cleanliness of his children

10.   This case was brought to the attention of the social worker by   10.____

   A.   government officials
   B.   teachers and school officials
   C.   the Department
   D.   Mr. Tunney

11.   In general, Mr. Tunney's attitude with regard to his children could BEST be described as   11.____

   A.   interested in correcting the obvious problems, but unable to do so alone
   B.   unwilling to follow the advice of those who are trying to help
   C.   concerned but unaware of the seriousness of these problems
   D.   interested in helping them, but afraid of taking the advice of the social worker

12. Which of the following actions has NOT been suggested as a possible step for the   12.____
Human Resources Aide to take?

    A. Help Helen to learn to care for herself by teaching her grooming skills
    B. Determine ways of improvement through information gathered on a home visit
    C. Discuss her own views on Helen's problems with school officials
    D. Ask Mr. Tunney in what ways he believes the physical care may be improved

13. According to the above memo, the Human Resources Aide is ESPECIALLY being asked   13.____
to observe and form her own opinions about

    A. the relationship between Mr. Tunney and the school officials
    B. Helen's attitude toward her classmates and teacher
    C. the sanitary conditions in the home
    D. the reasons Mr. Tunney is not cooperative with the agency

Questions 14-16.

DIRECTIONS: Questions 14 through 16 are to be answered SOLELY on the basis of the following paragraph.

In social work, professional responsibility and accountability extend to a larger segment of the general community than is true of the older professions which have more limited and more specialized areas of community responsibility and public trust. Advances in knowledge about both the nature of human institutions and the nature of the individual have placed social work in the center of a vast complex of interrelationships. The situations that come to the attention of the social worker, whatever his functions, may be the circumstances of an individual client or of a group or of a community which may or may not be socially sanctioned, and the proposed remedy may be considered desirable or questionable. When there is agreement between the client group and the community on the nature of the problem and on the validity of the proposed remedy, such agreement may lead to the establishment of social institutions. Complications arise when the client or client group, or the community, does not accept the need for change or is not in agreement with the social worker about the direction it should take. The social worker has the obligation to pursue his objective regardless of the difficulties. Even if social work, as it is practiced today, were to achieve the degree of acceptance afforded the older professions, it would still find itself, with every new development, holding unorthodox and not very respectable views on many aspects of personal and social relationships.

14. The MOST accurate of the following statements about the relationship between social   14.____
work and the other professions is:

    A. Advances in knowledge have placed social work in a central position among the professions
    B. Although younger, social work has become basic to the older professions in their responsibility and accountability in the community
    C. It is the responsibility of social workers to hold unorthodox views on social relationships
    D. The areas of responsibility of social work within the community are more extensive than those of the older professions

15. When, because of an existing problem, a social worker has advocated a change in a social institution which has been opposed by the community, the social worker should

    15.____

    A. attempt to surmount the opposition, continuing to seek to reach his objective
    B. change his position to gain the support of the community
    C. review the position that he has taken to see whether he cannot revise his objective to the point where it may gain community support
    D. work to achieve for his profession the degree of acceptance which is afforded the older professions

16. Of the following, the BEST title for the above paragraph is

    16.____

    A. DANGERS OF SOCIAL RESPONSIBILITY
    B. SOCIAL WORK AND THE OLDER PROFESSIONS COMPARED
    C. SOCIAL WORKERS' RESPONSIBILITY IN SOCIAL CHANGE
    D. UNORTHODOX SOCIAL WORK

Questions 17-19.

DIRECTIONS: Questions 17 through 19 are to be answered SOLELY on the basis of the following paragraph.

Toward the end of the 19th century, as social work principles and theories took form, areas of conflict between the responsibility of the social worker to the client group and to the status quo of social and economic institutions became highlighted. The lay public's attitude toward the individual poor was one of emphasis on betterment through the development of the individual's capacity for self-maintenance. They hoped to maintain this end both by helping the client to rely on his unused capacities for self-help and by facilitating his access to what were assumed to be the natural sources of help family, relatives, churches, and other charitable associations. Professional social workers were fast becoming aware of the need for social reform. They perceived that traditional methods of help were largely inadequate to cope with the factors that were creating poverty and maladjustment for a large number of the population faster than the charity societies could relieve such problems through individual effort. The critical view, held by social workers, of the character of many social institutions was not shared by other groups in the community who had not reached the same point of awareness about the deficiencies in the functioning of these institutions. Thus, the views of the social worker were beginning to differ, sometimes radically, from the basic views of large sections of the population.

17. The social workers of the late 19th century found themselves in conflict with the status quo CHIEFLY because they

    17.____

    A. had become professionalized through the development of a body of theory and principles
    B. became aware that many social ills could not be cured through existing institutions
    C. felt that traditional methods of helping the poor must be expanded regardless of the cost to the public
    D. believed that the right of the individual to be self-determining should be emphasized

18. It was becoming apparent, by the end of the 19th century, that in relation to the needs of the poor, existing social institutions

    18.____

A. did not sufficiently emphasize the ability of the poor to utilize their natural sources of help
B. were using the proper methods of helping the poor, but were hindered by the work of social workers who had broken with tradition
C. were no longer capable of meeting the needs of the poor because the causes of poverty had changed
D. were capable of meeting the needs of the poor, but needed more financial aid from the general public since the number of people in need had increased

19. Social workers at the end of the 19th century may be PROPERLY classified as   19._____

    A. growing in awareness that many social ills could be alleviated through social reform
    B. very perceptive individuals who realized that traditional methods of help were humiliating to the poor
    C. strong advocates of expanding the existing traditional sources of relief
    D. too radical because they favored easing life for the poor at the expense of increased taxation to the public at large

Questions 20-24.

DIRECTIONS: Questions 20 through 24 are to be answered SOLELY on the basis of the following paragraphs.

With the generation gap yawning before us, it is well to remember that 20 years ago teenagers produced a larger proportion of unwedlock births than today, and that the illegitimacy rate among teenagers is lower than among women in their twenties and thirties. In addition, the illegitimacy rate has risen less among teenagers than among older women.

It is helpful to note the difference between illegitimacy rate and illegitimacy ratio. The ratio is the number of illegitimate babies per 1,000 live births. The rate is the number of illegitimate births per 1,000 unmarried women of childbearing age. The ratio talks about babies; the rate talks about mothers. The ratio is useful for planning services, but worse than useless for considering trends since it depends on the age and marital <u>composition</u> of the population, illegitimacy rate, and the fertility of married women. For example, the ratio among girls under 18 is bound to be high in comparison with older women since few are married mothers. However, the illegitimacy rate is relatively low.

20. Of the following, the MOST suitable title for the above passage would be   20._____

    A. THE GENERATION GAP
    B. MORAL STANDARDS AND TEENAGE ILLEGITIMACY RATIO
    C. A COMPARISON OF ILLEGITIMACY RATE AND ILLEGITIMACY RATIO
    D. CAUSES OF HIGH ILLEGITIMACY RATES

21. According to the above passage, which of the following statements is CORRECT?   21._____
The illegitimacy

    A. rate has fallen among women in their thirties
    B. ratio is the number of illegitimate births per 1,000 unmarried women of childbearing age

C. ratio is partially dependent on the illegitimacy rate
D. rate is more useful than the ratio for planning services

22. According to the above passage, of the following age groups, the illegitimacy ratio would   22.____
     be expected to be HIGHEST in comparison with the other groups for the group aged

     A. 17   B. 21   C. 25   D. 29

23. According to the above passage, of the following age groups, the illegitimacy rate would   23.____
     be expected to be LOWEST in comparison with the other groups for the group aged

     A. 17   B. 21   C. 25   D. 29

24. As used in the above passage, the underlined word composition means MOST NEARLY   24.____

     A. essay   B. makeup
     C. security   D. happiness

25. A document was published by a public agency and distributed for discussion. The docu-   25.____
     ment contained data showing trends in the level of reading among freshmen college stu-
     dents and suggested that the high schools were not investing enough effort in
     overcoming retardation. It compared the costs of intensifying reading instruction in the
     secondary schools as compared to costs in colleges for such instruction.
     According to the above statement, it is REASONABLE to conclude that

     A. the document proposed new programs
     B. the college students read better than high school students
     C. some college students need remedial reading
     D. the study was done by a consultant

———

KEY (CORRECT ANSWERS)

1.	A		11.	C
2.	D		12.	C
3.	B		13.	C
4.	C		14.	D
5.	D		15.	A
6.	A		16.	C
7.	C		17.	B
8.	A		18.	C
9.	D		19.	A
10.	B		20.	C

21.	C
22.	A
23.	A
24.	B
25.	C

TEST 2

DIRECTIONS: Each question or incomplete statement is followed by several suggested answers or completions. Select the one that BEST answers the question or completes the statement. *PRINT THE LETTER OF THE CORRECT ANSWER IN THE SPACE AT THE RIGHT.*

Questions 1-4.

DIRECTIONS: Questions 1 through 4 are to be answered SOLELY on the basis of the following paragraph.

Form W-280 provides a uniform standard for estimating family expenses and is used as a basis for determining eligibility for the care of children at public expense. The extent to which legally responsible relatives can pay for the care of a child must be computed. The minimum amount of the payment required from legally responsible relatives shall be 50% of the budget surplus as computed on Form W-281, plus any governmental benefits, such as OASDI benefits, or Railroad Retirement benefits being paid to a family member for the child receiving care or services. Because of the kinds and quantities of services included in the budget schedule (W-280) and because only 50% of the budget surplus is required as payment, no allowances for special needs are made, except for verified payments into civil service pension funds, amounts paid to a garnishee, or amounts paid to another agency for the care of other relatives for whom the relative is legally responsible, or for other such expenses if approval has been granted after Form W-278 has been submitted. In determining the income of the legally responsible relative, income from wages, self-employment, unemployment insurance benefits, and any such portion of governmental benefits as is not specifically designated for children already receiving care is to be included. Should 50% of the family's surplus meet the child care expenses, the case shall not be processed. Form W-279, an agreement to support, shall be signed by the legally responsible relative when 50% of the surplus is $1.00 or more a week.

1. A family is required to sign an agreement to support   1.____

    A. whenever they are legally responsible for the support of the child under care
    B. before any care at public expense is given to the child
    C. when their income surplus is at least $2.00/week
    D. when 50% of their income surplus meets the full needs of the child

2. The reason for allowing a family to deduct only certain specified expenses when comput-   2.____
    ing the amount they are able to contribute to the support of a child being cared for at pub-
    lic expense is that the family

    A. should not be permitted to have a higher standard of living than the child being
        cared for
    B. the budget schedule is sufficiently generous and includes an allowance for other
        unusual expenses
    C. may not be able to verify their extraordinary expenses
    D. may meet other unusual expenses from the remainder of their surplus

3. Mrs. B wishes to have her daughter Mary cared for at public expense. Her income includes her wages and OASDI benefits of $250 a month, of which $50 a month is paid for Mary and $50 a month for another minor member of the family who is already being cared for at public expense. In order to determine the amount of Mrs. B's budget surplus, it is necessary to consider as income her wages and

    A. $ 50 of OASDI received for Mary
    B. $150 of the OASDI benefits
    C. $200 of the OASDI benefits
    D. $200 of the OASDI benefits if she is legally responsible for the care of the other child in placement

4. In order to determine a family's ability to contribute to the support of a child, the worker should

    A.   have the legally responsible member sign Form W-279 agreeing to support the child, and then compute the family surplus on W-281 in accordance with public assistance standards
    B.   compute the family's income in accordance with the allowance included on Form W-280 and the expenses included on Form W-278 and have Form W-279 signed if necessary
    C.   use Form W-278 to work out a budget schedule for the family and compute their surplus on W-281 and then have them sign W-279 if necessary
    D.   compute income and expenses on Form W-281, based on Form W-280, and have Form W-279 signed if necessary

Questions 5-10.

DIRECTIONS: Questions 5 through 10 are to be answered SOLELY on the basis of the following passage.

Too often in the past, society has accepted the existing social welfare programs, preferring to tinker with refinements when fundamental reform was in order. It has been a demeaning, degrading welfare system in which the instrument of government was wrongfully and ineptly used. It has been a system which has only alienated those forced to benefit from it and demoralized those who had to administer it at the level where the pain was clearly visible.

There is a need to put this nation on a course in which cash benefits, providing a basic level of support, are conferred in such a way as to intrude as little as possible into privacy and self-respect. It is difficult to define a basic level of support, no matter how high or low it might be set. In the end, however, the decision is not determined so much by how much is truly adequate for a family to meet all of its needs, but by the resources available to carry out the promise. That may be a harsh fact of life but it is also just that — a fact of life.

5. Of the following, the MOST suitable title for the above passage would be

    A.   THE NEED FOR GOVERNMENT CONTROL OF WELFARE
    B.   DETERMINING THE BASIC LEVEL OF SUPPORT
    C.   THE NEED FOR WELFARE REFORM
    D.   THE ELIMINATION OF WELFARE PROGRAMS

6. In the above passage, the author's GREATEST criticism of the welfare system is that it is too

    A. disrespectful of recipients
    B. expensive to administer
    C. limited by regulations
    D. widespread in application

6.____

7. According to the above passage, the BASIC level of support is actually determined by

    A. how much is required for a family to meet all of its needs
    B. the age of the recipients
    C. how difficult it is to administer the program
    D. the economic resources of the nation

7.____

8. In the above passage, the author does NOT argue for

    A. a work incentive system   B. a basic level of support
    C. cash benefits   D. the privacy of recipients

8.____

9. As used in the above passage, the underlined word demeaning means MOST NEARLY

    A. ineffective   B. expensive
    C. overburdened   D. humiliating

9.____

10. As used in the above passage, the underlined word ineptly means MOST NEARLY

    A. foolishly   B. unsuccessfully
    C. unskillfully   D. unhappily

10.____

Questions 11-14.

DIRECTIONS: Questions 11 through 14 are to be answered SOLELY on the basis of the following paragraph.

The unemployment rate, which counts those unemployed in the sense that they are actively looking for work and unable to find it, gives a relatively superficial index of economic conditions in a community. A better index is the subemployment rate which includes the unemployment rate and also includes those working part-time while they are trying to get full-time work; those heads of households under 65 years of age who earn less than $240 per week working full-time, and those individuals under 65 who are not heads of households and earn less than $224 per week in a full-time job; and an estimate of the males *not counted,* which is a very real concern in ghetto areas.

11. Of the following, the MOST suitable title for the above paragraph would be

    A. EMPLOYMENT IN THE UNITED STATES
    B. PART-TIME WORKERS AND THE ECONOMY
    C. THE LABOR MARKET AND THE COMMUNITY
    D. TWO INDICATORS OF ECONOMIC CONDITIONS

11.____

12. On the basis of the above paragraph, which of the following statements is CORRECT?

    A. The unemployment rate includes everyone who is not fully employed.
    B. The subemployment rate is higher than the unemployment rate.

12.____

C. The unemployment rate gives a more complete picture of the economic situation than the subemployment rate.

D. The subemployment rate indicates how many part-time workers are dissatisfied with the number of hours they work per week.

13. As used in the above paragraph, the underlined word <u>superficial</u> means MOST NEARLY   13.____

    A. exaggerated   B. official
    C. surface   D. current

14. According to the above paragraph, which of the following is included in the subemploy-   14.____
ment rate?

    A. Everyone who is unemployed
    B. All part-time workers
    C. Everyone under 65 who earns less than $220 per week in a full-time job
    D. All heads of households who earn less than $240 per week in a full-time job

Questions 15-16.

DIRECTIONS: Questions 15 and 16 are to be answered SOLELY on the basis of the following paragraphs.

The city's economy has its own dynamics, and there is only so much the government can do to shape it. But that margin is critically important. If the city uses its points of leverage, it can generate a large number of jobs – and good jobs, jobs that lead to advancement.

As a major employer itself, the city can upgrade the jobs it offers and greatly improve its services to the public if it does so. Since highly skilled professionals will always be in short supply, the city must train more paraprofessionals to take over routine tasks. Equally important, it must provide them with a realistic job ladder so they can move on up – nurse's aide to certified nurse, for example, teacher's aide to teacher. The training programs for such upgrading will require a substantial public investment but the cost-benefit return should be excellent.

As a major purchaser of goods and services, the city can stimulate business enterprise in the ghetto. The growth of Black and Puerto Rican firms will produce more local jobs; it will also create the kind of managerial talent the ghetto needs.

New kinds of enterprise can be set up. In housing, for example, there is a huge backlog of rehabilitation work to be done and a large pool of unskilled manpower to be trained for it. Corporations can be formed to take over tenements, remodel, maintain, and operate them, as in the Brownsville Home Maintenance Program. Grocery cooperatives to bring food prices down are another possibility.

15. According to the above paragraphs, the city is the major employer and by using its   15.____
capacity it can

    A. assist unskilled people with talent to move up on the job ladder
    B. create private enterprises that will renew all areas of the city in need of renewal
    C. eliminate poverty in the ghetto areas by selective purchase of goods and services
    D. have no influence on the economy of the city

16.　According to the above paragraph, one may REASONABLY conclude that　　　　　　16.____
　　　A.　the city has no power to influence the job market
　　　B.　a byproduct of strategic purchasing and employment and training practices can be
　　　　　the rehabilitation of housing and the lowering of food prices
　　　C.　highly skilled professions, which are now in short supply, will no longer be needed
　　　　　after paraprofes-sionals are trained to take over routine jobs
　　　D.　the city's major objective is to bring down food prices

Questions 17-21.

DIRECTIONS:　Questions 17 through 21 are statements based on the following paragraphs.
　　　　　　　For each question, there are two statements.

　　　　　　　Based on the information in the paragraphs, mark your answer A, B, or C, as
　　　　　　　follows.
　　　　　　　　A.　If only statement 1 is correct;
　　　　　　　　B.　If only statement 2 is correct;
　　　　　　　　C.　If both statements are correct.
　　　　　　　Mark your answer D if the excerpts do not contain sufficient evidence for con-
　　　　　　　cluding whether either or both statements are correct.

Upstate, 35% of the AFDC families lived in districts suburban to New York City, 43% in upstate urban districts, and 22% in the rest of upstate. Among white families, 28% resided in suburban districts, 40% in upstate urban districts, and 32% in the rest of upstate. Among non-white families, 43% lived in suburban districts, 47% in upstate urban districts, and 10% in the rest of upstate.

Upstate, 78.7% of the AFDC families resided in SMSA (Standard Metropolitan Statistical Area) counties, including 68.7% of the whites and 90.4% of the non-whites. In Buffalo, 83.3% of the families were non-white; in Rochester, 57.9% were non-whites; in cities of 100,000 to 250,000 (Albany, Syracuse, and Utica), 55.2% were white; and in the rest of the upstate urban counties, 86.5% were white.

The two most frequent underlying reasons for a family requiring AFDC were desertion of the father (31.3% of the cases) and *father not married to mother* (30.3%). Desertions were proportionately highest among Puerto Rican families (38.6%), compared with 29.4% for Blacks and 23.6% for white families. Unmarried mothers comprised 39.4% of the Black cases, compared with 26.6% for Puerto Ricans and 14.8% for white cases.

White families had substantially higher proportions in the separated and divorced cate-gories than non-whites. When the deserted, separated, and divorced categories are com-bined, marital breakdown occurred in 59% of the white AFDC families, compared with 52.3% for Puerto Ricans and 44.4% for Blacks.

Substantial ethnic differences existed in the proportions of incapacitated fathers; overall, the rate was 7.5%, but among white families the rate was 14.8%, compared with 9.4% for Puerto Ricans and only 3.0% for Blacks. Families where the father was deceased comprised 5.9% of the AFDC cases.

In New York City, desertion rates (35.3% of all cases) were substantially higher than upstate (18.9%), particularly among white families, as ethnic differences in New York City diminished considerably. Unmarried mother rates closely paralleled the statewide figures.

Incapacity of the father occurred more frequently among white families upstate (17.5%) than among white families in New York City (10.4%). Deceased fathers were proportionately highest among the New York City Black and Puerto Rican caseload, possibly reflecting fewer remarriage and employment opportunities among these groups in the event of the death of the father.

17. 1. The most frequent underlying reason for a family requiring AFDC was *father not
         married to mother*.   17._____
     2. Three-fourths of New York State's AFDC families lived in New York City.

18. 1. There were more cases of desertion among AFDC cases upstate than there were   18._____
         of incapacity of the father among white AFDC families upstate.
     2. There was a higher percentage of marital breakdowns among white AFDC families
         compared to Puerto Rican or Black families.

19. 1. Desertion of the father accounted for more AFDC cases than all other reasons   19._____
         combined.
     2. The proportion of incapacitated fathers in Puerto Rican families was higher than
         the overall rate of incapacitated fathers.

20. 1. Non-white families had substantially higher proportions in the divorced and sepa- 20._____
         rated categories than white families.
     2. Among AFDC families in New York State, there were more Puerto Ricans than
         Blacks in the combined deserted, separated, and divorced categories.

21. 1. In New York City, there was a higher percentage of unmarried mothers among   21._____
         Puerto Rican AFDC families than among white cases.
     2. Among white families, desertion rates were considerably higher upstate than in
         New York City.

Questions 22-25.

DIRECTIONS: Questions 22 through 25 are to be answered SOLELY on the basis of informa-
             tion given in the following paragraph.

The question of what material is relevant is not as simple as it might seem. Frequently, material which seems irrelevant to the inexperienced has, because of the common tendency to disguise and distort and misplace one's feelings, considerable significance. It may be necessary to let the client *ramble on* for a while in order to clear the decks, as it were, so that he may get down to things that really are on his mind. On the other hand, with an already disturbed person, it may be important for the interviewer to know when to discourage further elaboration of upsetting material. This is especially the case where the worker would be unable to do anything about it. An inexperienced interviewer might, for instance, be intrigued with the bizarre elaboration of material that the psychotic produces, but further elaboration of this might encourage the client in his instability. A too random discussion may indicate that the interviewee is not certain in what areas the interviewer is prepared to help him, and he may be seeking some direction. Or again, satisfying though it may be for the interviewer to have the interviewee tell him intimate details, such revelations sometimes need to be checked or encouraged only in small doses. An interviewee who has *talked too much* often reveals subsequent anxiety. This is illustrated by the fact that frequently after a *confessional* interview, the interviewee surprises the interviewer by being withdrawn, inarticulate, or hostile, or by breaking the next appointment.

22. Sometimes a client may reveal certain personal information to an interviewer and subsequently may feel anxious about this revelation.
    If, during an interview, a client begins to discuss very personal matters, it would be BEST to

    A. tell the client, in no uncertain terms, that you're not interested in personal details
    B. ignore the client at this point
    C. encourage the client to elaborate further on the details
    D. inform the client that the information seems to be very personal

22.____

23. The author indicates that clients with severe psychological disturbances pose an especially difficult problem for the inexperienced interviewer.
    The DIFFICULTY lies in the possibility of the client

    A. becoming physically violent and harming the interviewer
    B. *rambling on* for a while
    C. revealing irrelevant details which may be followed by cancelled appointments
    D. reverting to an unstable state as a result of interview material

23.____

24. An interviewer should be constantly alert to the possibility of obtaining clues from the client as to the problem areas.
    According to the above passage, a client who discusses topics at random may be

    A. unsure of what problems the interviewer can provide help
    B. reluctant to discuss intimate details
    C. trying to impress the interviewer with his knowledge
    D. deciding what relevant material to elaborate on

24.____

25. The evaluation of a client's responses may reveal substantial information that may aid the interviewer in assessing the problem areas that are of concern to the client. Responses that seemed irrelevant at the time of the interview may be of significance because

    A. considerable significance is attached to all irrelevant material
    B. emotional feelings are frequently masked
    C. an initial *rambling on* is often a prelude to what is actually bothering the client
    D. disturbed clients often reveal subsequent anxiety

25.____

KEY (CORRECT ANSWERS)

1.	C		11.	D
2.	D		12.	B
3.	B		13.	C
4.	D		14.	C
5.	C		15.	A
6.	A		16.	B
7.	D		17.	D
8.	A		18.	C
9.	D		19.	B
10.	C		20.	D

21.	A
22.	D
23.	D
24.	A
25.	B

WRITTEN ENGLISH EXPRESSION

EXAMINATION SECTION
TEST 1

DIRECTIONS: The following questions are designed to test your knowledge of grammar, sentence structure, correct usage, and punctuation. In each group, there is one sentence that contains an error. Select the letter of the INCORRECT sentence. *PRINT THE LETTER OF THE CORRECT ANSWER IN THE SPACE AT THE RIGHT.*

1. A. All things considered, he did unusually well.   1.____
    B. The poor boy takes everything too seriously.
    C. Our club sent two delegates, Ruth and I, to Oswego.
    D. I like him better than her.
    E. His eccentricities continually made good newspaper copy.

2. A. If we except Benton, no one in the club foresaw the changes.   2.____
    B. The two-year-old rosebushes are loaded with buds — and beetles!
    C. Though the pitcher had been broken by the cat, Teena was furious.
    D. Virginia got the cake recipe off of her grandmother.
    E. Neither one of the twins was able to get a summer vacation.

3. A. "What do you wish?" he asked, "may I help you?"   3.____
    B. Whose gloves are these?
    C. Has he drink all the orange juice?
    D. It was he who spoke to the manager of the store.
    E. Mary prefers this kind of evening dress.

4. A. Charles himself said it before the assembled peers of the realm.   4.____
    B. The wind stirred the rose petals laying on the floor.
    C. The storm beat hard on the frozen windowpanes.
    D. Worn out by the days of exposure and storm, the sailor clung pitifully to the puny raft.
    E. The day afterward he thought more kindly of the matter.

5. A. Between you and me, I think Henry is wrong.   5.____
    B. This is the more interesting of the two books.
    C. This is the most carefully written letter of all.
    D. During the opening course I read not only four plays but also three historical novels.
    E. This assortment of candies, nuts, and fruits are excellent.

6. A. According to your report card, you are not so clever as he.   6.____
    B. If he had kept his eyes open, he would not have fallen into that trap.
    C. We were certain that the horse had broken it's leg.
    D. The troop of scouts and the leader are headed for the North Woods.
    E. I knew it to be him by the knock at the door.

7.   A.   Being one of the earliest spring flowers, we welcome the crocus.   7.____
         B.   The cold running water became colder as time sped on.
         C.   Those boys need not have stood in line for lunch.
         D.   Can you, my friend, donate ten dollars to the cause?
         E.   Because it's a borrowed umbrella, return it in the morning.

8.   A.   If Walter would have planted earlier in the spring, the rosebushes would have sur-   8.____
             vived.
         B.   The flowers smell overpoweringly sweet.
         C.   There are three e's in dependent.
         D.   May I be excused at the end of the test?
         E.   Carl has three brothers-in-law.

9.   A.   We have bought neither the lumber nor the tools for the job.   9.____
         B.   Jefferson was re-elected despite certain powerful opposition.
         C.   The Misses Jackson were invited to the dance.
         D.   The letter is neither theirs nor yours.
         E.   The retail price for those items are far beyond the wholesale quotations.

10.   A.   To find peace of mind is to gain treasure beyond price.   10.____
         B.   Fred is cheerful, carefree; his brother is morose.
         C.   Whoever fails to understand the strategic importance of the Arctic fails to under-
             stand modern geography.
         D.   They came promptly at 8 o'clock on August 7, 1978, without prior notification.
         E.   Every one tried their best to guess the answer, but no one succeeded.

11.   A.   Is this hers or theirs?   11.____
         B.   Having been recognized, Frank took the floor.
         C.   Alex invited Sue; Paul, Marion; and Dan, Helen.
         D.   If I were able to do the task, you can be sure that I' d do it.
         E.   Stamp collecting, or philately as it is otherwise called is truly an international
             hobby.

12.   A.   He has proved himself to be reliable.   12.____
         B.   The fisherman had arisen before the sun.
         C.   By the time the truck arrived, I had put out the blaze.
         D.   The doctor with his colleagues were engaged in consultation.
         E.   I chose to try out a new method, but in spite of my efforts it failed.

13.   A.   He has drunk too much iced tea.   13.____
         B.   I appreciated him doing that job for me.
         C.   The royal family fled, but they were retaken.
         D.   The secretary and the treasurer were both present on Friday.
         E.   Iago protested his honesty, yet he continued to plot against Desdemona.

14.   A.   The family were all together at Easter.   14.____
         B.   It is altogether too fine a day for us to stay indoors.
         C.   However much you dislike him, you should treat him fairly.
         D.   The judges were already there when the contestants arrived.
         E.   The boy's mother reported that he was alright again after the accident.

15.   A. Ham and eggs is a substantial breakfast.   15.____
       B. By the end of the week the pond had frozen.
       C. I should appreciate any assistance you could offer me.
       D. Being that tomorrow is Sunday, we expect to close early.
       E. If he were to win the medal, I for one would be disturbed.

16.   A. Give the letter to whoever comes for it.   16.____
       B. He feels bad, but his sister is the one who looks sicker.
       C. He had an unbelievable large capacity for hard physical work.
       D. Earth has nothing more beautiful to offer than the autumn colors of this section of the country.
       E. Happily we all have hopes that the future will soon bring forth fruits of a lasting peace.

17.   A. This kind of apples is my favorite.   17.____
       B. Either of the players is capable of performing ably.
       C. Though trying my best to be calm, the choice was not an easy one for me.
       D. The nearest star is not several light years away; it is only 93,000,000 miles away.
       E. There were two things I still wished to do — to see the Lincoln Memorial and to climb up the Washington Monument.

18.   A. It is I who is to blame.   18.____
       B. That dress looks very good on Jane.
       C. People often take my brother to be me.
       D. I could but think she had deceived me.
       E. He himself told us that the story was true.

19.   A. They all went but Mabel and me.   19.____
       B. Has he ever swum across the river?
       C. We have a dozen other suggestions besides these.
       D. The Jones's are going to visit their friends in Chicago.
       E. The ideal that Arthur and his knights were in quest of was a better world order.

20.   A. Would I were able to be there with you!   20.____
       B. Whomever he desires to see should be admitted.
       C. It is not for such as we to follow fashion blindly.
       D. His causing the confusion seemed to affect him not at all.
       E. Please notify all those whom you think should have this information.

21.   A. She was not only competent but also friendly in nature.   21.____
       B. Not only must we visualize the play we are reading; we must actually hear it.
       C. The firm was not only acquiring a bad reputation but also indulging in illegal practices.
       D. The bank was not only uncooperative but also was indifferent to new business offered them.
       E. I know that a conscious effort was made not only to guard the material but also to keep it from being used.

22.   A.   How old shall you be on your next birthday?   22.____
         B.   I am sure that he has been here and did what was expected of him.
         C.   Near to the bank of the river, stood, secluded and still, the house of the hermit.
         D.   Because of its efficacy in treating many ailments, penicillin has become an important addition to the druggist's stock.
         E.   ROBINSON CRUSOE, which is a fairy tale to the child, is a work of social philosophy to the mature thinker.

23.   A.   We had no sooner started than it rained.   23.____
         B.   The fact that the prisoner is a minor will be taken into consideration.
         C.   Many parents think more of their older children than of their younger ones.
         D.   The boy laid a book, a knife and a fishing line on the table.
         E.   John is the tallest of any boy in his class.

24.   A.   Although we have been friends for many years, I must admit that May is most inconsiderate.   24.____
         B.   He is not able to run, not even to walk.
         C.   You will bear this pain as you have so many greater ones.
         D.   The harder the work, the more studious she became.
         E.   Too many "and's" in a sentence produce an immature style.

25.   A.   It would be preferable to have you submit questions after, not before, the lecture.   25.____
         B.   Plan your work; then work your plan.
         C.   At last John met his brother, who had been waiting two hours for him.
         D.   Should one penalize ones self for not trying?
         E.   There are other considerations besides this one.

KEY (CORRECT ANSWERS)

1.	C	11.	E
2.	D	12.	D
3.	A	13.	B
4.	B	14.	E
5.	E	15.	D
6.	C	16.	C
7.	A	17.	C
8.	A	18.	A
9.	E	19.	D
10.	E	20.	E

21.	D
22.	B
23.	E
24.	C
25.	D

TEST 2

DIRECTIONS: The following questions are designed to test your knowledge of grammar, sentence structure, correct usage, and punctuation. In each group there is one sentence that contains an error. Select the letter of the INCORRECT sentence. *PRINT THE LETTER OF THE CORRECT ANSWER IN THE SPACE AT THE RIGHT.*

1. A. "Halt!" cried the sentry, "Who goes there?"
   B. "It is in talk alone," said Robert Louis Stevenson, "that we can learn our period and ourselves."
   C. The world will long remember the "culture" of the Nazis.
   D. When duty says, "You must," the youth replies, "I can."
   E. Who said, "Give me liberty or give me death?"

   1.____

2. A. Why are you so quiet, Martha?
   B. Edward Jones, a banker who lives near us, expects to retire very soon.
   C. I picked up the solid-gold chain.
   D. Any boy, who refuses to tell the truth, will be punished.
   E. Yes, honey tastes sweet.

   2.____

3. A. I knew it to be him by the style of his clothes.
   B. No one saw him doing it.
   C. Her going away is a loss to the community.
   D. Mary objected to her being there.
   E. Illness prevented him graduating in June.

   3.____

4. A. Being tired, I stretched out on a grassy knoll.
   B. While we were rowing on the lake, a sudden squall almost capsized the boat.
   C. Entering the room, a strange mark on the floor attracted my attention.
   D. Mounting the curb, the empty car crossed the sidewalk and came to rest against a building.
   E. Sitting down, they watched him demonstrate his skill.

   4.____

5. A. The coming of peace effected a change in her way of life.
   B. Spain is as weak, if not weaker than, she was in 1900.
   C. In regard to that, I am not certain what my attitude will be.
   D. That unfortunate family faces the problem of adjusting itself to a new way of life.
   E. Fred Eastman states in his essay that one of the joys of reading lies in discovering courage.

   5.____

6. A. Not one in a thousand readers take the matter seriously.
   B. Let it lie there.
   C. You are not so tall as he.
   D. The people began to realize how much she had done.
   E. He was able partially to accomplish his purpose.

   6.____

7. A. In the case of members who are absent, a special letter will be sent.
   B. The visitors were all ready to see it.
   C. I like Burns's poem "To a Mountain Daisy."
   D. John told William that he was sure he had seen it.
   E. Both men are Yale alumni.

   7.____

8. A. The audience took their seats promptly.
    B. Each boy and girl must finish his examination this morning.
    C. Every person turned their eyes toward the door.
    D. Everyone has his own opinion.
    E. The club nominated its officers by secret ballot.

    8.____

9. A. I can do that more easily than you.
    B. This kind of weather is more healthful.
    C. Pick out the really important points.
    D. Because of his aggressive nature, he only plays the hardest games.
    E. He pleaded with me to let him go.

    9.____

10. A. It is I who am mistaken.
    B. Is it John or Susie who stand at the head of the class?
    C. He is one of those who always do their lessons.
    D. He is a man on whom I can depend in time of trouble.
    E. Had he known who it was, he would have come.

    10.____

11. A. Somebody has forgotten his umbrella.
    B. Please let Joe and me use the car.
    C. We thought the author to be he.
    D. Whoever they send will be welcome.
    E. They thought the intruders were we.

    11.____

12. A. If I had known that you were coming, I should have met you.
    B. All the girls but her were at the game.
    C. I expected to have heard the concert before the present time.
    D. Walter would not have said it if he had thought it would make her unhappy.
    E. I have always believed that cork is the best material for insulation.

    12.____

13. A. Their contributions amounted to the no insignificant sum of ten thousand dollars.
    B. None of them was there.
    C. Ten dollars is the amount I agreed to pay.
    D. Fewer than one hundred persons assembled.
    E. Exactly what many others have done and are doing, Frank did.

    13.____

14. A. Neither Jane or her sister has arrived.
    B. Either Richard or his brother is going to drive.
    C. Refilling storage batteries is the work of the youngest employee.
    D. Helen has to lie still for two weeks.
    E. Mother lay down for an hour yesterday.

    14.____

15. A. He is not the man whom you saw entering the house.
    B. He asked why I wouldn't come.
    C. This is the cow whose horns are the longest.
    D. Helen, this is a man I met on the train one day last February.
    E. He greeted every foreign representative which came to the conference.

    15.____

16. A. You, but not I, are invited.
    B. Guy's technique of service and return is masterly.
    C. Please pass me one of the books that are lying on the table.
    D. Mathematics is my most difficult subject.
    E. Unable to agree on a plan of organization, the class has departed in several directions.

16.____

17. A. He spoke to Gertrude and to me of the seriousness of the occasion.
    B. They seem to have decided to invite everyone except you and I.
    C. Your attitude is insulting to me who am your friend.
    D. He wished to know who our representative was.
    E. You may tell whomsoever you wish.

17.____

18. A. My favorite studies were Latin and science.
    B. The committee made its report.
    C. To get your work done promptly is better than leaving it until the last minute.
    D. That's what he would do if he were governor.
    E. He said that his chosen colors were red and blue.

18.____

19. A. Punish whoever disobeys orders.
    B. Come here, Henry; and sit with me.
    C. Has either of them his notebook?
    D. He talked as if he meant it.
    E. You did well; therefore you should be rewarded.

19.____

20. A. Many of us students were called to work.
    B. He shot the albatross with a crossbow.
    C. A house that is set on a hill is conspicuous.
    D. The wooden beams had raised slowly about a foot and then had settled back into place.
    E. Whom do you want to go with you?

20.____

21. A. He does not drive as he should.
    B. I can't hardly wait for the holidays.
    C. I like it less well than last week's.
    D. You were troubled by his coming.
    E. I don't know but that you are correct.

21.____

22. A. He was angry at both of us, her and me.
    B. When one enters the town, they see big crowds.
    C. They laid the tools on the ground every night.
    D. He is the only one of my friends who has written.
    E. He asked for a raise in wages.

22.____

23. A. None came with his excuse.
    B. Walking down the street, a house comes into view.
    C. "Never!" shouted the boy.
    D. Both are masters of their subject.
    E. His advice was to drive slowly.

23.____

24. A. There is both beef and lamb on the market.
     B. Either beans or beets are enough with potatoes.
     C. Where does your mother buy bananas?
     D. Dinners at the new restaurant are excellent.
     E. Each was rewarded according to his deeds.

24._____

25. A. Accordingly, we must prepare the food.
     B. The work, moreover, must be done today.
     C. Nevertheless, we must first have dinner.
     D. I always chose the most liveliest of the ponies.
     E. At six o'clock tomorrow the job will have been completed.

25._____

_____

KEY (CORRECT ANSWERS)

1.	E		11.	C
2.	D		12.	C
3.	E		13.	A
4.	C		14.	A
5.	B		15.	E
6.	A		16.	E
7.	C		17.	B
8.	C		18.	C
9.	D		19.	B
10.	B		20.	D

21.	B
22.	B
23.	B
24.	A
25.	D

_____

TEST 3

DIRECTIONS: In each group of five sentences below, one or more sentences contain an error in usage. Choose the lettered answer which indicates ALL the sentences containing errors in usage. *PRINT THE LETTER OF THE CORRECT ANSWER IN THE SPACE AT THE RIGHT.*

1.   I.   Shortly after the terms of the contract for the new road transpired, an aroused con-   1.____
            stituency showed its disapproval by voting the senator out of office.
   II. Neither father nor sons work for a living but spend their days in drinking and
           gambling at the pub.
   III. Like his Italian predecessor, Boccaccio, whose DECAMERON was used as a
           model, a company of people of various occupations and stations in life, brought
           together for a pilgrimage, are called upon to relate stories to help relieve the
           tedium of their journey.
   IV. Sarah hurried into the kitchen and after a half hour emerged with a nauseous
           brew which she called coffee.
   V. It was to the major that the people applied for redress and by his armed guards
           that they were driven away.

   A. I   B. III   C. I, II, III
   D. IV, III   E. II, III

2.   I.   As we approached the castle, which was illuminated suddenly by the full moon   2.____
            breaking through the clouds, we described a rider coming to meet us.
   II. The reason for his loss of interest in boxing, as far as I can see, was due to the
           pressure of his work and the distance of the local "Y" from his home.
   III. Accompanied by a handsome member of the British legation, Elsie was about to
           enter the luxuriously furnished salon to meet the countess.
   IV. In spite of all of John's gifts and attentions, little Rosalie, upon being asked to
           make a choice, said she liked me better than him.
   V. The scar of the clearing for the power line extended for a hundred miles over the
           mountains, and the great poles with fifty feet between each carried cables from
           Niagara to Albany.

   A. II, III   B. I, IV, III   C. I, II, IV, III
   D. II, V   E. III, V

3.   I.   The high wind had blown the roofs off several houses; the water supply had been   3.____
            contaminated by the floods; transportation to the business center had ground to a
           halt; but the mayor said there was no reason for alarm!
   II. Because there is a need to soften tragic or painful news, we resort to such
           euphuisms for the simple "to die" as "to pass away," "to go to a better world," or
           "to join the great majority."
   III. Hardly had the salient on the western shore of the river been obliterated than the
           one on the eastern bank crossed on a pontoon bridge and in boats of all sorts.
   IV. The distinction between the man who gives in a spirit of charity and him who
           gives for social recognition is often to be seen in the nature of the gift.
   V. After a few months in office, the new superintendent effected many changes, not
           all of them for the good, in the administration of the plant.

   A. II, III   B. II, III, IV   C. III, IV
   D. I, II, V   E. I, II, III

4.   I.   The defendants published an advertisement and notice giving information, directly   4.____
and indirectly, stating where, how, and when, and by what means and what pur-
ports to be the said book can be purchased.

      II.   In common with most Eskimos of her time, she had long spells of silence; and
nature, while endowing her with immense sagacity, had thrust on her a compel-
ling reticence.

   III.   The entire report was read in less than half an hour to the full committee, giving
no time for comment or question, and offered for vote.

   IV.   Students going through this course almost always find themselves becoming
critical of their own writing.

    V.   In his report of 1968, Mr. Jones states that his chief problem is the rapid turnover
of personnel which has prevailed to the moment of writing.

A. I, IV   B. II, III   C. III, IV, V
D. I, IV, V   E. I, III

5.   I.   The material was destroyed after it had served our purposes, and after portions of   5.____
it had been excluded and portions included in our report.

      II.   We checked our results very carefully, too carefully perhaps, for we spent several
hours on our task.

   III.   We should keep constantly in mind the fact that writing has no purpose save to
meet the needs of the reader.

   IV.   Not even discussed in October, when Lathrop flew in from the Coast, the problem of expense was settled at the June meeting.

    V.   Whether our facts were right or not, it was not necessary for you to rebuke him in
such a discourteous manner.

A. I *only*   B. I, IV   C. II, III
D. V *only*   E. I, V

6.   I.   At first the novel was interesting and liked by members of the class; but later the   6.____
long reading assignments dampened the pupils' enthusiasm.

      II.   Donnie had no love or confidence in his mother, who, when abandoned by her
husband, put the boy in an orphanage and seldom went to visit him.

   III.   Built during the Civil War, the house has a delicate air, supported as it is by iron
columns and rimmed by an iron railing.

   IV.   Recently a newspaper editor from the South returned from an eight-week trip
through the Caribbean and made a number of recommendations on what we
should do to counter the lack of accurate information about the United States.

    V.   The need is to be candid about our problems, to be informed on what we are
doing about them, and to resolve them as expeditiously as possible.

A. I, II   B. II, III   C. III, IV
D. I, V   E. I, III

7.   I.   "Man is flying too fast for a world that is round," he said. "Soon he will catch up with   7.____
himself in a great rear-end collision."

      II.   After the raid on the club, each of the men suspected of accepting racetrack
bets, along with the owner of the club, were held for questioning at police head-
quarters.

   III.   It seems to me that at the opening performance of the play the audience were of
different opinions about its merit and about its chances for a long run.

IV. Oak from the forests of Vermont and steel from the mills of Pittsburgh are the material of this magnificent modern structure.

V. The machine is subjected to severe strains which it must withstand and at the same time work easily and rapidly.

A. I, II   B. II, III   C. IV, V
D. I, V   E. II, V

8.   I. We don't have to worry about cutting down on expenses; money is no object in this venture.   8.____

II. And now, my dear, let you and I tell our guests of the plans we have for the future.

III. For all his errors of the past, no one can or has said that he did not turn out on this occasion a perfectpiece of work.

IV. Hercule Poirot, when looking for a suspect in the murder case never thought of its being me.

V. During the interpellation the minister refused to answer any questions concerning his predecessor's conduct of the war.

A. I, III   B. I, IV, V   C. II, III, IV
D. III, IV   E. II, III

9.   I. John Steinbeck received the Nobel Prize only a few years ago for his work of the thirties, work, which now, according to some critics, has lost its timeliness and which never had timelessness.   9.____

II. Respect is shown the flag by no matter when it is displayed, whether it be in the window of a private home or on the pole of a public building.

III. When dinner was over, we strolled through the garden and exclaimed at the beauty of the red gladioluses, the pride of the Jenkinses' gardener.

IV. Mrs. Cosgrove's gift of $100,000 to the hospitals is only the latest of the many acts of generosity by which she has before now benefited her fellow men.

V. Am I repeating your question exactly when I say, "How many of you are willing to join me in my attempt to rid America of the traitors who are threatening its freedom"?

A. I, II, III, IV   B. II, IV   C. II, III, IV
D. I, IV, V   E. I, II, IV

10.   I. Slashing the original 73 projects to 20 with little loss of subject matter in the consolidated schedule, a stalemate was avoided and the work of the Council speeded up.   10.____

II. I was particularly struck by the unselfishness of the American school children, many of whom willingly donating their allowances, because they felt that they should help the refugees.

III. As a result of Henry VIII's defiance of the Church of Rome, the ecclesiastical principle of government was substituted by the national.

IV. I wish you had invited me to the concert, for I should have liked particularly to hear Piatigorsky.

V. John will be in the best possible position for getting the most out of his vacation and of making business contacts in new markets.

A. I, II, III, IV   B. I, II, III, V
C. I, II, III   D. III, IV, V
E. I, II, III, IV, V

11.   I.   They took him to be me despite ever so many differences in our appearance and
          despite his addiction to loquacity.

      II. They may have more money, they may have more possessions, but they are not
          any happier than us, as we and they all know.

      III. Either Betty or Bob must have thought the teacher's remarks were addressed to
          him.

      IV. There was present at today's conference — and at next week's conference the
          same group is expected — representatives of many foreign countries, including
          Italy, France, England, and Germany.

      V.   The most important criteria in judging the performance of a pianist is not virtuos-
          ity but maturity of interpretation.

      A. I, IV   B. II, III, V   C. II, IV, V
      D. I, III   E. I, IV, V

11.____

12.   I.   Thoroughly exhausted after we had swum for six hours, we lay breathless on the
          sand and oblivious of anything but our utter fatigue.

      II. The jury seems in violent disagreement about the culpability of the defendant;
          such shouting as we hear from the jury room is most unusual among these halls.

      III. The difference between the class' average grades for the first week and those for
          the eighth week, on alternate forms of the same test, were quite insignificant,
          indicating, we thought, that instruction had been ineffective.

      IV. Each tree and each bush give forth a flaming hue such as we have not seen for
          many seasons in these climes.

      V.   We met a man whom we thought we had met many years since, when we lived
          in South Africa.

      A. III, IV, V   B. I, II, V   C. III, IV
      D. I, II   E. I, III, IV

12.____

13.   I.   That old friend, whom I met again last night after a lapse of many a year, stands
          head and shoulders above any person I have ever known.

      II. This is one of the finest pictures which have ever been put on canvas, bringing
          out rare qualities of tone-color, mature interpretation, and virtuosity in execution.

      III. Which of them would you prefer to have working for you, considering the inordi-
          nate physical and mental demands of the work, him or his brother?

      IV. Throughout Saturday and Sunday, the townsfolk took scarcely any notice of the
          absence of Jed Gorman, believing him to be off on a drunken spree; but on Mon-
          day a body was discovered in the river obviously that of the missing handyman.

      V.   Things being so pleasant as they were, we could not fathom the reason for John
          leaving so soon after he had started what we considered an excellent job with
          unlimited opportunities.

      A. I, V   B. II, III, V   C. II, III
      D. II, IV, V   E. I, IV, V

13.____

14.   I.   He is unfailingly polite not only to his superiors and his colleagues but even to
          those who are in subordinate positions, and, in general, to whoever else he thinks
          is deserving of kindly consideration.

      II. Without more ado, he took the books off the radiator, where they had lain quite
          neglected for several days and where their bindings were beginning to grow
          loose.

14.____

III. We can still include a discussion of the lunchroom situation among the topics, for the agenda have not yet been printed and will not be for another hour or two.

IV. We knew who would be at the party and who would take us home, but we didn't know who to expect to meet us at the station upon our arrival.

V. Despite his protestations, we know that the true reason why he was suffering such obvious anguish and failing to do his work was because of marital trouble.

A. I, III, IV   B. II, III, V   C. I, IV, V
D. I, II   E. IV, V

15. I. A difficult stretch of bad road in addition to a long detour which caused a series of minor motor mishaps, have much delayed our visitor's arrival and have created an awkward situation for us all.   15._____

II. To make the campaign effective, there is posted in every building, in full view of all entrants, one notice of the location of the shelter, and a second notice intended to boost morale and win cooperation.

III. One day while leading sheep in the desert and musing upon his people's future, the angel of the Lord appeared to Moses.

IV. Though he plead with the tongue of an angel, he will not ever alter her cold eyes nor trouble her calm fount of speech.

V. Despite continuous and well-advised and well-directed efforts by each of us, neither he nor I am able to improve the situation.

A. I, V   B. III, IV, V   C. I, II, III
D. II, III, IV   E. I, III

16. I. Though business has been brisk of late, this kind of appliances have not sold well at all, despite our continuous and concentrated efforts.   16._____

II. The return trip was a desperate one, with time of the essence; and partly blinded by the unexpected snowstorm, the trip was doubly hazardous.

III. I started on my journey by foot through forest and mountain, after a last warning to be careful about snake bites by my parents — a warning I knew I must heed on that dangerous terrain.

IV. That he was losing to a better man, a man who had worked diligently and a man of impeccable virtue, was a consideration of but small import to him.

V. The precarious state of affairs was aggravated by a new hazard, notwithstanding all our cautions to avoid any change in the situation.

A. I, III, V   B. II, IV   C. IV, V
D. I, II, III   E. II, III

17. I. Who's responsible for the feeding of his cat and its young, I'd like to know, we or they? If we, let's feed them.   17._____

II. The books that had lain on the desk for many weeks were laid in the bookcase, where they lay until picked up by the messenger from the second-handbook shop.

III. You say I merit the award for competence in my duties; but he deserves an award as well as I, for he is as good, without doubt, or even better than I.

IV. The Joneses' car was more luxurious than, but not necessarily as expensive as, the Browns'.

V. Slowly they tiptoed into the living room hoping not to be heard, but we were fully aware of it being they.

A. II, IV   B. I, III, IV   C. I, V
D. I, II, V   E. III, V

18.   I.   I shall lay the rug in the sun, where it has laid many times before; and I shall lie in   18._____
            the sun, too, as always I have lain at leisure while the rug has been drying.
        II. Though he knew a great deal about printing machinery, he thought, mistakenly,
            that the new machine could be made to cast type as well as setting it up.
        III. Knowledge in several major fields with sympathy for varied points of view make
            him an excellent choice for student adviser.
        IV. You will find the girls' equipment in the teachers' lounge where the boy's father
            left it at Professor Wills's suggestion.
        V.   I know that the Burnses have worked for the mill for generations, and that the
            Smiths have but recently removed from town, but does either of the Norton boys
            work here?

        A. I, II, III   B. II, III, IV   C. I, IV, V
        D. III, V   E. I, II, IV

19.   I.   I can put two and two together as quick as most men; but understanding how he, a   19._____
            slow-witted dolt, could achieve so notable a victory over his opponent is one of the
            things that puzzle and, forevermore, will puzzle me.
        II. Besides my two brothers, my sister, and I, there are a cousin and my father's
            nephew living at home with us.
        III. He has lived in the Reno for many years; previously he lived in Chicago for a
            short space, after he had come from Los Angeles.
        IV. Researchers have been baffled for a long time by this statistic, for it contradicts
            many of their most highly cherished hypotheses.
        V.   So intense was the heat near the furnace that all the men at work could not carry
            on; consequently, production came to a halt.

        A. I, II, IV   B. III, V   C. I, III, IV
        D. I, II, V   E. II, V

20.   I.   If we can escape from our desks for a brief interval, let's you, Henry, and I put in an   20._____
            appearance at the party.
        II. If you persevere in your ambitions, you are likely to achieve at least a modicum
            of success; if you malinger, you are liable to court failure.
        III. You may find conditions here congenial, but since I neither like the work nor the
            salary, it is to no avail for you to attempt to persuade me to stay.
        IV. He has never deigned to take a drink with us, his office colleagues, though we
            know him now for over fifteen years; and he takes an occasional drink, we know,
            at home and at his golf club.
        V.   Though the results of your investigation are at variance with the hypothesis we
            advanced, I believe you have interpreted these data in the only ways that have
            scientific validity.

        A. I, II, IV   B. I, II   C. IV, V
        D. II, III, V   E. I, III, IV

21.   I.   He can't hardly hear anything unless the room is completely quiet.   21.____
       II. His attitude seemed perfectly alright to me.
       III. One can't be too careful, can one?
       IV. He is one of those people who believe in the perfectability of man.
       V.   His uneasiness is reflected in his unwillingness to compromise on even the
            smallest point.

       A. II, III, V   B. I, III   C. I, IV, V
       D. I, II, IV   E. III, IV

22.   I.   "Have you found what you were looking for?" he asked.   22.____
       II. "I have never," she insisted, "Seen such careless disregard for the rights of
            oters."
       III. "I found this ticket on the step," he said. "Did you lose it?"
       IV. "In one way I'd like to enter the contest," said Anne; "in another way I'm not too
            eager."
       V.   Did he say, "I'm coming?"

       A. I, III, IV   B. II, V   C. III, V
       D. II, IV   E. I, II, IV

23.   I.   Were I the owner of the dog, I'd keep him muzzled.   23.____
       II. In the tennis match Don was paired with Bill; Ed, with Al.
       III. He was given an excellent trade-in allowance on his old car.
       IV. Why doesn't this window raise?
       V.   The prow of the vessel had almost completely sank by the time the rescuers
            arrived on the scene.

       A. I, II, V   B. I, IV, V   C. I, II, III
       D. II, V   E. IV, V

24.   I.   Turning the pages rapidly, his glance fell upon a peculiarly worded advertisement.   24.____
       II. Turning the pages rapidly, his eyes noticed a peculiarly worded advertisement.
       III. Turning the pages rapidly, he noticed a peculiarly worded advertisement.
       IV. Turning the pages rapidly made him more attentive to the unusual.
       V.   Turning the pages rapidly does not guarantee rapid comprehension.

       A. III, IV, V   B. I, II, IV   C. III, V
       D. I, II   E. I, II, III

25.   I.   They told us how they had suffered.   25.____
       II. It is interesting (a) to the student, (b) to the parent, and (c) to the teacher.
       III. There were blue, green and red banners.
       IV. "Will you help", he asked?
       V.   In addition to reproducibility, an attitude scale must meet various other require-
            ments characteristic of scale analysis procedures.

       A. I, II   B. II, III   C. I only
       D. IV only   E. IV, V

KEY (CORRECT ANSWERS)

1.	C	11.	C
2.	D	12.	C
3.	A	13.	D
4.	E	14.	E
5.	A	15.	C
6.	A	16.	D
7.	E	17.	C
8.	A	18.	A
9.	B	19.	E
10.	B	20.	A

21.	D
22.	B
23.	E
24.	D
25.	D

WRITTEN ENGLISH EXPRESSION
EXAMINATION SECTION
TEST 1

DIRECTIONS: The following questions are designed to test your knowledge of grammar, sentence structure, correct usage, and punctuation. In each group there is one sentence that contains no errors. Select the letter of the CORRECT sentence. *PRINT THE LETTER OF THE CORRECT ANSWER IN THE SPACE AT THE RIGHT.*

1.   A.   A low ceiling is when the atmospheric conditions make flying inadvisable.   1.____
     B.   They couldn't tell who the card was from.
     C.   No one but you and I are to help him.
     D.   What kind of a teacher would you like to be?
     E.   To him fall the duties of foster parent.

2.   A.   They couldn't tell whom the cable was from.   2.____
     B.   We like these better than those kind.
     C.   It is a test of you more than I.
     D.   The person in charge being him, there can be no change in policy.
     E.   Chicago is larger than any city in Illinois.

3.   A.   Do as we do for the celebration.   3.____
     B.   Do either of you care to join us?
     C.   A child's food requirements differ from the adult.
     D.   A large family including two uncles and four grandparents live at the hotel.
     E.   Due to bad weather, the game was postponed.

4.   A.   If they would have done that they might have succeeded.   4.____
     B.   Neither the hot days or the humid nights annoy our Southern visitor.
     C.   Some people do not gain favor because they are kind of tactless.
     D.   No sooner had the turning point come than a new issue arose.
     E.   I wish that I was in Florida now.

5.   A.   We haven't hardly enough tine.   5.____
     B.   Immigration is when people come into a foreign country to live.
     C.   After each side gave their version, the affair was over with.
     D.   Every one of the cars were tagged by the police.
     E.   He either will fail in his attempt or will seek other employment.

6.   A.   They can't seem to see it when I explain the theory.   6.____
     B.   It is difficult to find the genuine signature between all those submitted.
     C.   She can't understand why they don't remember who to give the letter to
     D.   Every man and woman in America is interested in his tax bill.
     E.   Honor as well as profit are to be gained by these studies.

7.
A. He arrived safe.
B. I do not have any faith in John running for office.
C. The musicians began to play tunefully and keeping the proper tempo indicated for the selection.
D. Mary's maid of honor bought the kind of an outfit suitable for an afternoon wedding.
E. If you would have studied the problem carefully you would have found the solution more quickly.

7.____

8.
A. The new plant is to be electric lighted.
B. The reason the speaker was offended was that the audience was inattentive.
C. There appears to be conditions that govern his behavior.
D. Either of the men are influential enough to control the situation.
E. The gallery with all its pictures were destroyed.

8.____

9.
A. If you would have listened more carefully, you would have heard your name called.
B. Did you inquire if your brother were returning soon?
C. We are likely to have rain before nightfall.
D. Let's you and I plan next summer's vacation together.
E. The man whom I thought was my friend deceived me.

9.____

10.
A. There's a man and his wife waiting for the doctor since early this morning.
B. The owner of the market with his assistants is applying the most modern principles of merchandise display.
C. Every one of the players on both of the competing teams were awarded a gold watch.
D. The records of the trial indicated that, even before attaining manhood, the murderer's parents were both dead.
E. We had no sooner entered the room when the bell rang.

10.____

11.
A. Why don't you start the play like I told you?
B. I didn't find the construction of the second house much different from that of the first one I saw.
C. "When", inquired the child, "Will we begin celebrating my birthday?"
D. There isn't nothing left to do but not to see him anymore.
E. There goes the last piece of cake and the last spoonful of ice cream.

11.____

12.
A. The child could find neither the shoe or the stocking.
B. The musicians began to play tunefully and keeping the proper tempo indicated for the selection.
C. The amount of curious people who turned out for Opening Night was beyond calculation.
D. I fully expected that the children would be at their desks and to find them ready to begin work,
E. "Indeed," mused the poll-taker, "the winning candidate is much happier than I."

12.____

13. A. Just as you said, I find myself gaining weight.
    B. A teacher should leave the capable pupils engage in creative activities.
    C. The teacher spoke continually during the entire lesson, which, of course, was poor procedure.
    D. We saw him steal into the room, pick up the letter, and tear it's contents to shreds.
    E. It is so dark that I can't hardly see.

13.____

14. A. The new schedule of working hours and rates was satis factory to both employees and employer.
    B. Many common people feel keenly about the injustices of Power Politics.
    C. Mr. and Mrs. Burns felt that their grandchild was awfully cute when he waved good-bye.
    D. The tallest of the twins was also the most intelligent,
    E. Please come here and try and help me finish this piece of work.

14.____

15. A. My younger brother insists that he is as tall as me.
    B. Suffering from a severe headache all day, one dose of the prescribed medicine relieved me,
    C. "Please let my brothers and I help you with your packages," said Frank to Mrs. Powers.
    D. Every one of the rooms we visited had displays of pupils' work in them.
    E. Do you intend bringing most of the refreshments yourself?

15.____

16. A. The telephone linesmen, working steadily at their task during the severe storm, the telephones soon began to ring again.
    B. Meat, as well as fruits and vegetables, is considered essential to a proper diet.
    C. He looked like a real good boxer that night in the ring.
    D. The man has worked steadily for fifteen years before he decided to open his own business.
    E. The winters were hard and dreary, nothing could live without shelter.

16.____

17. A. No one can foretell when I will have another opportunity like that one again.
    B. The last group of paintings shown appear really to have captured the most modern techniques,
    C. We searched high and low, both in the attic and cellar, but were unsuccessful in locating mementos.
    D. None of the guests was able to give the rules of the game accurately.
    E. When you go to the library tomorrow, please bring this book to the librarian in the reference room.

17.____

18. A. After the debate, every one of the speakers realized that, given another chance, he could have done better.
    B. The reason given by the physician for the patient's trouble was because of his poor eating habits.
    C. The fog was so thick that the driver couldn't hardly see more than ten feet ahead.
    D. I suggest that you present the medal to who you think best.
    E. I don't approve of him going along.

18.____

19. A. A decision made by a man without much deliberation is sometimes no different than a slow one.
    B. By the time Mr. Brown's son will graduate Dental School, he will be twenty-six years of age.
    C. Who did you predict would win the election?
    D. The auctioneer had less stamps to sell this year than last year.
    E. Being that he is occupied, I shall not disturb him.

20. A. Having pranced into the arena with little grace and unsteady hoof for the jumps ahead, the driver reined his horse.
    B. Once the dog wagged it's tail, you knew it was a friendly animal.
    C. Like a great many artists, his life was a tragedy.
    D. When asked to choose corn, cabbage, or potatoes, the diner selected the latter.
    E. The record of the winning team was among the most noteworthy of the season.

21. A. The maid wasn't so small that she couldn't reach the top window for cleaning.
    B. Many people feel that powdered coffee produces a really good flavor.
    C. Would you mind me trying that coat on for size?
    D. This chair looks much different than the chair we selected in the store.
    E. I wish that he would have talked to me about the lesson before he presented it.

22. A. After trying unsuccessfully to land a job in the city, Will located in the country on a farm.
    B. On the last attempt, the pole-vaulter came nearly to getting hurt.
    C. The observance of Armistice Day throughout the world offers an opportunity to reflect on the horrors of war.
    D. Outside of the mistakes in spelling, the child's letter was a very good one.
    E. The annual income of New York is far greater than Florida.

23. A. Scissors is always dangerous for a child to handle.
    B. I assure you that I will not yield to pressure to sell my interest.
    C. Ask him if he has recall of the incident which took place at our first meeting.
    D. The manager felt like as not to order his usher-captain to surrender his uniform.
    E. Everyone on the boat said their prayers when the storm grew worse.

24. A. The mother of the bride climaxed the occasion by exclaiming, "I want my children should be happy forever."
    B. We read in the papers where the prospects for peace are improving.
    C. "Can I share the cab with you?" was frequently heard during the period of gas rationing.
    D. The man was enamored with his friend"s sister.
    E. Had the police suspected the ruse, they would have taken proper precautions.

25. A. The teacher admonished the other students neither to speak to John, nor should they annoy him.
    B. Fortunately we had been told that there was but one service station in that area.
    C. An usher seldom rises above a theatre manager.
    D. The epic, "Gone With the Wind," is supposed to have taken place during the Civil War Era.
    E. Now that she has been graduated she should be encouraged to make her own choice as to the career she is to follow.

KEY (CORRECT ANSWERS)

1.	E		11.	B
2.	A		12.	E
3.	A		13.	A
4.	D		14.	A
5.	E		15.	E
6.	D		16.	B
7.	A		17.	D
8.	B		18.	A
9.	C		19.	C
10.	B		20.	E

21.	B
22.	C
23.	B
24.	E
25.	B

———

TEST 2

The following questions are designed to test your knowledge of grammar, sentence structure, correct usage, and punctuation. In each group, there is one sentence that contains no errors. Select the letter of the CORRECT sentence. *PRINT THE LETTER OF THE CORRECT ANSWER IN THE SPACE AT THE RIGHT.*

1.   A.   Shall you be at home, let us say, on Sunday at two o'clock?   1.____
      B.   We see Mr. Lewis take his car out of the garage daily, newly polished always.
      C.   We have no place to keep our rubbers, only in the hall closet.
      D.   Isn't it true what you told me about the best way to prepare for an examination?
      E.   Mathematics is among my favorite subjects.

2.   A.   The host thought the guests were of the hungry kinds so he prepared much food.   2.____
      B.   The museum is often visited by students who are fond of early inventions, and especially patent attorneys.
      C.   I rose to nominate the man who most of us felt was the most diligent worker in the group.
      D.   The child was sent to the store to purchase a bottle of milk, and brought home fresh rolls, too.
      E.   Hidden away in the closet, I found the long-lost purse.

3.   A.   The garden tool was sent to be sharpened, and a new handle to be put on.   3.____
      B.   At the end of her vacation, Joan came home with little money, but which systematic thrift soon overcame.
      C.   We people have opportunities to show the rest of the world how real democracy functions.
      D.   The guide paddled along, then fell in a reverie which he related the history of the region.
      E.   No sooner had the curtain dropped when the audience shouted its approval in chorus.

4.   A.   The data you need is to be made available shortly.   4.____
      B.   The first few strokes of the brush were enough to convince me that Tom could paint much better than me.
      C.   We inquired if we could see the owner of the store, after we waited for one hour.
      D.   The highly-strung parent was aggravated by the slightest noise that the baby made.
      E.   We should have investigated the cause of the noise by bringing the car to a halt.

5.   A.   The police, investigating the crime, were successful in discovering only one possibly valuable clue.   5.____
      B.   Due to an unexpected change in plans, the violin soloist did not perform.
      C.   Besides being awarded a Bachelor's degree at college, the scientist has since received many honorary degrees.
      D.   The data offered in advance of the recent Presidential election seems to have possessed elements of inaccuracy.
      E.   I don't believe your the only one who has been asked to come here.

6. A. I don't quite see that I will be able to completely finish the job in time.   6.____
    B. By my statement, I infer that you are guilty of the offense as charged.
    C. Wasn't it strange that they wouldn't let no one see the body?
    D. I hope that this is the kind of rolls you requested me to buy.
    E. The storekeeper distributed cigars as bonuses between his many customers.

7. A. He said he preferred the climate of Florida to California.   7.____
    B. Because of the excessive heat, a great amount of fruit juice was drunk by the
       guests.
    C. This week's dramatic presentation was neither as lively nor as entertaining as
       last week.
    D. The fashion expert believed that no one could develop new creations more suc-
       cessfully than him.
    E. A collection of Dicken's works is a "must" for every library.

8. A. There was such a large amount of books on the floor that I couldn't find a place for 8.____
       my rocking chair.
    B. Walking up the rickety stairs, the bottle slipped from his hands and smashed.
    C. The reason they granted his request was because he had a good record.
    D. Little Tommy was proud that the teacher always asked him to bring messages to
       the office.
    E. That kind of orange is grown only in Florida.

9. A. The new mayor is a resident of this city for thirty years.   9.____
    B. Do you mean to imply that had he not missed that shot he would have won?
    C. Next term I shall be studying French and history.
    D. I read in last night's paper where the sales tax is going to be abolished.
    E. In order to prevent breakage, she placed a sheet of paper between each of the
       plates when she packed them.

10. A. To have children vie against one another is psychologically unsound.   10.____
    B. Would anyone else care to discuss his baby?
    C. He was interested and aware of the problem.
    D. I sure would like to discover if he is motivating the lesson properly.
    E. The cloth was first lain on a flat surface; then it was pressed with a hot iron.

11. A. She graduated Barnard College twenty-five years ago.   11.____
    B. He studied the violin since he was seven.
    C. She is not so diligent a researcher as her classmate.
    D. He discovered that the new data corresponds with the facts disclosed by Werner.
    E. How could he enjoy the television program; the dog was barking and the baby
       was crying.

12. A. You have three alternatives: law, dentistry, or teaching.   12.____
    B. If I would have worked harder, I would have accomplished my purpose.
    C. He affected a rapid change of pace and his opponents were outdistanced.
    D. He looked prosperous, although he had been unemployed for a year.
    E. The engine not only furnishes power but light and heat as well.

13. A. The children shared one anothers toys and seemed quite happy.   13.___
     B. They lay in the sun for many hours, getting tanned.
     C. The reproduction arrived, and had been hung in the living room.
     D. First begin by calling the roll.
     E. Tell me where you hid it; no one shall ever find it.

14. A. Deliver these things to whomever arrives first.   14.___
     B. Everybody but she and me is going to the conference.
     C. If the number of patrons is small, we can serve them.
     D. When each of the contestants find their book, the debate may begin.
     E. Some people, farmers in particular, lament the substitution of butter by marga-
        rine.

15. A. After his illness, he stood in the country three weeks.   15.___
     B. If you wish to effect a change, submit your suggestions.
     C. It is silly to leave children play with knives.
     D. Play a trick on her by spilling water down her neck.
     E. There was such a crowd of people at the crossing we couldn't hardly get on the
        bus.

16. A. This is a time when all of us must show our faith and devotion to our country.   16.___
     B. Either you or I are certain to be elected president of the new club.
     C. The interpellation of the Minister of Finance forced him to explain his policies.
     D. After hoisting the anchor and removing the binnacle, the ship was ready to set
        sail.
     E. Please bring me a drink of cold water from the refrigerator.

17. A. Mistakes in English, when due to carelessness or haste, can easily be rectified.   17.___
     B. Mr. Jones is one of those persons who will try to keep a promise and usually
        does.
     C. Being very disturbed by what he had heard, Fred decided to postpone his deci-
        sion.
     D. There is a telephone at the other end of the corridor which is constantly in use.
     E. In his teaching, he always kept the childrens' interests and needs in mind.

18. A. The lazy pupil, of course, will tend to write the minimum amount of words accept-   18.___
        able.
     B. His success as a political leader consisted mainly of his ability to utter platitudes
        in a firm and convincing manner.
     C. To be cognizant of current affairs, a person must not only read newspapers and
        magazines but also recent books by recognized authorities.
     D. Although we intended to have gone fishing, the sudden outbreak of a storm
        caused us to change our plans.
     E. It is the colleges that must take the responsibility for encouraging greater flexibil-
        ity in the high-school curriculum.

19. A. "I am sorry," he said, "but John's answer was 'No'."   19.____
     B. A spirited argument followed between those who favored and opposed Marie's expulsion from the club.
     C. Whether a forward child should be humored or punished often depends upon the circumstances.
     D. Excessive alcoholism is certainly not conducive with efficient performance of one's work.
     E. Stroking his beard thoughtfully, an idea suddenly came to him.

20. A. "Take care, my children," he said sadly, "lest you not be deceived."   20.____
     B. Those continuous telephone calls are preventing Betty from completing her homework.
     C. They dug deep into the earth at the spot indicated on the map, but they found nothing.
     D. We petted and cozened the little girl until she finally stopped weeping.
     E. There was, in the mail, an inquiry for a house by a young couple with two or three bedrooms.

21. A. Please fill in the required information on the application form and return same by April 15.   21.____
     B. Tom was sitting there idly, watching the clouds scud across the sky.
     C. We started for home so that our parents would not suspect that anything out of the ordinary took place.
     D. The sudden abatement from the storm enabled the ladies to resume their journey.
     E. Each of the twelve members were agreed that the accused man was innocent.

22. A. The number of gifted students not continuing their education beyond secondary school present a nationwide problem.   22.____
     B. A man's animadversions against those he considers his enemies are usually reflections of his own inadequacies.
     C. The alembic of his fevered imagination produced some of the greatest romantic poetry of his era.
     D. The first case of smallpox dates back more than 3000 years and has gone unchecked until recently.
     E. He promised to go irregardless of the rain or snow.

23. A. The child picked up several of the coracles, which he had seen glittering in the sand, and brought them to his mother.   23.____
     B. He muttered in dejected tones – and no one contradicted him – "We have failed."
     C. A girl whom I believed to be she waved cheerily to me from a passing automobile.
     D. We discovered that she was a former resident of our own neighborhood who eloped some years ago with a milkman.
     E. It looks now like he will not be promoted after all.

24.   A. Mary is the kind of a person on whom you can depend in any emergency.   24.____
         B. I am sure that either applicant can fill the job you offer competently and effi-
             ciently.
         C. Although we searched the entire room, the scissors was not to be found.
         D. Being that you are here, we can proceed with the discussion.
         E. In spite of our warning whistle, the huge ship continued to sail athwart our
             course.

25.   A. The salaries earned by college graduates vary as much if not more than those   25.____
             earned by high school graduates.
         B. The apothegms that he felt to be so witty were all too often either trite or platitu-
             dinous.
         C. She read the letter carefully, took out one of the pages, and tore it into small
             pieces.
         D. A young man, who hopes to succeed, must be diligent in his work and alert to his
             opportunities.
         E. No one should plan a long journey for pleasure in these days.

———

KEY (CORRECT ANSWERS)

1.	A		11.	C
2.	C		12.	D
3.	C		13.	E
4.	E		14.	C
5.	A		15.	B
6.	D		16.	C
7.	B		17.	A
8.	E		18.	E
9.	B		19.	C
10.	B		20.	C

21.	B
22.	C
23.	B
24.	E
25.	B

English Expression
CHOICE OF EXPRESSION
COMMENTARY

One special form of the English Expression multiple-choice question in current use requires the candidate to select from among five (5) versions of a particular part of a sentence (or of an entire sentence), the one version that expresses the idea of the sentence most clearly, effectively, and accurately. Thus, the candidate is required not only to recognize errors, but also to choose the best way of phrasing a particular part of the sentence.

This is a test of choice of expression, which assays the candidate's ability to express himself correctly and effectively, including his sensitivity to the subleties and nuances of the language.

SAMPLE QUESTIONS

DIRECTIONS: In each of the following sentences some part of the sentence or the entire sentence is underlined. The underlined part presents a problem in the appropriate use of language. Beneath each sentence you will find five ways of writing the underlined part. The first of these indicates no change (that is, it repeats the original), but the other four are all different. If you think the original sentence is better than any of the suggested changes, you should choose answer A; otherwise you should mark one of the other choices. Select the best answer and blacken the corresponding space on the answer sheet.

This is a test of correctness and effectiveness of expression. In choosing answers, follow the requirements of standard written English; that is, pay attention to acceptable usage in grammar, diction (choice of words), sentence construction, and punctuation. Choose the answer that produces the most effective sentence - clear and exact, without awkwardness or ambiguity. Do not make a choice that changes the meaning of the original sentence.

SAMPLE QUESTION 1

Although these states now trade actively with the West, and although they are willing to exchange technological information, their arts and thoughts and social structure <u>remains substantially similar to what it has always been</u>.

    A. remains substantially similar to what it has always been
    B. remain substantially unchanged
    C. remains substantially unchanged
    D. remain substantially similar to what they have always been
    E. remain substantially without being changed

The purpose of questions of this type is to determine the candidate's ability to select the clearest and most effective means of expressing what the statement attempts to say. In this example, the phrasing in the statement, which is repeated in A, presents a problem of agreement between a subject and its verb <u>(their arts and thought and social structure</u> and <u>remains</u>), a problem of agreement between a pronoun and its antecedent <u>(their arts and thought and social structure</u> and <u>it</u>), and a problem of precise and concise phrasing <u>(remains substantially similar to what it has always been</u> for <u>remains substantially unchanged</u>). Each of the four remaining choices in some way corrects one or more of the faults in the sentence, but only one deals with all three problems satisfactorily. Although C presents a more careful and concise wording of the phrasing of the statement and, in the process, eliminates the problem of agreement between pronoun and antecedent, it fails to correct the problem of agreement between the subject and its verb. In D, the subject agrees with its verb and the pronoun agrees with its antecedent, but the phrasing is not so accurate as it should be. The same difficulty persists in E. Only in B are all the problems presented corrected satisfactorily. The question is not difficult.

SAMPLE QUESTION 2

Her latest novel is the largest in scope, the most accomplished in technique, and <u>it is more significant in theme than anything</u> she has written.

- A.   it is more significant in theme than anything
- B.   it is most significant in theme of anything
- C.   more significant in theme than anything
- D.   the most significant in theme than anything
- E.   the most significant in theme of anything

This question is of greater difficulty than the preceding one.

The problem posed in the sentence and repeated in A, is essentially one of parallelism: Does the underlined portion of the sentence follow the pattern established by the first two elements of the series <u>(the largest ... the most accomplished)?</u> It does not, for it introduces a pronoun and verb <u>(it is)</u> that the second term of the series indicates should be omitted and a degree of comparison <u>(more significant)</u> that is not in keeping with the superlatives used earlier in the sentence. B uses the superlative degree of <u>significant</u> but retains the unnecessary <u>it is</u>; C removes the <u>it is</u>. but retains the faulty comparative form of the adjective. D corrects both errors in parallelism, but introduces an error in idiom <u>(the most ...than)</u>. Only E corrects all the problems without introducing another fault.

SAMPLE QUESTION 3

Desiring to insure the continuity of their knowledge, <u>magical lore is transmitted by the chiefs</u> to their descendants.

- A.   magical lore is transmitted by the chiefs
- B.   transmission of magical lore is made by the chiefs
- C.   the chiefs' magical lore is transmitted
- D.   the chiefs transmit magical lore
- E.   the chiefs make transmission of magical lore

The CORRECT answer is D.

SAMPLE QUESTION 4

<u>As Malcolm walks quickly and confident</u> into the purser's office, the rest of the crew wondered whether he would be charged with the theft.

- A.   As Malcolm walks quickly and confident
- B.   As Malcolm was walking quick and confident
- C.   As Malcolm walked quickly and confident
- D.   As Malcolm walked quickly and confidently
- E.   As Malcolm walks quickly and confidently

The CORRECT answer is D.

SAMPLE QUESTION 5

The chairman, <u>granted the power to assign any duties to whoever he</u> wished, was still unable to prevent bickering.
- A. granted the power to assign any duties to whoever he wished
- B. granting the power to assign any duties to whoever he wished
- C. being granted the power to assign any duties to whoever he wished
- D. having been granted the power to assign any duties to whosoever he wished
- E. granted the power to assign any duties to whomever he wished

The CORRECT answer is E.

SAMPLE QUESTION 6

Certainly, well-seasoned products are more expensive, <u>but those kinds prove cheaper</u> in the end.
- A. but those kinds prove cheaper
- B. but these kinds prove cheaper
- C. but that kind proves cheaper
- D. but those kind prove cheaper
- E. but this kind proves cheaper

The CORRECT answer is A.

SAMPLE QUESTION 7

"We shall not," he shouted, "whatever the <u>difficulties." "lose faith in the success of our plan!"</u>
- A. difficulties," "lose faith in the success of our plan!"
- B. difficulties, "lose faith in the success of our plan"!
- C. "difficulties, lose faith in the success of our plan!"
- D. difficulties, lose faith in the success of our plan"!
- E. difficulties, lose faith in the success of our plan!"

The CORRECT answer is E.

SAMPLE QUESTION 8

<u>Climbing up the tree,</u> the lush foliage obscured the chattering monkeys.
- A. Climbing up the tree
- B. Having climbed up the tree
- C. Clambering up the tree
- D. After we had climbed up the tree
- E. As we climbed up the tree

The CORRECT answer is E.

EXAMINATION SECTION
TEST 1

DIRECTIONS: See DIRECTIONS for Sample Questions on page 1. *PRINT THE LETTER OF THE CORRECT ANSWER IN THE SPACE AT THE RIGHT.*

1. At the opening of the story, Charles Gilbert <u>has just come</u> to make his home with his two unmarried aunts.

    1._____

    A. No change
    D. had just come
    B. hadn't hardly come
    E. has hardly came
    C. has just came

2. The sisters, who are no longer young, <u>are use to living</u> quiet lives.

    2._____

    A. No change
    C. are use'd to living
    E. are use to live
    B. are used to live
    D. are used to living

3. They <u>willingly except</u> the child.

    3._____

    A. No change
    C. willingly accepted
    E. willingly accept
    B. willingly eccepted
    D. willingly acepted

4. As the months pass, Charles' presence <u>affects many changes</u> in their household.

    4._____

    A. No change
    C. effects many changes
    E. affected many changes
    B. affect many changes
    D. effect many changes

5. These changes <u>is not all together</u> to their liking.

    5._____

    A. No change
    C. are not all together
    E. is not alltogether
    B. is not altogether
    D. are not altogether

6. In fact, they have some difficulty in adapting <u>theirselves</u> to these changes.

    6._____

    A. No change
    C. in adopting themselves
    E. in adapting themselves
    B. in adopting theirselves
    D. in adapting theirselves

7. That is the man <u>whom I believe</u> was the driver of the car.

    7._____

    A. No change
    D. who to believe
    B. who I believed
    E. who I believe
    C. whom I believed

8. John's climb to fame was more rapid <u>than his brother's</u>.

    8._____

    A. No change
    C. than that of his brother's
    E. than the brother
    B. than his brother
    D. than for his brother

9. We knew that he <u>had formerly swam</u> on an Olympic team.

    9._____

    A. No change
    C. did formerly swum
    E. has formerly swam
    B. has formerly swum
    D. had formerly swum

10. Not one of us loyal supporters <u>ever get a pass</u> to a game

    10.____

  A. No change   B. ever did got a pass
  C. ever has get a pass   D. ever had get a pass
  E. ever gets a pass

11. He <u>was complemented</u> on having done a fine job.

    11.____

  A. No change   B. was compliminted
  C. was compleminted   D. was complimented
  E. did get complimented

12. This play is different from the one we <u>had seen</u> last night.

    12.____

  A. No change   B. have seen   C. had saw
  D. have saw   E. saw

13. A row of trees <u>was planted</u> in front of the house.

    13.____

  A. No change   B. was to be planted   C. were planted
  D. were to be planted   E. are planted

14. The house <u>looked its age</u> in spite of our attempts to beautify it.

    14.____

  A. No change   B. looks its age   C. looked its' age
  D. looked it's age   E. looked it age

15. I do not know <u>what to council</u> in this case.

    15.____

  A. No change   B. where to council
  C. when to councel   D. what to counsel
  E. what to counsil

16. She is more capable <u>than any other girl</u> in the office.

    16.____

  A. No change   B. than any girl
  C. than any other girls   D. than other girl
  E. than other girls

17. At the picnic the young children <u>behaved very good</u>.

    17.____

  A. No change   B. behave very good
  C. behaved better   D. behave very well
  E. behaved very well

18. I resolved <u>to go irregardless of</u> the consequences.

    18.____

  A. No change   B. to depart irregardless of
  C. to go regarding of   D. to go regardingly of
  E. to go regardless of

19. The new movie has a number of actors <u>which have been famous</u> on Broadway.

    19.____

  A. No change   B. which had been famous
  C. who had been famous   D. that are famous
  E. who have been famous

20. I am certain that these books <u>are not our's</u>.   20._____

    A. No change   B. have not been ours'
    C. have not been our's   D. are not ours
    E. are not ours'

21. <u>Each of your papers is filed</u> for future reference.   21._____

    A. No change
    B. Each of your papers are filed
    C. Each of your papers have been filed
    D. Each of your papers are to be filed
    E. Each of your paper is filed

22. I wish that <u>he would take his work more serious</u>.   22._____

    A. No change
    B. he took his work more serious
    C. he will take his work more serious
    D. he shall take his work more seriously
    E. he would take his work more seriously

23. <u>After the treasurer report had been read</u>, the chairman called for the reports of the committees.   23._____

    A. No change
    B. After the treasure's report had been read
    C. After the treasurers' report had been read
    D. After the treasurerer's report had been read
    E. After the treasurer's report had been read

24. Last night the stranger <u>lead us down the mountain</u>.   24._____

    A. No change
    B. leaded us down the mountain
    C. let us down the mountain
    D. led us down the mountain
    E. had led us down the mountain

25. It would not be safe <u>for either you or I</u> to travel in Viet Nam.   25._____

    A. No change   B. for either you or me
    C. for either I or you   D. for either of you or I
    E. for either of I or you

KEY (CORRECT ANSWERS)

1.	A		11.	D
2.	D		12.	E
3.	E		13.	A
4.	C		14.	A
5.	D		15.	D
6.	E		16.	A
7.	E		17.	E
8.	A		18.	E
9.	D		19.	E
10.	E		20.	D

21.	A
22.	E
23.	E
24.	D
25.	B

———

TEST 2

DIRECTIONS: See DIRECTIONS for Sample Questions on page 1. *PRINT THE LETTER OF THE CORRECT ANSWER IN THE SPACE AT THE RIGHT.*

1. Both the body and the mind <u>needs exercise</u>.   1.____

    A. No change   B. have needs of exercise
    C. is needful of exercise   D. needed exercise
    E. need exercise

2. <u>It's paw injured</u>, the animal limped down the road.   2.____

    A. No change   B. It's paw injured
    C. Its paw injured   D. Its' paw injured
    E. Its paw injure

3. The butter <u>tastes rancidly</u>.   3.____

    A. No change   B. tastes rancid
    C. tasted rancidly   D. taste rancidly
    E. taste rancid

4. <u>Who do you think</u> has sent me a letter?   4.____

    A. No change   B. Whom do you think
    C. Whome do you think   D. Who did you think
    E. Whom can you think

5. If more nations <u>would have fought</u> against tyranny, the course of history would have been   5.____
different.

    A. No change   B. would fight
    C. could have fought   D. fought
    E. had fought

6. Radio and television programs, along with other media of communication, <u>helps us to</u>   6.____
<u>appreciate the arts and to keep informed</u>.

    A. No change
    B. helps us to appreciate the arts and to be informed
    C. helps us to be appreciative of the arts and to keep informed
    D. helps us to be appreciative of the arts and to be informed
    E. help us to appreciate the arts and to keep informed

7. Music, <u>for example most always</u> has listening and viewing audiences numbering in the   7.____
hundreds of thousands.

    A. No change   B. for example, most always
    C. for example, almost always   D. for example nearly always
    E. for example, near always

8. When operas are performed on radio or television, <u>they effect the listener</u>.   8.____

    A. No change   B. they inflict the listener
    C. these effect the listeners   D. they affects the listeners
    E. they affect the listener

9. <u>After hearing then the listener wants</u> to buy recordings of the music.   9._____

    A. No change
    B. After hearing them, the listener wants
    C. After hearing them, the listener want
    D. By hearing them the listener wants
    E. By hearing them, the listener wants

10. <u>To we Americans</u> the daily news program has become important.   10._____

    A. No change   B. To we the Americans
    C. To us Americans   D. To us the Americans
    E. To we and us Americans

11. This has resulted from <u>it's coverage of a days' events</u>.   11._____

    A. No change
    B. from its coverage of a days' events
    C. from it's coverage of a day's events
    D. from its' coverage of a day's events
    E. from its coverage of a day's events

12. In schools, <u>teachers advice their students</u> to listen to or to view certain programs.   12._____

    A. No change
    B. teachers advise there students
    C. teachers advise their students
    D. the teacher advises their students
    E. teachers advise his students

13. In these ways <u>we are preceding toward the goal</u> of an educated and an informed public.   13._____

    A. No change
    B. we are preeceding toward the goal
    C. we are proceeding toward the goal
    D. we are preceding toward the goal
    E. we are proceeding toward the goal

14. The cost of living <u>is raising again</u>.   14._____

    A. No change   B. are raising again
    C. is rising again   D. are rising again
    E. is risen again

15. We did not realize that the boys' father <u>had forbidden them to keep there puppy</u>.   15._____

    A. No change
    B. had forbade them to keep there puppy
    C. had forbade them to keep their puppy
    D. has forbidden them to keep their puppy
    E. had forbidden them to keep their puppy

16. <u>Her willingness to help others'</u> was her outstanding characteristic.   16._____

    A. No change
    B. Her willingness to help other's,

C. Her willingness to help others's
D. Her willingness to help others
E. Her willingness to help each other

17. Because he did not have an invitation, <u>the girls objected</u> to him going,   17.____

A. No change
B. the girls object to him going
C. the girls objected to him's going
D. the girls objected to his going
E. the girls object to his going

18. Weekly dances <u>have become a popular accepted feature</u> of the summer schedule.   18.____

A. No change
B. have become a popular accepted feature
C. have become a popular excepted feature
D. have become a popularly excepted feature
E. have become a popularly accepted feature

19. I <u>couldn't hardly believe</u> that he would desert our party.   19.____

A. No change   B. would hardly believe
C. didn't hardly believe   D. should hardly believe
E. could hardly believe

20. I found the place in the book <u>more readily than she</u>.   20.____

A. No change   B. more readily than her
C. more ready than she   D. more quickly than her
E. more ready than her

21. A good example of American outdoor activities <u>are sports</u>.   21.____

A. No change   B. is sports   C. are sport
D. are sports events E. are to be found in sports

22. My point of view is <u>much different from your's</u>.   22.____

A. No change
B. much different than your's
C. much different than yours
D. much different from yours
E. much different than yours'

23. The cook <u>was suppose to use two spoonfuls</u> of dressing for each serving.   23.____

A. No change
B. was supposed to use two spoonsful
C. was suppose to use two spoonsful
D. was supposed to use two spoonsfuls
E. was supposed to use two spoonfuls

24. If anyone has any doubt about the values of the tour, <u>refer him to me</u>.   24.____

A. No change   B. refer him to I   C. refer me to he
D. refer them to me   E. refer he to I

25. We expect that the affects of <u>the trip will be beneficial</u>.   25.____

    A. No change
    B. the effects of the trip will be beneficial
    C. the effects of the trip should be beneficial
    D. the affects of the trip would be beneficial
    E. the effects of the trip will be benificial

KEY (CORRECT ANSWERS)

1.	E		11.	E
2.	C		12.	C
3.	B		13.	E
4.	A		14.	C
5.	E		15.	E
6.	E		16.	D
7.	C		17.	D
8.	E		18.	E
9.	B		19.	E
10.	C		20.	A

21.	B
22.	D
23.	E
24.	A
25.	B

TEST 3

DIRECTIONS: See DIRECTIONS for Sample Questions on page 1. *PRINT THE LETTER OF THE CORRECT ANSWER IN THE SPACE AT THE RIGHT.*

1. <u>That, my friend</u> is not the proper attitude.   1._____

   A. No change   B. That my friend
   C. That my friend,   D. That -- my friend
   E. That, my friend,

2. The girl refused <u>to admit that the not was her's</u>.   2._____

   A. No change   B. that the note were her's
   C. that the note was hers'   D. that the note was hers
   E. that the note might be hers

3. There <u>were fewer candidates that we had been lead</u> to expect.   3._____

   A. No change
   B. was fewer candidates than we had been lead
   C. were fewer candidates than we had been lead
   D. was fewer candidates than we had been led
   E. were fewer candidates than we had been led

4. When I first saw the car, <u>its steering wheel was broke</u>.   4._____

   A. No change
   B. its' steering wheel was broken
   C. it's steering wheel had been broken
   D. its steering wheel were broken
   E. its steering wheel was broken

5. I find that the essential spirit for <u>we beginners is missing</u>.   5._____

   A. No change
   B. we who begin are missing
   C. us beginners are missing
   D. us beginners is missing
   E. we beginners are missing

6. I believe that <u>you had ought</u> to study harder.   6._____

   A. No change   B. you should have ought
   C. you had better   D. you ought to have
   E. you ought

7. This is <u>Tom, whom I am sure</u>, will be glad to help you.   7._____

   A. No change   B. Tom whom, I am sure,
   C. Tom, whom I am sure,   D. Tom who I am sure,
   E. Tom, who, I am sure,

8. His father or his mother <u>has read to him</u> every night since he was very small.   8._____

   A. No change   B. did read to him
   C. have been reading to him   D. had read to him
   E. have read to him

9. He <u>become</u> an authority on the theater and its great personalities.　　　　9.____

    A. No change　　　　　　　　　B. becomed an authority
    C. become the authority　　　　　D. became an authority
    E. becamed an authority

10. I know of no other person in the club <u>who is more kind-hearted than her</u>.　　　　10.____

    A. No change
    B. who are more kind-hearted than they
    C. who are more kind-hearted than them
    D. whom are more kind-hearted than she
    E. who is more kind-hearted than she

11. After Bill <u>had ran the mile</u>, he was breathless.　　　　11.____

    A. No change　　　　　　　　　B. had runned the mile
    C. has ran the mile　　　　　　　D. had ranned the mile
    E. had run the mile

12. Wilson <u>has scarcely no equal</u> as a pitcher.　　　　12.____

    A. No change　　　　　　　　　B. has scarcely an equal
    C. has hardly no equal　　　　　D. had scarcely no equal
    E. has scarcely any equals

13. It <u>was the worse storm</u> that the inhabitants of the island could remember.　　　　13.____

    A. No change　　　　　　　　　B. were the worse storm
    C. was the worst storm　　　　　D. was the worsest storm
    E. was the most worse storm

14. If only <u>we had began</u> before it was too late'.　　　　14.____

    A. No change　　　　　　　　　B. we had began
    C. we would have begun　　　　　D. we had begun
    E. we had beginned

15. <u>Lets evaluate</u> our year's work.　　　　15.____

    A. No change　　　　　　　　　B. Let us' evaluate
    C. Lets' evaluate　　　　　　　　D. Lets' us evaluate
    E. Let's evaluate

16. This is an organization <u>with which I wouldn't want to be associated with</u>.　　　　16.____

    A. No change
    B. with whom I wouldn't want to be associated with
    C. that I wouldn't want to be associated
    D. with which I would want not to be associated with
    E. with which I wouldn't want to be associated

17. The enemy fled in many directions, <u>leaving there weapons</u> on the field.　　　　17.____

    A. No change　　　　　　　　　B. leaving its weapons
    C. letting their weapons　　　　　D. leaving alone there weapons
    E. leaving their weapons

18. I hoped that John <u>could effect a compromise between</u> the approved forces.   18.____

    A. No change
    B. could accept a compromise between
    C. could except a compromise between
    D. would have effected a compromise among
    E. could effect a compromise among

19. I was surprised to learn <u>that he has not always spoke English</u> fluently.   19.____

    A. No change
    B. that he had not always spoke English
    C. that he did not always speak English
    D. that he has not always spoken English
    E. that he could not always speak English

20. The lawyer promised <u>to notify my father and I</u> of his plans for a new trial.   20.____

    A. No change
    B. to notify I and my father
    C. to notify me and our father
    D. to notify my father and me
    E. to notify mine father and me

21. The most important feature of the series of tennis lessons <u>were the large amount</u> of strokes taught.   21.____

    A. No change
    B. were the large number
    C. was the large amount
    D. was the largeness of the amount
    E. was the large number

22. That the prize proved to be beyond her reach <u>did not surprise him</u>.   22.____

    A. No change
    B. has not surprised him
    C. had not ought to have surprised him
    D. should not surprise him
    E. would not have surprised him

23. I am not <u>all together in agreement</u> with the author's point of view.   23.____

    A. No change   B. all together of agreement
    C. all together for agreement   D. altogether with agreement
    E. altogether in agreement

24. Windstorms have recently established a record which meteorologists hope <u>will not be equal</u> for many years to come.   24.____

    A. No change   B. will be equal
    C. will not be equalized   D. will be equaled
    E. will not be equaled

25. A large number of Shakespeare's soliloquies must be considered <u>as representing thought</u>, not speech.

    25.____

    A. No change
    B. as representative of speech, not thought
    C. as represented by thought, not speech
    D. as indicating thought, not speech
    E. as representative of thought, more than speech

———

KEY (CORRECT ANSWERS)

1.	E	11.	E
2.	D	12.	B
3.	E	13.	C
4.	E	14.	D
5.	D	15.	E
6.	E	16.	E
7.	E	17.	E
8.	A	18.	A
9.	D	19.	D
10.	E	20.	D

21.	E
22.	A
23.	E
24.	E
25.	A

———

TEST 4

DIRECTIONS: See DIRECTIONS for Sample Questions on page 1. *PRINT THE LETTER OF THE CORRECT ANSWER IN THE SPACE AT THE RIGHT.*

1. A sight to inspire fear <u>are wild animals on the lose</u>.   1._____

   A.   No change
   B.   are wild animals on the loose
   C.   is wild animals on the loose
   D.   is wild animals on the lose
   E.   are wild animals loose

2. For many years, the settlers <u>had been seeking to workship as they please</u>.   2._____

   A.   No change
   B.   had seeked to workship as they pleased
   C.   sought to workship as they please
   D.   sought to have worshiped as they pleased
   E.   had been seeking to worship as they pleased

3. The girls stated that the dresses were <u>their's</u>.   3._____

   A.   No change   B.   there's   C.   theirs   D.   theirs'   E.   there own

4. <u>Please fellows</u> don't drop the ball.   4._____

   A.   No change   B.   Please, fellows   C.   Please fellows;
   D.   Please, fellows,   E.   Please! fellows

5. Your sweater <u>has laid</u> on the floor for a week.   5._____

   A.   No change   B.   has been laying
   C.   has been lying   D.   laid
   E.   has been lain

6. I wonder whether <u>you're sure that scheme of yours</u>' will work.   6._____

   A.   No change
   B.   your sure that scheme of your's
   C.   you're sure that scheme of yours
   D.   your sure that scheme of yours
   E.   you're sure that your scheme's

7. Please let <u>her and me</u> do it.   7._____

   A.   No change   B.   she and I   C.   she and me
   D.   her and I   E.   her and him

8. I expected him to be angry <u>and to scold</u> her.   8._____

   A.   No change   B.   and that he would scold
   C.   and that he might scold   D.   and that he should scold
   E.   , scolding

9. Knowing little about algebra, <u>it was difficult to solve the equation</u>.   9._____

A. No change
B. the equation was difficult to solve
C. the solution to the equation was difficult to find
D. I found it difficult to solve the equation
E. it being difficult to solve the equation

10. He <u>worked more diligent</u> now that he had become vice president of the company.   10.____

    A. No change   B. works more diligent
    C. works more diligently   D. began to work more diligent
    E. worked more diligently

11. <u>Flinging himself at the barricade</u> he pounded on it furiously.   11.____

A. No change
B. Flinging himself at the barricade: he
C. Flinging himself at the barricade - he
D. Flinging himself at the barricade; he
E.   Flinging himself at the barricade, he

12. When he <u>begun to give us advise</u>, we stopped listening.   12.____

    A. No change   B. began to give us advise
    C. begun to give us advice   D. began to give us advice
    E. begin to give us advice

13. John was only one of the boys whom as you know was not eligible.   13.____

    A. No change   B. who as you know were
    C. whom as you know were   D. who as you know was
    E. who as you know is

14. Why was Jane and he permitted to go?   14.____

    A. No change   B. was Jane and him
    C. were Jane and he   D. were Jane and him
    E. weren't Jane and he

15. <u>Take courage Tom: we</u> all make mistakes.   15.____

    A. No change   B. Take courage Tom - we
    C. Take courage, Tom; we   D. Take courage, Tom we
    E. Take courage! Tom: we

16. Henderson, the president of the class and <u>who is also captain of the team</u>, will lead the   16.____
    rally.

A. No change
B. since he is captain of the team
C. captain of the team
D. also being captain of the team
E. who be also captain of the team

17. Our car has always <u>run good</u> on that kind of gasoline.   17.____

    A. No change   B. run well   C. ran good
    D. ran well   E. done good

18. There was a serious difference of opinion <u>among her and I</u>.

    A. No change   B. among she and I
    C. between her and I   D. between her and me
    E. among her and me

18.____

19. "This is most unusual," said <u>Helen, "the</u> mailman has never been this late before."

    A. No change   B. Helen, "The   C. Helen - "The
    D. Helen; "The   E. Helen." The

19.____

20. The three main characters in the story are Johnny Hobart a <u>teenager, his mother a widow, and</u> the local druggist.

    A. No change
    B. teenager; his mother, a widow; and
    C. teenager; his mother a widow; and
    D. teenager, his mother, a widow and
    E. teenager, his mother, a widow; and

20.____

21. How much <u>has food costs raised</u> during the past year?

    A. No change
    B. have food costs rose
    C. have food costs risen
    D. has food costs risen
    E. have food costs been raised

21.____

22. "Will you come <u>too" she pleaded</u>?

    A. No change   B. too,?"she pleaded.
    C. too?" she pleaded.   D. too," she pleaded?
    E. too, she pleaded?"

22.____

23. If he <u>would have drank</u> more milk, his health would have been better.

    A. No change   B. would drink   C. had drank
    D. had he drunk   E. had drunk

23.____

24. Jack had <u>no sooner laid down and fallen asleep when</u> the alarm sounded.

    A. No change
    B. no sooner lain down and fallen asleep than
    C. no sooner lay down and fell asleep when
    D. no sooner laid down and fell asleep than
    E. no sooner lain down than he fell asleep when

24.____

25. Jackson is <u>one of the few Sophomores, who has</u> ever made the varsity team.

    A. No change
    B. one of the few Sophomores, who have
    C. one of the few sophomores, who has
    D. one of the few sophomores who have
    E. one of the few sophomores who has

25.____

KEY (CORRECT ANSWERS)

1.	C		11.	E
2.	E		12.	D
3.	C		13.	B
4.	D		14.	C
5.	C		15.	C
6.	C		16.	C
7.	A		17.	B
8.	A		18.	D
9.	D		19.	E
10.	E		20.	B

21.	C
22.	C
23.	E
24.	B
25.	D

———

TEST 5

DIRECTIONS: See DIRECTIONS for Sample Questions on page 1. *PRINT THE LETTER OF THE CORRECT ANSWER IN THE SPACE AT THE RIGHT.*

1. The lieutenant had ridden almost a kilometer when the scattering shells <u>begin landing</u> uncomfortably close.   1._____

   A. No change   B. beginning to land   C. began to land
   D. having begun to land   E. begin to land

2. <u>Having studied eight weeks</u>, he now feels sufficiently prepared for the examination.   2._____

   A. No change
   B. For eight weeks he studies so
   C. Due to eight weeks of study
   D. After eight weeks of studying
   E. Since he's been spending the last eight weeks in study

3. <u>Coming from the Greek, and the word "democracy" means government by the people.</u>   3._____

   A. No change
   B. "Democracy," the word which comes from the Greek, means government by the people.
   C. Meaning government by the people, the word "democracy" comes from the Greek.
   D. Its meaning being government by the people in Greek, the word is "democracy."
   E. The word "democracy" comes from the Greek and means government by the people.

4. Moslem universities were one of the chief agencies <u>in the development</u> and spreading Arabic civilization.   4._____

   A. No change   B. in the development of
   C. to develop   D. in developing
   E. for the developing of

5. The water of Bering Strait <u>were closing</u> to navigation by ice early in the fall.   5._____

   A. No change   B. has closed   C. have closed
   D. had been closed   E. closed

6. The man, <u>since he grew up</u> on the block, felt sentimental when returning to it.   6._____

   A. No change   B. having grown up
   C. growing up   D. since he had grown up
   E. whose growth had been

7. <u>Jack and Jill watched the canoe to take their parents out of sight round the bend of the creek</u>.   7._____

   A. No change
   B. The canoe, taking their parents out of sight, rounds the bend as Jack and Jill watch.
   C. Jack and Jill watched the canoe round the bend of the creek, taking their parents out of sight.

D. The canoe rounded the bend of the creek as it took their parents out of sight, Jack and Jill watching.
E. Jack and Jill watching, the canoe is rounding the bend of the creek to take their parents out of sight.

8. Chaucer's best-known work is THE CANTERBURY TALES, a collection of stories which he tells with a group of pilgrims as they travel to the town of Canterbury.   8.____

   A. No change   B. which he tells through   C. who tell
   D. told by   E. told through

9. The Estates-General, the old feudal assembly of France, had not met for one hundred and sevety-five years when it convened in 1789.   9.____

   A. No change   B. has not met   C. has not been meeting
   D. had no meeting   E. has no meeting

10. Just forty years ago, there had been fewer than one hundred symphony orchestras in the United States.   10.____

    A. No change   B. there had   C. there were
    D. there was   E. there existed

11. Mrs. Smith complained that her son's temper tantrums aggragravated her and caused her to have a headache.   11.____

    A. No change   B. gave her aggravation
    C. were aggravating to her   D. aggravated her condition
    E. instigated

12. A girl like I would never be seen in a place like that.   12.____

    A. No change B. as I   C. as me   D. like I am   E. like me

13. Between you and me. my opinion is that this room is certainly nicer than the first one we saw.   13.____

    A. No change   B. between you and I   C. among you and me
    D. betwixt you and I   E. between we

14. It is important to know for what kind of a person you are working.   14.____

    A. No change
    B. what kind of a person for whom you are working
    C. what kind of person you are working
    D. what kind of person you are working for
    E. what kind of a person you are working for

15. I had all ready finished the book before you came in.   15.____

    A. No change B. already   C. previously D. allready   E. all

16. Ask not for who the bell tolls, it tolls for thee.   16.____

    A. No change
    B. Ask not for whom the bell tolls, it tolls for thee.
    C. Ask not whom the bell tolls for; it tolls for thee.

D. Ask not for whom the bell tolls; it tolls for thee.
E. Ask not who the bell tolls for: It tolls for thee.

17. It is a far better thing I do, than <u>ever I did</u> before.   17.____

     A. No change   B. never I did   C. I have ever did
     D. I have ever been done   E. ever have I done

18. <u>Ending a sentence with a preposition is something up with which I will not put</u>.   18.____

     A. No change
     B. Ending a sentence with a preposition is something with which I will not put up.
     C. To end a sentence with a preposition is that which I will not put up with.
     D. Ending a sentence with a preposition is something of which I will not put up.
     E. Something I will not put up with is ending a sentence with a preposition.

19. Everyone <u>took off their hats and stand up</u> to sing the national anthem.   19.____

     A. No change
     B. took off their hats and stood up
     C. take off their hats and stand up
     D. took off his hat and stood up
     E. have taken off their hats and standing up

20. <u>She promised me that if she had the opportunity she would have came irregardless of the weather</u>.   20.____

     A. No change
     B. She promised me that if she had the opportunity she would have come regardless of the weather.
     C. She assured me that had she had the opportunity she would have come regardless of the weather.
     D. She assured me that if she would have had the opportunity she would have come regardless of the weather.
     E. She promised me that if she had had the opportunity she would have came irregardless of the weather.

21. The man decided it would be advisable to marry a girl <u>somewhat younger than him</u>.   21.____

     A. No change   B. somehow younger than him
     C. some younger than him   D. somewhat younger from him
     E. somewhat younger than he

22. Sitting near the campfire, the old man told <u>John and I about many exciting adventures he had had</u>.   22.____

     A. No change
     B. John and me about many exciting adventures he had.
     C. John and I about much exciting adventure which he'd had.
     D. John and me about many exciting adventures he had had.
     E. John and me about many exciting adventures he has had.

23. <u>If you had stood at home and done your homework</u>, you would not have failed the   23.____
course.

    A. No change
    B. If you had stood at home and done you're homework,
    C. If you had staid at home and done your homework,
    D. Had you stayed at home and done your homework,
    E. Had you stood at home and done your homework,

24. The children didn't, as a rule, <u>do anything beyond</u> what they were told to do.   24.____

    A. No change   B. do hardly anything beyond
    C. do anything except   D. do hardly anything except for
    E. do nothing beyond

25. <u>Either the girls or him is</u> right.   25.____

    A. No change
    B. Either the girls or he is
    C. Either the girls or him are
    D. Either the girls or he are
    E. Either the girls nor he is

KEY (CORRECT ANSWERS)

1.	C		11.	D
2.	A		12.	E
3.	E		13.	A
4.	D		14.	C
5.	D		15.	B
6.	B		16.	D
7.	C		17.	E
8.	D		18.	E
9.	A		19.	D
10.	C		20.	C

21.	E
22.	D
23.	D
24.	A
25.	B

CPSIA information can be obtained
at www.ICGtesting.com
Printed in the USA
BVHW010902140220
572397BV00014B/266